Safer Hospital Care
Strategies for Continuous Quality Innovation

Safer Hospital Care
Strategies for Continuous Quality Innovation

Second Edition

Dev Raheja

Routledge
Taylor & Francis Group

A PRODUCTIVITY PRESS BOOK

Productivity Press
Taylor & Francis Group
270 Madison Avenue
New York, NY 10016

International Standard Book Number: 978-0-367-17848-2 (Paperback)
International Standard Book Number: 978-0-367-17849-9 (Hardback)

Library of Congress Cataloging-in-Publication Data

Names: Raheja, Dev, author.
Title: Safer hospital care : strategies for continuous improvement / Dev Raheja.
Description: 2nd edition. | Boca Raton : Taylor & Francis, 2019. | Includes bibliographical references and index.
Identifiers: LCCN 2019001326 (print) | LCCN 2019005415 (ebook) | ISBN 9780429058042 (e-Book) | ISBN 9780367178482 (pbk. : alk. paper) | ISBN 9780367178499 (hardback : alk. paper)
Subjects: LCSH: Hospitals—Safety measures.
Classification: LCC RA969.9 (ebook) | LCC RA969.9 .R34 2019 (print) | DDC 362.11068/4—dc23
LC record available at https://lccn.loc.gov/2019001326

Visit the Taylor & Francis Web site at
http://www.taylorandfrancis.com

and the Productivity Press Web site at
http://www.productivitypress.com

Dedicated to all physicians, nurses, and caregivers who are doing their best to prevent adverse and "never" events.

Contents

Introduction

Dr Lucian Leape, who cofounded the patient-safety movement more than a decade ago, is confident that healthcare is moving in the right direction, but the progress to date is dismal. He sums it up: "Despite some successes, I think it's safe to say the patient-safety movement also has been a great failure. No one to my knowledge has implemented all 34 protocols from the National Quality Forum. Why not? Why isn't that priority number 1 for all hospitals in America?" He said this at the annual meeting of the American Organization of Nurse Executives, which attracted an audience of more than 2,200 to the Indianapolis Convention Center from April 9–13, 2010.

Dr Mark Chassin, president of the Joint Commission, has similar views: "The problem is that we need to generate new knowledge." He adds, "We have imperfect tools to assess exactly what happened in the course of an adverse event. Then, once we understand where the weak defenses are, we have imperfect analytic tools to tell us which one to fix first."

The purpose of this volume is precisely to address these issues with the use of evidence-based safety theories and tools used in other ultra-high safety industries, such as the aerospace, nuclear, and chemical industries. With my engineering background, experience with these industries as a consultant, and medical writing background, I am able to blend the state of the art into patient safety. I have done safety training for NASA and the U.S. Navy several times. The tools from these organizations can be and must be used in patient care if we want to prevent adverse, sentinel, and "never" events. The book offers a systematic way to learn the science of safe care, how to do the right things at the right time, where to use safeguards, and how to identify the combination of root causes that result in an adverse event. The current method of root-cause analysis assumes that a single event can cause an adverse event; according to Dr Chassin, the name is a misnomer, because there is never a single cause in an adverse event.

Dr Chassin sums up the argument candidly: "The analytic methods we have are from a different generation. We need to develop the next generation of those tools to achieve the goal of high reliability." This volume offers methods that are not new to aerospace but are new to many industries, including healthcare.

We need a paradigm shift. We need it in a hurry! As Rabindranath Tagore said, "You can't cross the sea merely by standing and staring at the water." Do not be afraid to take a big step if one is needed. No noble thing can be done without risks.

This book is not just theory. It is about the lessons learned from my experience of more than 30 years in safety in the fields of medical device, aerospace, healthcare, nuclear power, subways, consumer products, and pharmaceuticals. These are enriched by evidence-based practices for more than 40 years in aerospace and nuclear industries. If healthcare can adopt translocation of such practices, it can fulfill the dreams of the patients in which nothing bad happens to them! This is precisely the aim of this book.

Safe hospital care is neither a science nor an art. It is a practice just like the practice by a doctor who combines hindsight of experience and foresight of imagination to come up with an outsight of the best interventions and best protocols. Over time, the doctor standardizes the process but is vigilant to any unique requirements of each patient. Such an approach in patient safety is called *hazard analysis* and *mitigation process*, and is covered in this book. And, this book goes one big step further: it covers innovation strategies which ensure safety improvements result in a high value to the hospital, patients, and other stakeholders.

Acknowledgment

I am grateful to Dr Peter Pronovost, intensive care physician and medical director of the Center for Innovation in Quality Patient Care at Johns Hopkins Hospital, for his help and suggestions, and for making it possible for me to present several topics from this book to the members of the Quality and Safety Research Group (QSRG); also to Dr Tom Scaletta, chairman of Emergency Medicine at Edward Hospital; and to David Marshall, CEO of Safer Healthcare. My special thanks also to physicians and healthcare professionals Dr David Brown, Dr Maria Escano (coauthor of several of my articles), Dr Nirmal Saini, Lauren Fishkin, Michelle Self, Gauri Raheja, and Carli Philips for their valuable suggestions. Thanks also to members of the National Capital Healthcare Executives Chapter of the American College of Healthcare Executives who gave positive feedback on my four articles published in their quarterly newsletters and constantly requested for more articles.

Author

Dev Raheja, MS, CSP, has been an international risk management and quality assurance consultant to the healthcare, medical device, and aerospace industries for more than 25 years. He applies evidence-based safety techniques from a variety of industries to healthcare.

He is a trainer and author, and shows clients how to come up with elegant solutions using creativity and innovation. Being a true international consultant, he has conducted training in several countries, including Sweden, Australia, Japan, Germany, the United Kingdom, Singapore, Taiwan, South Africa, and Brazil. He helped a major Midwest company from going out of business to becoming a world leader by eliminating safety mishaps.

Prior to becoming a consultant in 1982, he worked at GE Healthcare as supervisor of quality assurance and manager of manufacturing, and at Booz-Allen Hamilton Inc. as risk management consultant to nuclear and mass transportation industries.

He has served as adjunct professor at the University of Maryland for 5 years in its PhD program in reliability engineering. Currently, he is an adjunct professor at the Florida Institute of Technology (Florida Tech) for its BBA degree in healthcare management, has authored two books, *Assurance Technologies Principles and Practices* and *Zen and the Art of Breakthrough Quality Management*, and is associate editor of healthcare safety for the *Journal of System Safety*. He is a medical writer for the National Capital Healthcare Executives newsletters. He has received several industry awards, including the Scientific Achievement Award and the Educator of the Year Award from the System Safety Society.

He is a former National Malcolm Baldrige Quality Award Examiner and has frequently lectured for the Johns Hopkins Quality and Safety Research Group.

He majored in human factors engineering to earn his master's degree in industrial engineering; is a certified safety professional through the Board of Certified Safety Professionals; took training in "Perfecting Patient Care" through the Pittsburgh Regional Health Initiative, an organization supported by 40 hospitals; and is a member of the American College of Healthcare Executives.

He teaches healthcare management courses at the Florida Institute of Technology. He is also a charter member of the Improvement Science Research Center at the University of Texas Health Science Center.

Chapter 1

The Etiologies of Unsafe Healthcare

Medicine arose out of the primal sympathy of man with man; out of the desire to help those in sorrow, need, and sickness.

—**William Osier**

Introduction

"Despite some successes, I think it's safe to say the patient-safety movement also has been a great failure," said Lucian Leape, the father of the patient-safety movement. "No one to my knowledge has implemented all 34 protocols from the National Quality Forum," he told thousands of nurse executives who gathered to hear him deliver one of the big-tent speeches at the 43rd Annual Meeting of the American Organization of Nurse Executives, which attracted 2,200 healthcare professionals to the Indianapolis Convention Center April 9–13, 2010 [1].

Inadequate systems, not inadequate people, usually cause accidents. People are only an element in a system, which can be defined as an integration of interfacing and interdependent entities working together to accomplish a mission. It includes facility, environment, all hospital staff, and services, including support personnel, suppliers, patients, families, and equipment.

Human errors are bound to happen in a system of many microsystems, such as a hospital. The physician treats from a list of differential diagnoses. This is the nature of the treatment process where there are conflicting symptoms, multiple symptoms, false-positive and false-negative test results, constant distractions, and insufficient information on the patient history. Even the most conscious safety professionals make mistakes. But this does not mean that errors can be ignored. They must be minimized through robust system designs and individual accountability.

Some errors may be unpreventable, but preventing a mishap is often an option. This is the core message in this book for hospital professionals who must work as a team to produce high return on investment and to deliver safer care.

Even though some progress has been made over the last decade, hospital care still needs a very significant amount of transformation. Would you go to a hospital where there is an excellent surgery department but where several medication errors take place every day? You may be surprised that this actually happens in many medical facilities and is not as rare as one might think. A simple math calculation will illustrate the seriousness. The Institute of Medicine estimated the medication error rate to be between 3% and 5% [2]. A hospital with 600 beds with about five medications per patient administers about 3,000 medications per day. Even with the most conservative estimate of 3% errors, the number of errors works out to be 90 errors per day!

Considering that the average length of stay in U.S. hospitals is between 3 and 4 days, the range of medication errors for this period works out to be between 270 and 360. In other words, nearly half of the available 600 beds could theoretically witness a medication error during an average patient stay. While this is scary and unacceptable, there is some hope. Not all these errors are linked or cause harm or reach the bedside of the patient. This is because some of these errors are intercepted before they reach the bedside, and, in some instances, the human body responds well to antidotes or other medications used to nullify their effect.

To clarify further, these errors are the sum total of all errors, such as in pharmacy (stocking, dilutions, compounding), handoffs (shift changes, doctor changes), prescriptions, intensive care units (surgical, pediatric, neonatal), general care units (oncology, HIV, palliative), emergency departments (EDs), operating room (anesthesia, antibiotics), lab testing, medication administration, electronic health records, and patient discharge. The errors that are not intercepted may result in adverse events.

Equally shocking are several other statistics. A Johns Hopkins research paper [3] shows about 40,000–80,000 patients are misdiagnosed every year. Another study [4] found that diagnostic error accounted for 17% of preventable errors in hospitalized patients, and about 9% of patients experienced a major diagnostic error that went undetected while the patient was alive. The purpose of this book is to explain why such errors happen and how to innovate elegant solutions that address the issues at a system level. Failure in healthcare is not an option.

Failure Is Not an Option

Concern for errors is a universal problem and not just limited to hospitals. Errors happen in aerospace, and even at Toyota car company, which is the world standard for quality. Like aerospace, failure is not an option in hospital care. Errors happen in larger proportions because of complexity of systems of interactions, highly variable conditions, complex handoffs, too many handoffs, very frequent emergencies, and too many opportunities for communication errors. Table 1.1 provides an idea on the rationale for how there are greater chances for errors in hospitals because of the iterative process in decision-making and care delivery. Since there is an intrinsic value in every human being, they can make extraordinary transformations in systems if they work as teams. The most important message that leadership must believe and convey is that when an error occurs, it is a process issue. The leadership must create a system of urgency to fix the process.

An Unconventional Way to Manage Risks

This book will start in an unconventional way. We will first define unsafe work in order to have an appreciation of what is safe work. *The premise is that if we stop doing unsafe work, the ideas for safer*

Table 1.1 Why the Chance of Error Is Higher in Hospitals

	Aerospace	*Automotive*	*Hospitals*
Production level of variability	Planned (streamlined)	Planned (streamlined)	Planned+emergency
	Design-led assembly Specialists perform specific task (usually in sequence)	Design-led assembly Specialists perform specific task (usually in sequence)	Patient condition characteristic driven Specialists+others perform tasks simultaneously
	Demand usually known	Demand usually known	Demand anticipated but variable
Level of handoffs	Few	Few	Many
Design to output flow	Streamlined/ structured	Streamlined/structured	Streamlined but subject to significant variation, depending on intermediate patient outcomes during stay

care will automatically blossom. This is human nature. We will begin with a quote from Professor Harry Frankfurt of Princeton University [5]:

> One of the most salient features of our culture is that there is so much bullshit. Everyone knows this. Each of us contributes his share. But we tend to take the situation for granted. Most people are rather confident of their ability to recognize bullshit and to avoid being taken in by it. So the phenomenon has not aroused much deliberate concern, nor attracted much sustained inquiry. In consequence, we have no clear understanding of what bullshit is, why there is so much of it, or what functions it serves. And we lack a conscientiously developed appreciation of what it means to us.

In my experience of more than 30 years as a consultant to the aerospace, medical device, and healthcare industries, a major source of unsafe work is Frankfurt's description of bullshit. Again, let us be clear that it is a global phenomenon, and hospitals are simply a participant in the phenomenon. I regret the use of the word *bullshit*, but nothing else easily conveys the same meaning. The hope is that we will awaken to the wisdom of Harry Frankfurt and avoid huge amounts of inadequate, unsafe, and marginal work.

Defining Unsafe Work

Frankfurt admits that the term "bullshit" is loosely used and offers no clear definition. He offers an excellent example with the intent of what to do about it:

> In the old days, craftsmen did not cut corners. They worked carefully, and they took care with every aspect of their work. Every part of the product was considered, and each was designed and made to be exactly as it should be. These craftsmen did not

relax their thoughtful self-discipline even with respect to features of their work that would ordinarily not be visible. Although no one will notice if those features were not quite right, the craftsmen would be bothered by their consciences. So nothing was swept under the rug. Or, one might perhaps say, there was no bullshit.

If we accept this notion of craftsmanship as a foundation of safe work, we can say that any work linked to a potential harm to the patient can be an unsafe work if done without sufficient understanding or with an attitude of indifference. The attitude of indifference needs explanation. A driver speeding on a highway knows speeding is unsafe and yet he/she keeps doing it day in and day out. He/she has justification in the interest of efficiency and time. Like most of us, they believe that the chance "it will happen to me" is very small. In addition, he/she has very little guilt, because almost everyone else is doing it. Since an unsafe act is an option on a highway but not in healthcare, I want to make everyone aware of such a phenomenon. Allow me to use a new word "indifferencity" to emphasize the impact of such an act on safe care. It refers to performance without passion or "due concern," or a performance diligently done in a substandard way. We can then say that any medical intervention done with inadequate knowledge or indifferencity can be unsafe.

Unsafe work can be defined as:
- Performance without adequate knowledge
- Performance with indifferencity

Chapter 3 is devoted to the expansion of the concept of indifferencity. It includes examples and some remedies.

How Unsafe Work Propagates Unknowingly

According to a Gallup poll nationally [6], engaged employees made up only 29% of the workforce (an engaged employee is one who is willing to go the extra mile to help the organization do the right things). The remaining employees were either not engaged (56%) or actively disengaged (15%). Sometimes they are referred to as "warm bodies" that just fill a position. Not engaged and actively disengaged employees tend to be accident prone. A vice president of human resources once said: Hire for attitude and train for skill when you can. With a great attitude you could get the requisite skills but without a great attitude it is hard.

For employees to be engaged, the organization must create interesting and meaningful work, a variety of responsibilities, capable and similarly committed colleagues, and respectful and respected managers who will welcome investment in safety as a business strategy instead of a necessary cost. A system of disengaged employees is a source of unsafe work. Richard Hackman and Greg Oldham in their book *Work Redesign* proposed a job design model that would motivate workers to be more engaged and improve overall organizational performance. They proposed core dimensions for evaluating the immediate work environment. These core dimensions turned out to be associated significantly with job satisfaction and a high sense of workers' motivation. The work environment source consisted of five dimensions, namely, those of skill variety, task identity, task significance, autonomy, and feedback. Three key psychological states are produced when you focus on these five job design characteristics. Employees experienced meaningfulness of their work, responsibility for the outcomes of their work, and knowledge of the actual results of their work. These in turn increase the likelihood of positive personal and work outcomes.

Let us make this theory a bit more real with an example. The example here is of a carpenter in the "olden days," who conceptualized the design of a table, used the wood to create the top of the table and the four legs, and put it together, finishing it with varnish/polish. This carpenter then worked on chairs and other pieces of furniture. The high skill variety (working on different parts of the table and furniture), task identity, task significance associated with creating the whole table, and autonomy (deciding the shape, design, etc.), according to Hackman and Oldham, provide greater job satisfaction and a high degree of motivation and engagement. Now imagine if this carpenter were just involved in making the legs of the table? How engaged or motivated do you think he is likely to be in his work?

In healthcare, we have created "warm bodies" unconsciously who work like robots. We have done this by splitting tasks and creating superspecializations. Nurses, who form a very important role in the care of every patient, often perform repetitive tasks each day and, at times, are not aware of the overall plan of care for the patient. In many instances, the patient is transferred to another unit or ward, and they may not get to see the results of their work directly. Compare this with the work that Florence Nightingale performed. As a nurse attending to patients' injuries from war, she often had to make the decisions and would be involved with the care from the start to the end. Nurses today can specialize and work in units (e.g., ICU nurse, pediatric intensive care nurse).

Concern on volume and outcome relationship certainly created the need for specialization and encouraging professionals to specialize within medical disciplines. However, this has created a sort of compartmentalization. This compartmentalization creates task monotony and sometimes boredom that creates "warm bodies" who are not engaged—in part because they're not aware of the results of their work.

Organizations, especially the large ones, want inflexible tools, procedures, and processes so that everyone thinks the same way, the opposite of creativity. In other words, they are asking employees to limit their thinking and work with insufficient knowledge, a typical case of unsafe work. Managers have often rejected their own intuitive guidance and opted for methods that are popular with other hospitals under the garb of so-called best practices. Then they don't have to justify anything. It is like receiving a blessing from the Pope. These best practices, such as Six Sigma quality and root-cause analysis, are usually more than 30 years old. They are developed by emulating the gurus and other companies of that time. If airlines depended only on Six Sigma, there would be about 11 crashes per week at the Chicago airport alone. Usually, it takes about 4 years for a hospital to buy into a traditional Six Sigma program. It takes another 10 years to achieve the Six Sigma level. Assuming all the hospitals achieve Six Sigma levels, the following scenarios can still exist [7]:

■ 76 newborn babies in the United States would be given to wrong parents each month.
■ At least 1,000 patients would be getting wrong medications per week.
■ 107 incorrect medical procedures would be performed every day.
■ No electricity would be available for 10 minutes each week.

Traditional tools such as Six Sigma have value in solving traditional problems and improving operational efficiency, but they are highly inadequate for preventing adverse, never, or sentinel events. Marginal innovations will not be sufficient. There is an urgent need for disruptive innovations if we have an interest in preventing these very highly disruptive events!

Dr Mark Chassin, president of the Joint Commission, expresses this concern clearly about the most best practices such as the root-cause analysis:

> What we call root cause analysis, I think is a misnomer since there is never a single cause in an adverse event. There aren't usually even two or three. Five, eight, or ten

defenses fail in many of these adverse events. The analytic methods we have are from a different generation. We need to develop the next generation of those tools to achieve the goal of high reliability [8].

Usually, the bandwagon followers are also satisfied with a low return on investment (ROI) of 10% or even less when they could be getting an ROI of several 100% as shown in many examples in this book. The hospitals competing for funds must face changing realities and unchanging truths. This book is an attempt to show you how you can sniff out unsafe work practices in hospitals and innovate elegant solutions for yourself—usually at very low or no cost.

To satisfy the reader's curiosity, I will give an example of an unsafe work practice. A homicide charge was filed against a hospital ED in Illinois because of the following incident [9]. A 49-year-old woman, Beatrice Vance, complaining of chest pain was triaged as semi-urgent but sent back to the waiting room. When called back after 2 hours for evaluation, she was already dead. In another hospital in New York, Esmin Green [10] died while waiting for more than 24 hours. She fell to the floor and the whole episode was captured on the hospital's video recording. The medical examiner's office concluded she was killed by pulmonary thrombo-emboli, blood clots that form in the legs and travel through the bloodstream to the lungs, due to physical inactivity.

Most hospitals would say a 2-hours wait time is not too bad. The nationwide wait time is about 3 hours and 42 minutes [11] to see an emergency physician. Obviously, making patients wait this long to see a doctor is an unsafe work practice. There is a high chance of patient harm and even fatality. The right thing to do is to use innovative techniques to reduce the waiting time to about 15 minutes in the ED. If Singapore General Hospital can limit the wait time to see a doctor to 10 minutes, why can't other hospitals learn from them?

The cause of long waits may be not enough ED capacity. But it's not all doom and gloom everywhere. Some hospitals are finding low-cost solutions to make their EDs more efficient while maintaining safety. Hospitals such as Cooper Hospital–University Medical Center in Camden, New Jersey, are forming "fast-track" areas in their EDs to more quickly treat patients with minor illnesses and injuries, such as small cuts or ankle sprains. Often, these areas are staffed by physician assistants or nurse practitioners, leaving the doctors to treat more serious problems. Dr Wechsler, president of Emergency Excellence and medical director of Edward Hospital in Illinois, has several innovative solutions such as the following [12]:

- Charge emergency department leaders to set a door-to-doctor (D2D) goal of less than 30 minutes.
- Adhere to a rapid (1-minute), first-stage triage process. This discourages patients from leaving without being seen (LWBS), which could harm patients even more, in addition to loss of revenue to the hospital.
- Encourage temporary double parking in the hallway of the clinical area when there is shortage of beds.
- Initiate standardized nurse-activated protocols (SNAPs) in triage to expedite patient testing and comfort measures.
- Position a mid-level practitioner in triage to prepare initial orders and discharge quick cases.
- Utilize a greeter to update waiting patients with their status and advocate for their comfort.
- Challenge a multidisciplinary team to reduce boarding hours by admitted patients, which reclaims space and staff in a cost-free manner.
- Have your ED callback clerk check on the well-being of all LWBS cases the next day. And determine the factors that caused them to walk out so that these can be discussed at monthly ED leadership meetings.

Through the Emergency Excellence network, Dr Wechsler has made a very significant reduction in D2D wait times. Figure 1.1 shows the graph of improvements with the following results:

Best EDs	15 minutes
Notable threshold	40 minutes
Average of all EDs	60 minutes

How Does Unsafe Work Originate?

Unsafe work happens in many ways. Since the list is very long, I will share only some of it. Examples are as follows:

■ Excessive work for clinicians
■ Too many unnecessary reports and requirements
■ Overdependence on technology

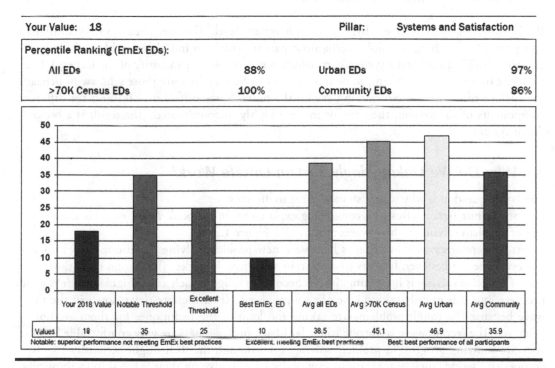

Door-to-Doctor Time

Emergency Excellence

How many minutes from patient arrival until the patient is seen by a physician (or midlevel provider)?

Your Value: 18		Pillar:	Systems and Satisfaction

Percentile Ranking (EmEx EDs):

All EDs	88%	Urban EDs	97%
>70K Census EDs	100%	Community EDs	86%

	Your 2018 Value	Notable Threshold	Excellent Threshold	Best EmEx ED	Avg all EDs	Avg >70K Census	Avg Urban	Avg Community
Values	18	35	25	10	38.5	45.1	46.9	35.9

Notable: superior performance not meeting EmEx best practices   Excellent: meeting EmEx best practices   Best: best performance of all participants

Figure 1.1 Graph showing comparison of waiting time in the emergency department of a hospital and the benchmarks.

- Conflict between the need for professional autonomy and establishing the dynamically changing best process
- Each department interested in only their own work, resulting in lack of teamwork (care deliver silos)
- Constant distractions and interruptions
- Too many policies and procedures—tendency to follow marginally effective methods
- Overreliance on electronic medical tracking instead of bedside discussions with patients
- Inattention to details
- Lack of motivation or resources for a second opinion
- Quick diagnosis based on past observations
- Inadequate attention to dangers of medical equipment
- Insufficient effort in infection prevention
- People pretend the negative would not happen to them
- Hospitals may be looking for quick profit
- Questionable alternate boards exist to certify physicians who may not be qualified
- A lack of passion for work
- Unfavorable workflow such as the lab located far from the emergency department
- Lack of clarity over what is required to ensure patient safety
- Too much consensus in the teams instead of challenging the quality of intervention
- Organization of healthcare professionals tends to be based on professional training, for example, doctors report to doctors, nurses to nurses (sometimes to doctors), paramedics to the chief paramedic, and pharmacists to the chief pharmacist. They train separately and then are put together to work as a team.

Ranjit Singh et al. [13] have a hypothesis at a system level. They see patient safety similar to two parts of an iceberg: a visible mechanistic part in which an individual is blamed for errors (the tip of the iceberg) and a system part, which is not visible (the majority of the iceberg). If an iceberg can be seen as a system, some of its parts can be seen by only those who swim beneath the surface of the water. No one can see all the parts. Since different swimmers see different components of the system, the components are highly uncoordinated. The result is a broken-down system.

So, Why Do We Unknowingly Sustain Unsafe Work?

The larger question is why we are so indifferent to unsafe work.

Joel Arthur Barker gives us a convincing explanation in his book *Paradigms*. He divides the rate of problem solving in three waves as shown in Figure 1.2.

At first, progress is slow. That is because a new problem-solving technique comes up and not everyone is a believer. It takes time to train and prove it works. The second wave shows the rate of problem solving is increasing; it now becomes a religion such as Six Sigma. There is good progress, but it is mainly taking care of easy problems. Then the rate slows down in the third wave because the tough problems are taking too long or the techniques for them are not in place yet. The second wave is the one where laid-back professionals are very comfortable because they are showing progress in problem solving, even though the ROI might be hardly 5%. In a competitive world, such organizations eventually have to give up their leadership to those who break the rules and create a new paradigm as shown in Figure 1.3. Joel calls them "paradigm pioneers."

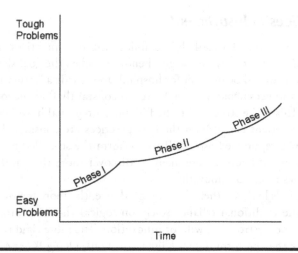

Figure 1.2 Three phases of problem solving.

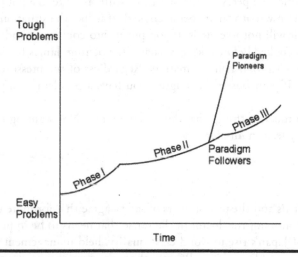

Figure 1.3 The paradigm pioneers break out and capture the market.

Hospitals can get stuck in the second wave by default, because patients need to go to the nearest hospital during emergencies. The federal and state governments have the authority to shut them down, but this happens rarely.

Despite the limited competition, there are paradigm pioneers even in healthcare. Three such examples are Geisinger Health System, Johns Hopkins Hospital, and Allegheny General Hospital. I will describe how they did it in Chapter 11.

Paradigm pioneers have another quality, which distinguishes them from those who are satisfied with the status quo, says Barker, "The paradigm pioneer must have courage as well as intuition." He has a point. Traditional techniques depend on logic and data analyses. One can argue that you always need data. The point is that the paradigm pioneers, who often rely on intuition, do not need the complete data. They try to see flaws in the system and constantly look outside the box for solutions.

Using Best Practices Is Insufficient

It is understandable that every hospital should follow the best practices from other hospitals. Since what was best at one time may not be good enough today, the goal should be to constantly improve the processes. It would be prudent for hospitals to provide a "structure" that allows using best-known practices and yet encourages employees to constantly find the loopholes in them and improve the process. This is the structure in the Pittsburgh regional hospitals that use the Toyota production system for patient care. Often the best practices are considered best simply because they are being used by a reputable hospital. If we perform the so-called healthcare failure mode and effects analysis (covered later), we are likely to discover more than 100 flaws even in a best practice. There is always room for innovation.

The more the hospitals look to others for their guidance, the more removed they become from their own wisdom. The traditional reliance solely on logical thinking promoted by rigid rules promotes inflexibility and destroys the will for innovation. The more rigid rules people create, the more low-quality work they perform. James Kilts in his book *Doing What Matters* has this advice for new employees: Usually, in your first day on a new job, you spot a number of things that don't make sense. Some seem inefficient and ill conceived. Two weeks later wrong things seem perfectly fine because your experienced peers are OK with this stuff. You are in a pot that has been heating slowly and you don't know that you are being cooked. It is like the situation of a frog. If you put it into boiling water, it will not tolerate it. If you put it into cool water and slowly raise the temperature, the frog gets cooked before it knows what is happening. James Kilts advises: Willingness to view the reflection with total honesty matters. Regardless of the pressure, understand exactly what you need to do. If your bosses don't agree, you have a problem, and your future might be better elsewhere.

You will spot a number of things that don't make sense. Not wanting to view the reflection with total honesty may lead to unsafe work.

There Is Hope

Most management gurus and the practitioners of safety agree that for more than 85% of medical errors, it is the system and not the doctor or the nurse that needs to be improved. Dr W. Edward Deming, the father of Japan's rise to world-class quality, held management responsible for more than 85% of the quality problems. James Reason, the proponent of the famous Swiss cheese theory of mishaps (Appendix A), also says that people on the front line are not so much the initiators of bad events. It is the long-term system's failings.

Dr Deming discouraged the use of the very popular best practice called *management by objectives*. Most hospitals use this practice to improve the performance of each function, such as surgery, oncology, and emergency medicine. The danger with this technique is that it is linked to the departmental silo goals instead of the system goal of safe healthcare. The managers contend that if every component of the healthcare system performs its best, the patient will be safe. This thinking is inherently flawed because healthcare safety is not a function of components only. It is also a dynamic function of complex system interactions, complex influences of components throughout the system, and equally complex communications among interfaces such as patient handoffs, electronic health records, and unreported medical errors. Chapter 3 covers more details on this topic.

The management by objectives can be practiced with efficiency and speed if implemented by a team with the goal of flawless execution in the interest of the patient. It should be for measuring the performance of teams that provide a certain class of care rather than individuals. An individual is helpless most of the time, not knowing what else can affect his/her work. For example, a different doctor on a new shift may change the medication frequency or dosage, and if the nurse did not know in time to administer the medicine, the patient may be harmed. This nurse and this doctor should be on the same team even though they work on different shifts. They should be jointly responsible for avoiding any harm. Such a near miss should be documented as an incident report. Unfortunately, more than 52% employees don't report any medical error according to the 2009 AHRQ survey report on 198,000 hospital staff. Obviously, they are interested in personal performance instead of team performance. In addition, there should be a real-time problem-solving process with a prevention system for similar events. Actions to prevent harm should be immediate and should not wait for months of data collection. The objectives for individuals can be there, but they should be subservient to the team objectives.

The caregivers must also understand that the healthcare system is a dynamic and moving target. The patients' conditions change, doctors' opinions change, employees' behaviors change, and shift priorities change, in addition to disruptions and fatigue. Each of these affects the complex whole. To implement flawless execution, management must provide a structure

> Safety is not a function of individual components only. It is also a function of complex system interactions and complex influences of components throughout the system.

for doing the work with full understanding, an architecture for ultra-high safety, and an up-front budget for preventing mishaps. The architecture should include creativity, innovation, system requirements analysis for safety, technical gap analysis, and management gap analysis on the difference between ideal and actual performance. Schumacher, the author of *Small Is Beautiful*, suggests such a structure for large organizations where individuals and teams can be creative and yet conform to broad policies and criteria. It is like a person holding a lot of balloons where the balloons can float in different directions, but they are still held together by the person (system) holding the threads.

The Lessons Learned

Bruce Pasternack and Albert Viscio, the founding partners of Booz Allen Hamilton, Inc., have studied many large corporations and their chief executives [14]. They conclude that the current paradigm under which businesses are built and run is a century

> Any work that produces little or no value to the patient is likely to be unsafe.

old. They add, "While there is value in something that is tried and true, there is no value in something that is obsolete!" In my experience, any program that produces less than 5% ROI breeds shoddy work. Why go for 5% ROI when you could go for 500% ROI? Aiming at higher goals breeds innovation. You will see many examples of 500% or more ROI in this book, even on patient safety.

Summary

The latest American College of Healthcare Executives Survey of CEOs found that the percentage who said quality and safety were a "top concern" *fell* from 43% to 32% [14]. This shows the safe care is still not safe. Urgency and innovations are badly needed in healthcare.

This chapter presented the ways unsafe work can be defined. Safe hospital care is not just about doing things right but also about *doing the right things*. You will discover more right things to do once you cease doing the wrong things. That is a sign of innovation and a path to ultra-high-quality care. The two wrong things, as just learned, are insufficient understanding and indifferencity.

The next two chapters show examples and some remedies for these attributes of unsafe care. The remaining chapters are on strategies for leading to change. The World Health Organization estimates one in ten people receiving healthcare will suffer preventable harm [15]. Let us not let that happen!

References

1. Carlson, J., 2010. Leape Sees Potential for Change, ModernHealthcare.com, April 13, www.modernhealthcare.com/apps/pbcs.dll/article?AID=/20100413/NEWS/304139985#.
2. The Institute of Medicine (IOM) Report, 2006. Report on Emergency Medical Services, June 14. The report cited 1.5 million people are harmed annually by medication errors that include incorrect administration of medication, and failure to prescribe or administer medication.
3. Newman-Toker, D., and Pronovost, P., 2009. Diagnostics errors the next frontier for patient safety, *JAMA*, 301(10): 1060–1062.
4. Agency for Healthcare Research and Quality (AHRQ) Web site, 2010. Diagnostic Errors, retrieved on may 28, http://psnet.ahrq.gov/primer.aspx?primerID=12.
5. Frankfurt, H., 2005. *On Bullshit*, Princeton University Press, Princeton, NJ.
6. Gallup Management Journal, 2006. Gallup Study: Engaged Employees Inspire Company Innovation, October 12, http://gmj.gallup.com/content/24880/gal-lup-study-engaged-employees-inspire-company.aspx.
7. Maryland Hospital Association, 2009. Six Sigma Green Belt Training Manual. The source of data on the number of incorrect medical procedures at 3.4 defects per million opportunities is when a hospital meets Six Sigma requirements on a process.
8. Chassin, M., 2009. Chassin's Comments were on Issue of AHRQ WebM&M site, April, http://webmm.ahrq.gov/perspective.aspx?perspectiveID=73.
9. ABC News, 2006. Illinois Woman's ER Wait Death Ruled Homicide, September 17, http://abcnews.go.com/GMA/Health/story?id=2454685&page=1.
10. New York Daily News, 2008. Esmin Green, Who Died on Brooklyn Hospital Floor, Perished from Sitting, July 11, www.nydailynews.com/ny_local/brooklyn/2008/07/11/2008-07-11_esmin_green_who_died_on_brooklyn_hospita.html.
11. Costello, T., 2006. Hospitals work to improve ER wait times, *NBC Nightly News*, November 20, www.msnbc.msn.com/id/15817906/.
12. Wechsler, S., 2018, Emergency Excellence, LLC.
13. Singh, R., et al., 2006. Building learning practices with self empowered teams for improving patient safety, *Journal of Health Management*, 8, 91.
14. Viscio, B., and Pasternack, A., 1999. *The Centerless Corporation—Transforming Your Organization for Growth and Prosperity*, Simon & Schuster, New York.
15. Patient Safety Monitor, 2009. India to Have National Patient Safety Policy, September 14, www.thaindian.com/newsportal/health1/india-to-have-national-patient-safety-policy-azad_100247361.html.

Chapter 2

Sufficient Understanding Is a Prerequisite to Safe Care

If you know that you don't know, then you know.

—Ancient proverb

Introduction

What we don't know can result in harm. Adverse events can happen from insufficient understanding. High inherent radiation risks, unnecessary CT scans, and inaccurately working CT scan machines used in 2007 were expected to cause 29,000 new diagnoses of cancers from overexposure to radiation, and may kill nearly 15,000 Americans, according to the Archives of Internal Medicine [1]. Even a treatment gets changed a third of the time if you seek a second opinion [2]. There are at least five classes of insufficient understanding as follows:

A. **Insufficient understanding of system vulnerability.** A prevalent form of insufficient understanding is to accept the notion that human errors cause accidents. This is never true! Accidents can only happen when hazards already exist in a system (e.g., an infected wheelchair or poor enforcement of sanitization policy), and a trigger event (an active error) is initiated such as a human error (using the infected wheelchair to transport a patient or a technician keeps using a certain MRI, knowing that it is inaccurate).

B. **Insufficient understanding of what is preventable.** A frequent misunderstanding is the notion that many mishaps such as infections are unpreventable because of the complexity of healthcare interactions, pressures, and unsuccessful attempts in the past. Wrong hypothesis again! Error may indeed be unpreventable, *but usually preventing a mishap is an option!*

C. **Insufficient understanding from myopia or shortsightedness.** It is the inability to see the forest for the trees. This dysfunction is usual in practically all industries. Healthcare is not an exception. Myopic practitioners tend to focus on

> Myopic practitioners tend to create unsafe environments for decision-making.

fire fighting and overlook tectonic changes reshaping the industry [3]. Such shortsightedness is the frequent cause of band-aid solutions and weak interventions.

D. **Insufficient understanding of oversights and omissions.** This is different from myopia. It is not from shortsightedness. It is usually from lack of sanity checks, task urgency, and distractions. It can happen to even cool and balanced professionals. It also happens from not knowing anything about the paths not taken, knowing only about the outcome of the paths taken.

E. **Insufficient understanding of variation.** The minimum and maximum number of patients who may get wrong medications is predictable based on variations observed in the past. The range of waiting time in an emergency room (ER) is similarly predictable from historical data in a hospital. Quality improvement teams can act on the root causes of variation and reduce it. As we will see later in this chapter, reducing variability requires understanding the difference between common causes and special causes.

Insufficient Understanding of System Vulnerability

The Institute for Safe Medication Practices (ISMP) cited a report about the death of a patient who was accidentally injected with *topical* epinephrine. The attending surgeon and nurse mistakenly thought the syringe they were using contained lidocaine with epinephrine 1:100,000 [4].

How can two professionals make the same mistake? The reason is system vulnerability. The latent hazards in the system and an active error on their part (trigger event) caused the mishap. It is like triggering a loaded gun. If the gun was not loaded with bullets (hazards) in the first place, the accident could not have happened. Both these professionals did not seem to be fully aware of the vulnerability of the system. The loaded bullets were (1) the bottles for injection solution and topical solution looked alike and (2) their method of delivery can be mistaken such that the topical solution can be given as an injection. To prevent this hazard, the topical solution should have come in a pour bottle such that it cannot be mistakenly used for injecting.

The same ISMP alert reported a death of a child from cardiac arrest after his ear was infiltrated with a syringe containing epinephrine 1:1,000. The physician mistakenly assumed that the solution in an open cup contained lidocaine with epinephrine 1:100,000. One hazard was that the solution should have been in a standard container instead of an open cup. Another hazard was that the cup was not labeled.

Both these examples show that the system was vulnerable to accidents. Physicians should have been aware of the loaded gun. In addition, someone should have been in charge of eliminating the hazard or introducing safeguards.

One could make an argument that the physicians' job is to assume that they are supplied with the right medication, especially when they are short of time. The answer is that this assumption is very unreasonable in light of hundreds of medication errors occurring every week in hospitals. Making such an assumption is in itself an insufficient understanding.

One of the very significant components of system vulnerability is equipment vulnerability. It can fail prematurely from manufacturing errors, or fail suddenly from aging. It can also perform inaccurately. While a physician has no control on the equipment vulnerability, the system must be designed to have checks prior to a time-critical intervention. In November 2009, the operating room surgical navigation systems for orthopedic surgeries were recalled because they could result in the screen freezing, the system updating at a slow rate, or not responding. The potential harms associated with this failure are delay in surgery, reschedule of the procedure resulting in an additional surgery, risk of infection, increased morbidity, potential neurological deficits, or injury due to the surgeon operating in an unintended area [5].

Insufficient Understanding of What Is Preventable

Many professionals often make a judgment that some harmful incidences are inevitable because of too many complex events occurring in patient care. Hospital-acquired infections used to be in this category. Bloodstream infections, which attack about 80,000 patients annually in intensive care units in the United States, are such an example. But Dr Peter Pronovost at Johns Hopkins lifted the veil from this kind of misunderstanding. A *Wall Street Journal* article details how he changed the minds of his peers [6]. Later he changed minds in more than 100 hospitals.

He started with a simple checklist covered in the article: The list prescribed steps doctors and nurses in the intensive care unit should take when performing a common procedure—inserting a catheter into a vein just outside the patient's heart to allow easy delivery of intravenous drugs and fluids. The steps are simple: washing hands, cleaning the patient's skin with a disinfectant called chlorhexidine, wearing a cap and gown and using a surgical drape during the procedure, inserting the catheter through parts of the body other than the groin when possible, and removing unnecessary catheters. The Michigan study, which included more than 100 intensive care units, found that putting the checklist in place lowered the rate of bloodstream infections related to catheter use by 66%.

Some hospitals have been able to bring down the infection rates close to zero, proving that the unpreventable label was a myth for decades. This example is not unique. The World Health Organization has encountered similar successes with a surgical checklist also. Gawande [7] presents several other examples of what was thought to be unpreventable that became preventable.

We need to apply similar thinking to all hospital mishaps. We can only do this by starting with the assumption that *all mishaps are preventable* until proven otherwise. Not preventing them is usually a result of insufficient understanding if we analyze the accountability of the systems, not just that of the individual caregivers. For example, the Joint Commission and the United States Pharmacopeia acknowledge that interruptions contribute to preventable medical errors and a study submitted to them through MEDMARX attributes 43% of medication errors to workplace distractions [8]. Distractions are a system issue.

It may take a long time and we may never be able to prevent all the harm, but giving up on the effort is not the answer. If we aim at preventing all the potential mishaps and monitor prevention efforts, we can come closer to our goal.

> Start with the assumption that all adverse, sentinel, and never events are preventable. Then test your assumptions.

Insufficient Understanding from Myopia

Shortsightedness can easily lead to potential wrong decisions. Turning away patients from an ER because of shortage of personnel can be shortsighted in terms of increased potential harm to the patients and in loss of income. I gave a presentation at a famous hospital on a special technique for preventing adverse events. The response was that they had hundreds of known problems, and they had to take care of them first. They failed to see that adverse and sentinel events destroy the reputation of the hospital, result in very costly legal actions, and turn away customers. They wanted to concentrate on firefighting and overlooked the opportunity to make changes that matter the most.

Shortsightedness often stems from overconfidence in the form of diagnosis errors. Schiff [9] points out a cause of such an oversight to an open-loop system, also called a "non-feedback-controlled" system. He says:

> This approach does not use feedback to calibrate its output or determine if the desired goal is achieved. Because open-loop systems do not observe the output of the process they are controlling, they cannot engage in learning.

He relates the open-loop system to diagnosis errors:

> To an unacceptably large extent, clinical diagnosis is an open-loop system. Typically clinicians learn about their diagnostic successes or failures in various ad hoc ways (e.g., a knock on the door from a server with a malpractice subpoena). Physicians lack systematic methods for calibrating diagnostic decisions based on feedback from their outcomes.

David Newman-Toker and Peter Pronovost [10] report that an estimated 40,000–80,000 hospital deaths per year are due to misdiagnosis—defined as diagnoses that are missed, wrong, or delayed. Typically, they note, diagnostic errors were thought to originate with individual doctors lacking proper training and skills they should have, and physicians were blamed who haven't produced solutions. As with successful approaches to reducing treatment errors, they point out that reducing diagnostic errors will likely require a focus on larger "system" failures that affect medical practice overall. This is a critical area where more understanding is required.

We also need to understand that preventing adverse events requires more advanced approaches such as the fault tree analysis [11] and tools from successful industries, such as aerospace and nuclear, that help in identifying the chain of events that can result in an adverse event. These tools are hardly mentioned in the healthcare literature. Preventing adverse events results in profitability and high quality when one considers the cost of negligence and refusal of reimbursements from Medicare. This book is an attempt to convince readers that safety results in a high return on investment if a culture of continuous innovation is implemented instead of the culture of marginal quality improvements.

One question is why hospitals have not developed or adopted the evidence-based techniques for preventing adverse, sentinel, and "never" events from other industries? An answer seems to be that, with so many problems every day, hospitals tend to pick only the low-hanging fruit on the trees. The need for long-term excellence is often postponed.

> We have to go beyond the Six Sigma program to prevent adverse, sentinel, and "never" events.

McFarland [3] offers a method to avoid falling prey to myopia. He found a common thread among the breakthrough companies he studied. They encouraged people to question the fundamental assumptions behind major decisions and buck the system. His team found so many people bucking the system during interviews that they started calling these people "insultants." He defines an insultant as someone willing to ask the tough questions that cause an organization to think critically about its fundamental assumptions and will go to great lengths to get their organizations to reevaluate the position.

Fred Lee, in his book *If Disney Ran Your Hospital: 9½ Things You Would Do Differently*, gives a common example of shortsightedness. In an effort to increase patient satisfaction scores, managers often adopt programs that are shortsighted and superficial, he claims. He recommends a shift in emphasis from caregiver service to patient experience. His measure of a good patient experience: nothing bad happens during the hospital stay!

Insufficient Understanding of Oversights and Omissions

Wrong-site surgery often happens from incomplete information due to oversights and omissions. A patient-safety blog had the following example of insufficient understanding from incomplete information [12].

Here is an example of what has been reported and the initial changes made as a result of Massachusetts hospitals' analyses of "serious reportable events," as required in the new Chapter 305 state law.

> A Spanish-speaking-only patient was admitted for surgery to release a left "trigger finger," a condition where the finger catches in a bent position and straightens with a snap. Instead, she had a carpal tunnel release, a completely different operation on the wrist and not the finger. This mistake was not discovered by the team in the operating room, but by the doctor when he returned to his office and looked at the patient's medical record.
>
> To avoid this error from recurring, the hospital changed its policy from having the surgeon sign the site of operation to requiring the surgeon to sign the actual incision site. Also in this case, not all team members participated in the time-out. In response, two more important issues were addressed by the facility: first, the policy was changed to require the presence of an interpreter for non-English-speaking patients, so they could answer questions about the operation and verify the site, as required by the Universal protocol; and second, a revised hand-off routine was instituted to accommodate changes in staff immediately before and during the operation.

Another similar accident took place in Minnesota [13] as follows:

> Doctors at Methodist Hospital in a suburb of Minneapolis–St. Paul mistakenly removed the only healthy kidney from a patient who had kidney cancer.
>
> Instead of removing the cancerous kidney, they took out the healthy one. The mistake was only noted after the removed kidney was examined by a pathologist, and it was found to have no cancer. The tragic error occurred even after careful protocol was observed in the operating room in which the chart was double-checked and every member of the surgical team reviewed the case.
>
> The error was traced back to a note in the patient's chart made weeks before the surgery, when a surgeon marked the wrong kidney on the chart. "This is a tragic error on our part and we accept full responsibility for this," said Dr Samuel Carlson, the chief medical officer for Park Nicollet Health Services, which operates Methodist Hospital. While mistakes of this nature are generally not widely publicized, the hospital decided to go to the press in the interest of transparency and patient safety. Minnesota health records reveal that 24 "wrong site" errors occurred between 2006 and 2007, two of them at Methodist Hospital.

> **Work done without challenge is likely to be the work done without sufficient understanding.**

Another source of oversights and omissions is the lack of patient contact. With electronic patient management systems, the bedside discussion with patients is becoming a lost art. The following incidence is a symptom of the current state of the patient as a stakeholder. This incidence was reported by Dr Dena Rifkin ("Impersonal Hospital Care," *New York Times*, November 17, 2009) on his own family member who was a patient:

> A close family member was recently hospitalized after nearly collapsing at home. He was promptly checked in, and an EKG was done within 15 minutes. He was given a bar-coded armband, his pain level was assessed, blood was drawn, x-rays and stress tests were performed, and he was discharged 24 hours later with a revised medication list after being offered a pneumonia vaccine and an opportunity to fill out a living will.
>
> The only problem was an utter lack of human attention. An ER physician admitted him to a hospital service that rapidly evaluates patients for potential heart attacks. No one noted the blood tests that suggested severe dehydration or took enough history to figure out why he might be fatigued.
>
> A doctor was present for a few minutes at the beginning of his stay, and fewer the next day. Even my presence, as a family member and physician, did not change the cursory attitude of the doctors and nurses we met.
>
> Yet his hospitalization met all the current standards for quality care.
>
> As a profession, we are paying attention to the details of medical errors—to ambiguous chart abbreviations, to vaccination practices and hand-washing, and many other important, or at least quantifiable, matters.
>
> But as we bustle from one well-documented chart to the next, no one is counting whether we are still paying attention to the human beings. No one is counting whether we admit that the best source of information, the best protection from medical error, the best opportunity to make a difference—that all of these things have been here all along.
>
> The answers are with the patients, and we must remember the unquantifiable value of asking the right questions. The lessons learned from these findings are that we need to understand the system issues and understand the needs of the customer.

Insufficient Understanding of Variation

The cause of cancer from MRI mentioned at the beginning of this chapter is an example of insufficient understanding of variation. All equipment performances, including MRI, perform in a range of values. The actual delivered values are usually different from what is indicated on the visual display. An MRI will deliver more radiation than chosen or less than chosen, depending on the inherent variability in the equipment. The variation can come from internal causes such as the design of the equipment itself, as well as from external causes such as a repair technician forgetting to calibrate or making an error in calibration. Variation also applies to the number of patients exposed to higher risk such as cancer. The more unnecessary the tests, the more the variation in the incidence of cancer. Redberg [1], who wrote a commentary on the studies, said "U.S. doctors' enthusiasm for the tests has led to an explosion in their use that is putting patients at risk. While certainly some of the scans are incredibly important and lifesaving, it is also certain that some of them were not necessary."

The internal variation is called *common cause variation* because the cause is inherent in the design of the system until it is removed. It occurs randomly, which explains why some patients get attention right away and others wait for hours to get the attention of the doctor. External variation is called the *special cause variation*. This not inherent in the process. For example, a patient waits for hours in the ER because the MRI machine suddenly breaks down, or a patient monitoring device does not measure vital signs accurately on that particular day. Special cause variation can be traced to the source eliminated while common cause variation can only be reduced by improving the underlying process [14]. We must be vigilant of how much variation exists in a day-to-day task. If a variation is excessive and can result in patient harm, it must be reduced using quality improvement methods.

Some Remedies

To gain sufficient understanding, employees should be encouraged to think outside the box and yet find a balance with what has always worked well. Since failure seems punitive, employees are afraid to try elegant solutions. Then they try to fit a square peg into someone else's outdated round hole. Some very useful strategies can be:

a. Aim at zero defects for all "never," adverse, and sentinel events. Chapter 8 on translocating aerospace system safety techniques will illustrate some proven methods. They have been successfully implemented for more than 40 years in the nuclear, chemical, and automotive industries.

b. Use innovation techniques for managing complex problems. A successful industry practice is to allow a very short time for solutions instead of months in traditional quality assurance and patient-safety processes. When we create a sense of urgency, employees think differently. They come up with complete, comprehensive, and cheap solutions. That is the standard strategy at organizations such as Apple Computer, Microsoft, and Google.

c. The best way to promote understanding is to stop doing wrong things. Then the right things will start to emerge. Start by asking questions in the Socratic style. Ask peers questions such as the following:
   - Can the lab test results be flawed?
   - Can we do anything to prevent false negatives and false positives?
   - Are the adverse events reported preventable?
   - Do employees report all the incidences and near misses?
   - Are near misses analyzed to improve the system?
   - What percent of patients are impressed by the care? Ask why they are impressed?
   - How can we prevent the "never" events?
   - Do the doctors and nurses challenge each other? Why not?
   - What is it that the patients and families are not telling?

My experience of 25 years of solving very complex problems suggests that the solutions come intuitively if you keep asking questions with creative brainstorming and use innovative thinking. This method of brainstorming is covered in Chapter 4. Below are some considerations.

a. *Brainstorm on unknown-unknowns.* Many healthcare professionals know some things do not make sense, but they are afraid to speak up. Others have seen many near misses such as changing a diagnosis for a patient, administering the wrong dose of medication, missing a dose, not knowing what other medications a patient is taking, realizing that a wrong limb might be amputated minutes prior to the surgery, switching x-rays between patients, giving a baby to the wrong parents—the list seems endless. Many have not erred themselves but they have seen their colleagues do it. But they cannot report the mistakes of their colleagues and peers. Since this information on hazards is critical and so secret, it is unavailable by traditional means. The aviation industry calls such faults and hazards "unknown-unknowns." But many can be known. Here is one way:

The Federal Aviation Authority (FAA) had about 130 ways listed for near misses of aircraft accidents in their database. They wanted American Airlines employees to be aware of them. American Airlines was not impressed by only 130 ways a near miss can take place. It suggested asking the employees, with full anonymity. The employees did not have to declare their name nor the names of colleagues and peers. They were asked to report on any mistake anyone could make. Since this survey was not punitive, the employees came up with about 12,000 potential ways! [15] A similar incidence took place when I was in charge of safety for the Baltimore subway design. Our team came up with only about 50 things that could go wrong after the trains are deployed. I interviewed employees and repair crews of the San Francisco Bay Area Rapid Transit (BART); they gave me a list of about 2,000 potential problems! If you want to know the unknown-unknowns in a hospital, ask employees, patients, their families, housekeepers, and social workers.

If we ask each employee of a hospital about unpublished and potential incidences, each employee can probably have at least 20 suggestions. Some will have more than 100 issues on the list. Hospital environment and complexity may be unique, but people are not afraid to speak if they do not have to disclose their identity. What may keep them from reporting is when they see too many failed solutions, or their suggestions are not being implemented, or the safety and efficacy processes do not have sufficient teeth in them.

The unknown-unknowns include cognitive errors, which are rarely reported. The AHRQ patient safety website [16] shows the following matrix of biases and diagnosis errors (Table 2.1):

Table 2.1 Matrix of Biases in Diagnostic Intervention

Cognitive Bias	Definition	Example
Availability heuristic	Diagnosis of current patient biased by experience with past cases	A patient with crushing chest pain was incorrectly treated for a myocardial infarction, despite indications that an aortic dissection was present.
Anchoring heuristic (premature closure)	Relying on initial diagnostic impression, despite subsequent information to the contrary	Repeated positive blood cultures with *Corynebacterium* were dismissed as contaminants; the patient was eventually diagnosed with *Corynebacterium endocarditis*.
Framing effects	Diagnostic decision-making unduly biased by subtle cues and collateral information	A heroin-addicted patient with abdominal pain was treated for opiate withdrawal, but proved to have a bowel perforation.
Blind obedience	Placing undue reliance on test results or "expert" opinion	A false-negative rapid test for *Streptococcus pharyngitis* resulted in a delay in diagnosis.

It may be difficult to put safeguards against many diagnostics errors. Being aware of the bias during diagnosis is the first step toward adequate knowledge. There is a famous saying: If you know that you don't know, then you know.

> If you want to uncover the problems under the rug, ask employees, patients, their families, housekeepers, and social workers with full anonymity.

b. This section applies to decision processes when a team decision is required, such as developing a new process or solving complex problems in a quality improvement team. Understand that consensus can be a shoddy practice. The leaders pride themselves in building consensus during important decisions. What we need is conflicts instead. Without different viewpoints, the uninformed decisions will be made. For example, someone discusses a new surgical procedure and everyone likes it without knowing the pros and cons. I was a consultant for therapeutic x-ray equipment. It could deliver regular chest radiation if the med technician pressed the numeral 1 on the computer keyboard and 40 times more radiation if the technician pressed the numeral 2 on the keyboard. The supplier trained the hospital staff. The procedure was so simple, everyone accepted it without any question and paid compliments to the supplier for making it so simple. In the first week alone, ten different hospitals killed ten patients! The FDA forced the supplier to recall all the devices.

What went wrong? The hospital had too much consensus without challenge. All the accidents happened because the med techs inadvertently pressed the numeral 2 because it was next to the numeral 1. No one in the hospital realized that someone can accidentally

> If everyone votes YES without providing justification, your decision should be NO.

press 1 instead of 2. The lesson learned: Never accept consensus until there is some challenge. If no one challenges, accidents are likely.

Of course, once someone challenges, the conflicts must be resolved. The solution should be convincing to the person who brought up the conflict. I was facilitating a team in which a hybrid vehicle design included a 340-volt electrical circuit. A manufacturing engineer brought up a conflict. He claimed that the driver of the vehicle can get electrocuted if the vehicle had to go through high water in heavy rain. All the seven design engineers tried to convince him that the high voltage will cut off before the current becomes fatal. He was not sure if the circuits would work safely under all conditions for the entire life of the vehicle. Ordinarily, he would have been voted down or ridiculed by the majority. Being a part of the team, I took his side since I myself had a doubt. We spent an hour on discussion. Suddenly, the manufacturing engineer had an "aha" moment. He told the engineers that if they were so confident of its safety, he wanted one of them to actually drive the vehicle through a large water puddle available for this test. None of the engineers volunteered! We wound up using redundant circuits as a safeguard. Had we gone by the consensus or majority vote, this new product could have been a disaster.

So, how do you know that you have no real consensus? Most people just want to vote yes so they can go back to their text messages on phones and pagers. Others may be doing their work on laptops while you are trying to get their attention. These situations are common. Going by the consensus is often a mistake. It is better to select a person who can be trusted for crafty work to make the final decisions *after* hearing everyone. Even better, have a team of two to make the decisions, the second person being an outsider who has no vested interest in the hospital.

Summary

It is hoped the reader has a good feel now for what are the wrong practices. The question one may have is how can we start doing the right things? The best way to start doing right things is to stop doing wrong things!

The best way to start doing right things is to stop doing wrong things!

Once we start doing right things, we also need to do them efficiently. If the execution is shoddy, we still cannot control the risks. Flawless execution is the key. The next chapter is the key to flawless execution.

References

1. Reuter News On MSNBC, 2009. 15,000 Will Die from CT Scans Done in 1 Year, December 14, www.msnbc.msn.com/id/34420356/ns/health-cancer/.
2. Oz, M., 2009. Dr. Oz on *Dr. Oz Show*, *NBC Television*, December 14.
3. McFarland, K., 2008. *The Breakthrough Company*, Crown Publishing, New York.
4. FDA Patient Safety News, 2009. Patient Deaths from Injection of Topical Epinephrine, September, www.accessdata.fda.gov/scripts/cdrh/cfdocs/psn/transcript.cfm?show=90.
5. FDA Recall Notice, 2009. FDA.org, November 28, www.fda.gov/Safety/Recalls/ucm192003.htm.
6. Goldstein, J., 2009. As easy as 1-2-3?, Article in *Wall Street Journal*, October 27.
7. Gawande, A., 2002. *Complications: A Surgeon's Notes on an Imperfect Science*, Metropolitan Books, New York.
8. Brixey, J., et al., 2005. Interruptions in workflow for RNs in a level one trauma center, In *American Medical Informatics Association Symposium Proceedings*, www.ncbi.nlm.nih.gov/pmc/articles/PMC1560877/pdf/amia2005_0086.pdf.
9. Schiff, G., 2008. Minimizing diagnostic error: The importance of follow-up and feedback, *The American Journal of Medicine*, 121(5A): 538–542.
10. Newman-Toker, D., and Pronovost, P., 2009. Diagnostics errors the next frontier for patient safety, *JAMA*, 301(10): 1060–1062.
11. Raheja, D., and Escano, M., 2009. Patient safety-reducing healthcare risks through fault tree analysis, *Journal of System Safety*, 45(5): 13–15.
12. Patient Safety Blog-Telling Our Stories, 2009. Write on the Incision Site: Wrong Site Wrist/Finger Surgery, September, http://patientadvocare.blogspot.com/2009/09/write-on-incision-site-wrong-site.html.
13. Austin, A., 2008. Minnesota Hospital Removes Healthy Kidney from Cancer, Patient, Buzzle.com, www.buzzle.com/articles/minnesota-hospital-removes-healthy-kidney-from-cancer-patient.html.
14. McLaughlin, C., and Kaluzny, A., 2006. *Continuous Quality Improvement in Healthcare*, Jones and Bartlett, Sudbury, MA.
15. Speech by Dr. Douglas R. Farrow, Fifth International Workshop on Risk Analysis and Performance Measurement in Aviation sponsored by FAA and NASA, Baltimore, August 19–21, 2003.
16. The AHRQ Website, 2010. Diagnostics Errors, retrieved on May 26, http://psnet.ahrq.gov/primer.aspx?primerID=12.

Chapter 3

Preventing "Indifferencity" to Enhance Patient Safety

Some people grin and bear it; others smile and change it.

—Source unknown

Introduction

Each patient is unique. For a flawless execution of safety, each caregiver has to plan the implementation with some unique steps that matter to each patient. The care has to be patient-centered. When caregivers are not engaged to this goal, the seeds of indifference germinate. In Chapter 1, we defined "indifferencity" as performance without passion, or without due concern or done diligently in a substandard manner. Functional departments must work together to sustain the foundation of safe care.

This chapter explores the symptoms of indifferencity and their causes. The rest of the chapters cover the methods and strategies to eradicate these symptoms and formulate effective solutions. A good safe care program transcends personal biases and utilizes all the tools of innovation. Table 3.1 summarizes the identified symptoms and some major causes, based on my experience of more than 30 years in safety in the medical device, aerospace, and healthcare fields.

Performance without Passion

Safety requires doing right things the right way, at all times! This can only happen with the right attitude and the right environment, with full support from the senior management. The following root causes must be treated.

Table 3.1 The Symptoms and Causes of Indifferencity

	Major Symptoms	Potential Causes
Causes of Indifferencity (Substandard Care)		
I	Performance without passion	Not learning from mistakes
		Inattention to the voice of the patient
		Making premature judgments without critical thinking
		Lack of teamwork
		Lack of feedback and follow-up
II	Performance without due concern	Lack of accountability
		Encouraging substandard work
		Reacting to unsafe incidences instead of proactively seeking them
		Inattention to clinical systems
		Difference between management and caregivers
		Poor risk management
III	Performance diligently done in a substandard manner	Doing substandard work, knowing it is substandard
		Ignoring bad behavior
		Inattention to quality

Not Learning from Mistakes

When healthcare professionals do not report errors, the opportunity to improve the system is missed and potentially unsafe patient care can take place, which could lead to patient deterioration. This becomes a case of indifferencity because patient care continues to be potentially unsafe. Even worse, not learning from mistakes eventually results in even bigger mistakes.

A journal of patient safety on a survey [1] summarizes the seriousness of this dangerous precedence: Physicians have traditionally been reluctant to report errors, due in part to logistical barriers but also due to cultural barriers that inhibit error reporting. This survey of practicing obstetrician/gynecologists found that only slightly more than half of respondents felt comfortable reporting errors they had witnessed. Interestingly, physicians who had themselves been the victim of an error, or who had a family member injured as a result of an error, were more likely to both report errors and describe witnessing errors in their own practice.

Inattention to the Voice of the Patient

As more and more hospitals are adopting computerized patient tracking systems, the bedside contact with a patient is becoming progressively less and less. Doctors have to spend more and more time with computers on tasks such as electronic medical records, resulting in less time for the patients. More importantly, the doctors are interrupted frequently especially in the emergency departments. A study of three teaching urban hospitals [2] where each physician was tracked for 180 minutes showed that the average number of interruptions was 30.9 and average number of breaks in task was 20.7. The number of interruptions and breaks works out to be 60.6 or 20.2 per hour. An interruption was defined as an event that briefly required the attention of the physician. A break in task was defined as an event requiring attention of more than 10 seconds and resulted in subsequently changing the task. The patient can hardly get time to communicate, with the doctor listening to him or her. Many doctors are overworked. Sometimes they ask the patients, "How are you?" and quickly have to turn to other patients.

With the technological edge to the practice of medicine today, people contact is getting marginalized even by the physicians. As a result, the patient is almost ignored on a routine basis and best treatment approaches are hardly discussed with the patients. Fortunately, there are still many physicians who ask every patient: "Would you like to tell me anything that may help you?"

> Not listening to what the patient is trying to say is performance without passion.

Making Premature Judgments without Critical Thinking

Sometimes we make familiar diagnoses on the symptoms that seem familiar, overlooking the need to know more. Mark Graber, Chief, Medical Service, Veterans Administration Medical Center in New York, equates this to falling in love with the first puppy [3]. He blames this type of premature closure on cognitive errors that can result from faulty synthesis, faulty knowledge, or faulty data gathering. When the decisions are made on high-risk intervention, critical thinking can be a good mitigation strategy. It can be defined as "the careful, deliberate determination of whether one should accept, reject, or suspend judgment [4]." An international panel of expert nurses identified ten habits of the mind for critical thinking and seven skills of critical thinking in nursing [5]. They are as follows:

- Confidence
- Contextual perspective
- Creativity
- Flexibility
- Inquisitiveness
- Intellectual integrity
- Intuition
- Open-mindedness
- Perseverance
- Reflection

The list is generic. It applies to all healthcare decisions. Unfortunately, in the interest of reaching a consensus, the caregivers often make a mistake of going with "the process," called *groupthink*. It is a phenomenon of a group to minimize conflict and reach consensus. Often it results in ignoring most of the components of critical thinking mentioned above. People routinely try to please their peers in a group situation and tend not to disagree, resulting in substandard care. Wikipedia adds this insight on a groupthink process:

> During groupthink, members of the group avoid promoting viewpoints outside the comfort zone of consensus thinking. A variety of motives for this may exist, such as

a desire to avoid being seen as foolish, or a desire to avoid embarrassing or angering other members of the group.

Such a groupthink phenomenon is often the backbone of standards and regulations in which a minimum standard is set such that all in the group can agree. Therefore, all standards should be viewed as a standard of minimum conduct—not the best practice!

Lack of Teamwork

There are processes, systems, and goals in healthcare where teamwork is absolutely essential. They require multifunctional participation with a patient-centered goal. Appropriate communications and teamwork can be a major precursor of optimal healthcare practice. Instead, the familiar protocol is that each function has its own goal to excel in with its own chosen agenda. Usually the family members of patients, who often represent the voice of the patient, are left out of the team such as in the case of baby Josie King [6] where her mother Sorrel was totally ignored in spite of her screaming attempts to get the attention of the doctors and nurses while Josie was dying from dehydration. Josie was a little over 1 year old when she was hospitalized for 60% burns on her body from very hot boiling water in a bathtub. The hospital treated her in a reasonable time. The doctors issued the discharge papers and the family and friends were preparing for a celebration. Suddenly the situation took a 180° turn! Josie was dehydrating terribly. Sorrel tried to confront doctors and nurses but almost everyone ignored her, according to her. Josie received a dose of narcotic painkiller methadone instead of badly needed fluids. Sorrel tried to protest the use of wrong and dangerous medication, but she could not convince the staff to take her seriously. The doctors and nurses did not seem to work as a team either because they did not discuss Josie's dehydration with one another. One thing led to another, and Josie died from cardiac arrest. Since then, Sorrel has started a crusade for promoting patient safety to help others and wrote the book *Josie's Story* describing the entire episode.

A roadblock to good teamwork can be the physicians on pay-for-service. They cannot devote much time to teams. Their resistance for involvement may leave a big gap between what the team should do and what they can actually accomplish. Other functions get involved but they are also usually short of time. Teams become dysfunctional in such an environment. They lack efficacy and synergy. A Veterans Health Administration (VA) study published in the Archives of Surgery [7] concludes that poor communication among surgical team members is the leading cause of wrong surgeries, including wrong procedures, wrong patients, wrong body parts, and wrong implants. The study also includes the following conclusion:

> About 20 percent of adverse events between 2001 and 2006 reported by the VA were caused by communication failures, such as poor handoffs of critical information. More than 15 percent were caused by problems with the preoperative timeout process, which involves redundant checks on patient's identity, test results, and other vital information. One in every 18,955 surgeries involves a wrong surgery, and the VA found 209 adverse events and 314 close calls in which mistakes were discovered before patients were harmed. There were no adverse events reported when the procedures were followed, says James P. Bagian, MD, a co-author of the study.

It is not all doom and gloom. There are bright spots. Almost all Pittsburgh regional hospitals use the Toyota Production System, thanks to the former Secretary of Treasury Paul O'Neil who introduced the concept. In this system, a team is formed as soon as a quality or safety problem arises. Many hospitals across the United States are using it. The team is encouraged to stop the process (safely) until the problem is fixed and a prevention plan is developed. If any person on the team feels a patient is in the way of harm and the team is unable to mitigate it, he or she is encouraged to speak to a high-level executive in charge through a phone line dedicated for this purpose. This ensures efficiency and speed of right action, not a band-aid. The team then is accountable for validating the improved process [8].

Lack of Feedback and Follow-Up

Since a physician's role is central to diagnosis and treatment, they are the ones that need most feedback. But there are still many barriers that need to be removed. Some barriers require research. Others require systematical thinking, analysis, and senior management support. Schiff [9] highlights these in a very candid way:

- Physician's lack of time and systematic approaches for obtaining the follow-up
- High frequency of symptoms for which no definite diagnosis is ever established
- Threatening nature of critical feedback makes MDs defensive
- Fragmentation and discontinuities of care
- Reliance on patient return for follow-up
- Managed care discourages access
- Information breakage

Sanders [10] presents the cases of successful diagnosis in complex ailments. She goes into extraordinary detail as to why trials and errors lead to a wrong diagnosis. She suggests that doctors who arrive at the right diagnosis quickly are the ones who use the irreplaceable tools: a phone call and a friend who may view it from a different angle!

Performance without Due Concern

Lack of Accountability

Errors are committed even by those who try to do the right things. Therefore, many hospitals adopted the "no blame" policy. But systems can have limitations. A no-blame policy without accountability can result in laxity in enforcing safe practices, ignoring unsafe behavior, and looking the other way when high risks are obvious. Such inactions on part of the hospitals can introduce even higher risks. In most cases, the system can be changed to prevent opportunities for making errors, or mitigated in a way to intercept them or avoid harm to patients. Physicians Wachter and Pronovost, the famous icons of patient safety, suggest a balance between "no blame" and accountability [11]. They credit patient-safety pioneer Lucian Leape for creating the awareness that we need a more aggressive approach to poorly performing physicians who have more autonomy. They describe some system barriers to physician accountability:

- A given safety practice may be supported by weak evidence.
- Providers may worry about unexpected consequences for their patients.
- Providers may not know what behavior is expected, what the underlying rationale for the behavior is, or how the behavior is being audited.
- There may be a dysfunctional system where administrators lack essential training in human factors and systems engineering.

They point out that accountability is not the issue of what happens to the busy or distracted caregiver who forgets to clean hands or fails to perform a timeout once. It is the issue of what should happen to those who do it habitually and willfully, despite education, counseling, and system improvements. Ignoring it is "indifferencity." A reasonable redemption should be encouraged, such as asking the team that skipped timeout before a surgery to implement an improved process to prevent such incidences. Reprimands such as no privilege to do no surgery for two weeks may be unnecessary.

Encouraging Substandard Work

Healthcare professionals are not immune to substandard work. In many instances, the management encourages substandard performance and care for various reasons, including financial, and the patient and physicians, may be ignored and marginalized, resulting in litigation.

A newly hired radiologist in a California hospital discovered that staffing, training, and supervision were so deficient that they represented a hazard to patients. The staff resisted his efforts to improve the process. He reprimanded several technologists for unsatisfactory performance. As a result he ran into problems with his clinical supervisors. Ultimately, he was accused of racism and sexual harassment that the jury rejected. The radiologist won $11.4 million judgment against the hospital [12].

In a hospital in California, Dr Angelique Campen's daughter, born premature, acquired irreversible brain damage from substandard work [13]. While in the neonatal unit Dr Campen noticed that her baby's heart rate was extremely slow and at times she actually stopped breathing. She complained, but the staff in the neonatal center attributed the symptoms to the anesthetic used when a catheter was removed a few days before. Despite her protests, it was 11 hours before the baby was treated with antibiotics. In the meantime, toxins did irreversible damage. She sued the hospital. The jury awarded her a $7,379,000 verdict.

Such examples indicate that even healthcare professionals are not immune from substandard work. The symptoms obviously point to a widespread phenomenon.

Reacting to Unsafe Incidences Instead of Proactively Seeking Them

A survey on the use of incident reports to document medical errors was sent to a random sample of 200 physicians and nurses at a large children's hospital [14]. The statistics in the following results are likely to apply to many hospitals.

A total of 140 surveys were returned, including 74 from physicians and 66 by nurses. Overall, 34.8% of respondents indicated that they had reported <20% of their perceived medical errors in the previous 12 months. Commonly listed reasons for underreporting included lack of certainty about what is considered an error and concerns about implicating others.

Suggestions included the following:

■ Education about which errors should be reported.
■ Feedback on a regular basis about the errors reported and about individual events.
■ Evidence of system changes because of reports of errors.
■ Specific changes in the incident report system could lead to more reporting by physicians and nurses.

The report concluded that medical errors in pediatric patients are significantly underreported in incident report systems, particularly by physicians.

The lack of incidence reporting can be compensated by using "What if" analyses with formal tools such as failure mode and effects analysis (FMEA), fault tree analysis (FTA), and event tree analysis (ETA). Most patient-safety officers and managers agree that quality processes are reactive rather than using a proactive approach. The number of hospitals that proactively use tools for what else can go wrong is very small. The Joint Commission requires using FMEA at least once a year on a critical process. The question is why not for all the critical processes? It is hoped this tool will be a standard on every critical process. Those who work only to react to problems apparently are prone to "indifferencity" and overlook preventing many more future mishaps. Healthcare safety and quality cannot be trusted to those who do only firefighting.

Besides safety and quality, most of the clinical teams are also reactive when they should be proactive. At morbidity and mortality (M&M) conferences, one discovers that surgeons/physicians discuss causes and are open to suggestions. But they rarely go back and change the system to prevent future mishaps. The solution lies in reengineering the system. Dr Leo Gordon, associate director of Surgical Education at Cedars-Sinai Medical Center, is an exception. He uses the M&M conferences proactively. In his article "Rediscovering the Power of the Surgical M&M Conference," he says [15]:

> There is a slumbering giant—one that carries the potential to transform surgical safety—merely waiting to be awakened and freshened up. Now how, you may ask, can a transformation of this tired old remnant of days past help us create a safer medical environment? How can an assembly of surgeons, cloistered in a meeting steeped in the ABCs (abuse, berate, and chastise) of traditional surgical education, help us reach our safety goals by reinventing itself?
>
> The answer lies in the evolving recognition by medical educators, department chiefs, program directors, and patient safety officers that this conference can be transformed into a vibrant patient safety curriculum. To understand the transformation, we must begin by considering today's typical M&M conference—the quintessential "one-shot" deal:
>
> ■ The collective wisdom of the department assembles.
> ■ Critical issues of patient safety are discussed. Somewhere in these discussions are the essential patient-safety lessons so necessary to the education of the physician; however, these are often glossed over or ignored.
> ■ The meeting ends.

What is done to preserve those essential patient-safety and error-reducing points—even when they have been raised and debated? The answer is usually straightforward: nothing is done. It is as if a culture arose that never developed a written language—never took the time to memorialize its most important error-reducing insights. This culture—the culture of medicine—never canonized patient safety.

Dr Gordon has initiated a proactive tool called M+M Matrix in which all the information from the M&M discussion fed into a matrix for curriculum improvements. All the interns, nurses, and residents are trained on lessons learned and taught on how to avoid the mishaps. A moderator is assigned to constantly incorporate lessons learned into the curriculum. We all can learn to be proactive using this simple approach.

Inattention to Clinical Systems

A system has to be understood in the context of subsystems. Each subsystem is also a system in its right. It can be called a microsystem. It is one of several subsystems of a larger system integral to system performance [16]. An analogy would be a human body where the whole body is a system and the nervous system or the respiratory system is a microsystem. The microsystems are inter-related to each other as well as to the system performance. One reason many teams are marginal in performance because they are organized by *ad hoc* choices instead of from the power of clinical microsystems that affect a system of a group of patients. For example, the manner in which a pharmacy microsystem functions affects the intensive care microsystems and vice versa. They both in turn affect the patient outcome system.

Finding time to improve care can be difficult, but the only way to improve and maintain quality, safety, efficiency, and flexibility is by blending analysis, change, measuring, and rede-signing into the regular patterns and the daily habits of frontline clinicians and staff. With the absence of the intelligent and dedicated improvement work by all staff in all units, the quality, efficiency, and pride in work will not be sustained. An important principle of clinical microsys-tems is that the effectiveness of a healthcare system cannot be better than the microsystems that make up the system [17]. The Institute of Health Improvement adds [18]: "A general clinical microsystem includes, in addition to doctors and nurses, other clinicians, some administrative support and a small population of patients, with information and information technology as criti-cal 'participants.'"

Difference in Mind-Set between Management and Employees

In almost every organization, there are technical gaps and the management gaps. A techni-cal gap is the difference between what employees do versus what is the state of the art. A management gap is the difference between what management preaches and the state of the art in management for the applicable environment. For example, most management gurus say that management is responsible for about 85% mishaps, and employees may be responsible for a good portion of the rest [19]. If management actions support their claim, then there is no gap. If not, then there is a gap between the mindset of management and the employees. Usually, independent surveys by an outside agency are an effective tool to determine the difference and the symptoms.

One company, General Electric, has demonstrated that this gap can be minimized. It has an architecture that remains intact even though the top leaders change. The structure consists of the president training vice presidents at a remote corporate training site. Being offsite, the training is the only focus. There are open discussions both ways. Then the vice presidents train their senior leadership the same way, not necessarily offsite. There is a feedback both ways. This structure con-tinues all the way to the lowest level of management. Usually employee surveys are done to serve as an audit.

Organizations that cultivate the leader's mindset can succeed over the long term because indi-viduals are expected to think for themselves. Even as the organization grows larger, it continues to be effective because individuals at all levels are thinking about how they can effectively achieve the desired result.

Poor Risk Management

Risk management process in most hospitals is broken based on my interviews with more than 100 healthcare executives. They simply react to yesterday's events, which is the opposite of risk man-agement. It is only a damage control process. A risk is something intangible, something that can happen in the future. Its probability is elusive. It is an art and a science of measuring the value of the intangibles and making an appropriate mitigation plan that still produces positive return on investment. It is like an investment in health insurance. If you do not get sick, you may think that you wasted money but you can sleep securely at night. If you do become catastrophically disabled, the return on investment is very high. Either way you win. The details of risk management can be found in Chapter 8.

Performance Diligently Done in a Substandard Manner

Continuing to Do Substandard Work, Knowing It Is Substandard

Doctors, nurses, and other support sometimes continue to do substandard work in the interest of providing timely service. Under emergency circumstances such actions may be acceptable but should be prevented in extended time.

Not all doctors sanitize their hands prior to seeing a patient. Research has shown that healthcare workers clean their hands effectively only about 50% of the time according to Katherine Greider [20], a medical writer. Every year over two million patients get infections from the hospital and about 90,000 die. Doctors, their gowns, and stethoscopes are not the only source of infection. It can come from furniture, bed rails, call buttons, mobile phones, handshakes, wheel chairs, ventilation, from a patient in the room, drapes, TVs, bathrooms, faucets, and improper room sanitization by housekeepers after a discharge of a previous patient.

A family friend's father had a brain tumor. The MRI completely missed it because it was not working right that day. He was given the wrong diagnosis resulting in the overgrowth of the tumor. When the tumor was finally diagnosed in another hospital, the family discovered through doctor-to-doctor communication that the MRI was not working right in the first hospital. Should not someone have challenged the diagnosis when the MRI was not working right? Faulty equipment can also cause disastrous results. Some patients at the VA hospitals were exposed to overdose and others to underdose in a nuclear medicine treatment over a year. The staff was aware that the equipment was not working right according to a report [21]. The *New York Times'* examination of the prostate cancer unit at the hospital also found that the errors resulted from a system-wide regulatory failure, in which none of the safeguards intended to protect veterans from poor medical care had worked [22]. This report further adds:

> Medical malpractice is now considered between the fifth and eighth leading cause of death in the United States, according to the Henry J. Kaiser Family Foundation. Researchers report that roughly 5% to 10% of all patients admitted to hospitals this year will fall victim to medical negligence, whether in the form of a surgical mistake, wrong prescription, birth injury, or other type of error. Based on these hospitals' track records, this sounds about right: annually, up to 98,000 people die from preventable medical errors, two million patients contract infections in hospitals, and approximately 90,000 die from infections caused by inadequate sanitation methods (such as infrequent hand washing).

Ignoring Bad Behavior

Most of the healthcare professionals and staff are in this field because they are passionate about making a difference in the lives of others. Yet bad behavior is not rare. A Joint Commission

Sentinel Event Alert, "Behaviors That Undermine a Culture of Safety" [23], includes the following findings:

> Intimidating and disruptive behaviors include overt actions such as verbal outbursts and physical threats, as well as passive activities such as refusing to perform assigned tasks or quietly exhibiting uncooperative attitudes during routine activities. Intimidating and disruptive behaviors are often manifested by healthcare professionals in positions of power. Such behaviors include reluctance or refusal to answer questions, return phone calls or pages; condescending language or voice intonation; and impatience with questions. Overt and passive behaviors undermine team effectiveness and can compromise the safety of patients.
>
> Intimidating and disruptive behaviors in healthcare organizations are not rare. A survey on intimidation conducted by the Institute for Safe Medication Practices found that 40% of clinicians have kept quiet or remained passive during patient care events rather than question a known intimidator. While most formal research centers on intimidating and disruptive behaviors among physicians and nurses, there is evidence that these behaviors occur among other healthcare professionals, such as pharmacists, therapists, and support staff, as well as among administrators. Several surveys have found that most care providers have experienced or witnessed intimidating or disruptive behaviors.

In January 2009, the Joint Commission issued a Leadership Standard (LD.03.01.01) that addresses disruptive and inappropriate behaviors. It suggests, as a part of the accreditation, that the hospitals have a code of conduct that defines acceptable and disruptive and inappropriate behaviors. In addition, the leaders create and implement a process for managing disruptive and inappropriate behaviors. Included in the alert are related details such as the following:

1. Educate all team members—both physicians and nonphysician staff. The code and education should emphasize respect. Include training in basic business etiquette (particularly phone skills) and people skills.
2. Hold all team members accountable for modeling desirable behaviors, and enforce the code consistently and equitably among all staff regardless of seniority or clinical discipline in a positive fashion through reinforcement as well as punishment.
3. Develop and implement policies and procedures/processes appropriate for the organization that address:
   - "Zero tolerance" for intimidating and/or disruptive behaviors. Incorporate the zero tolerance policy into medical staff by laws and employment agreements.
   - Reducing fear of intimidation or retribution and protecting those who report or cooperate in the investigation of intimidating, disruptive, and other unprofessional behavior.
   - Responding to patients and/or their families who are involved in or witness intimidating and/or disruptive behaviors. The response should include hearing and empathizing with their concerns, thanking them for sharing those concerns, and apologizing.
   - How and when to begin disciplinary actions (such as suspension, termination, loss of clinical privileges, reports to professional licensure bodies).

4. Develop an organizational process for addressing intimidating and disruptive behaviors (LD.3.10 EP 5) that solicits and integrates substantial input from an interprofessional team.

5. Provide skills-based training and coaching for all leaders and managers in relationship-building and collaborative practice, including skills for giving feedback on unprofessional behavior and conflict resolution.
6. Develop and implement a system for assessing staff perceptions of the seriousness and extent of instances of unprofessional behaviors and the risk of harm to patients.
7. Develop and implement a reporting/surveillance system (possibly anonymous) for detecting unprofessional behavior.
8. Support surveillance with tiered, nonconfrontational interventional strategies, starting with informal "cup of coffee" conversations directly addressing the problem and moving toward detailed action plans and progressive discipline, if patterns persist. These interventions should initially be non-adversarial in nature, with the focus on building trust, placing accountability on and rehabilitating the offending individual, and protecting patient safety.
9. Encourage interprofessional dialogues across a variety of forums as a proactive way of addressing ongoing conflicts, overcoming them, and moving forward through improved collaboration and communication.
10. Document all attempts to address intimidating and disruptive behaviors.

The following excerpt by Jonel Aleccia "Hospital Bullies Take a Toll on Patient Safety: Bad Behavior by Doctors and Others Undercuts Morale, Leads to Errors" [24] says what no healthcare provider wants to say openly. It is about hospitals ignoring bad behavior.

> They're the bullies of the operating room, the browbeaters of bedside manner: doctors, nurses and other clinicians who make a habit of behaving badly.
>
> They yell, they cuss, they throw things. Or they engage in more subversive behaviors: ignoring questions, acting impatient, insulting colleagues or speaking to them in condescending tones.
>
> "It can go from verbal abuse to sexual harassment and physical assault," said Dianne Felblinger, an associate professor of nursing at the University of Cincinnati who studies medical intimidation.
>
> The acts are bad enough when they affect staff morale, leading to greater turnover and less job satisfaction. But the Joint Commission, a national hospital accrediting agency, warned Wednesday that there's mounting evidence that such disruptive behaviors are tied to medical errors that can cause patient harm—and that hospitals across the country should no longer tolerate it.
>
> The Joint Commission wants hospitals to establish codes of conduct that define inappropriate behaviors and create plans for dealing with them. Suggested actions include better systems to detect and deter unprofessional behavior; more civil responses to patients and families who witness bad acts; and overall training in "basic business etiquette," including phone skills and people skills for all employees.
>
> "The data is clear that certain members of the team don't play so well with other members of the medical team," said Hickson. "We've dealt more effectively with drugs and alcohol than we have dealt with the kicking, spitting and cussing."
>
> Dr Mark Chassin, president of the Joint Commission, said growing emphasis on preventing medical errors has made it clear that a culture of intimidation contributes to the mistakes.
>
> "It's a problem that goes underreported, threatens patient safety and has become so ingrained in healthcare that it's rarely talked about," Chassin told reporters.

Nearly everyone who has worked in hospitals can recount a tale of bad behavior. Hickson recalled a doctor who hurled a table across a room, sending shards flying back at co-workers. Felblinger remembered when a doctor threw a used needle at a nurse, piercing her skin.

Ignoring bad behavior has potentially serious consequences for patients, said Felblinger, author of an analysis of studies on medical bullying published this spring in the journal of *Obstetric, Gynecologic and Neonatal Nursing*.

About 70% of nurses studied believe there's a link between disruptive behavior and adverse outcomes, and nearly 25% said there was a direct tie between the bad acts and patient mortality, she said.

A 2004 study of workplace intimidation by the Institute for Safe Medication Practices (ISMP) in Horsham, Pennsylvania, found that nearly 40% of clinicians have kept quiet or ignored concerns about improper medication rather than talk to an intimidating colleague.

In the ISMP study of about 2,000 clinicians, more than 90% said they'd experienced condescending language or voice intonation; nearly 60% had experienced strong verbal abuse and nearly half had encountered negative or threatening body language.

"Some people are intimidated because they think the doctor has the higher authority," said Renee Setteducato, 55, a nurse at Lutheran Medical Center in Brooklyn, N.Y.

It's important to note that bad behavior is not limited to doctors, said Dr Joseph Heyman, chair of the board of directors for the American Medical Association. The Joint Commission warning also covers nurses, pharmacists, and other clinicians, he noted.

Setteducato observed her share of tantrums and slammed phones in 37 years of nursing. But it's not just doctors bullying nurses, she said. Nurses do their share of intimidation, too. "The experienced nurses are not patient with the new doctors," she observed.

> Ignoring bad behavior is shoddy work.

Inattention to Quality

Quality of service has been defined in several ways. It varies widely among organizations. The American National Standards Institute (ANSI) and the American Society for Quality (ASQ) standardized the definition [25] as the totality of features and characteristics of a product or service that bears on its ability to satisfy given needs. This definition did not become popular, being too generic. The most popular definition used currently is "meeting or exceeding customer expectations." This definition seems very appropriate for healthcare but most healthcare organizations are far from achieving this goal according to the Leapfrog Group [26].

The 2008 Leapfrog Group survey found that "hospitals have a long way to go to fully implement the organization's recommendations for improving the safety and efficiency of patient care." The survey of about 1,300 hospitals discovered that only 7% of the responding hospitals met the organization's current standards for using computerized prescriber-order-entry (CPOE) systems. This system has error prevention features in it that can exceed customer expectations.

Of course, there are many hospitals that do an outstanding job of quality also, according to the survey. But the report adds: the overall survey results "are simply not adequate for the most expensive healthcare system in the world." Chapter 4 is an approach to improve quality rapidly.

Summary

In this chapter, we learned how unwanted practices happen. Most of the caregivers are aware but unable to speak up or change the system. Most of the changes needed are beyond their control. There is still hope—the power of one. If individuals change their behavior, chances are colleagues working with them will change. As you move upward, the people reporting to you will change. And when you move to the top, everyone will change. This is what happened to Japan. They were known for shoddy quality. Then, Dr Edward Deming was sent by General McArthur to help improve quality systems. The management looked the other way, but he managed to teach right things to the lowest-level employees. Eventually, they rose to the top, and Japan became the best in the world. Some hospitals in the Pittsburgh region, especially University of Pittsburgh Medical Center and Allegheny General, are using Japanese techniques imported from Toyota.

References

1. Anderson, B., et al., 2006. Medical error reporting, patient safety, and the physician, *Journal of Patient Safety*, 5: 176–179, http://psnet.ahrq.gov/resource.aspx?resourceID=11659.
2. Carey, D., 2008. Emergency department workplace interruptions are emergency physicians "interrupt-driven" and "multitasking"? *Academic Emergency Medicine*, 7(11): 1239–1243, published Online: www3.interscience.wiley.com/journal/119827055/abstract?CRETRY=1&SRETRY=0.
3. Graber, M., 2009. *Addressing Diagnostic Error in Medicine, There's a Job for Everyone*, Annual National Patient Safety Congress, Washington, DC.
4. Noel, B., and Parker, R., 2005. *Critical Thinking*, McGraw-Hill, New York.
5. Scheffer, B., and Rubenfeld, M., 2000. A consensus statement on critical thinking in nursing, *Journal of Nursing Education*, 39(8): 352–359, www.ncbi.nlm.nih.gov/pubmed/11103973.
6. King, S., 2009. *Josie's Story*, Atlantic Monthly Press, New York.
7. O'Reilly, K., 2009. Wrong surgeries a product of poor communication, *American Medical News*, December 12.
8. Gruden, N., 2007. *The Pittsburgh Way to Efficient Healthcare: Improving Patient Care Using Toyota Based Methods*, Productivity Press, Boca Raton, FL.
9. Schiff, G., 2008. Minimizing diagnostic error: The importance of follow-up and feedback, *The American Journal of Medicine*, 121(5A), S38–S42, http://download.journals.elsevierhealth.com/pdfs/journals/0002-9343/PIIS0002934308001551.pdf.
10. Sanders, L., 2009. *Every Patient Tells a Story*, Broadway Books, Portland, OR.
11. Wachter, R., and Pronovost, P., 2009, Balancing "no blame" with accountability in patient safety, *New England Journal of Medicine*, 361(14): 1401–1406.
12. Domino, D., and Brice, J., 2009. Radiologist Wins $11.4 Million Judgment against Kaiser in Retaliation resource.html?rurl=http%3A%2F%2Fwww.diagnosticimaging.com%2Fimaging-trends-advances%2Fcardiovascular-imaging%2Farticle%2F113619%2F1382443&q=february+25+2009+kaiser+permanente&c=ra&ss=diagnosticImagingLink&p=Convera&fr=true&ds=0&srid=1.
13. Craig, B., 2009. Doctor Sues Hospital for Daughter's Substandard Care, LawyersandSettlements.com, December 24, www.lawyersandsettlements.com/articles/13328/diane-corwin-medical-malpractice.html?ref=rss.
14. Taylor, J., et al., 2004. Use of incident reports by physicians and nurses to document medical errors in pediatric patients, *Journal of the American Academy of Pediatrics*, 114(3): 729–735, http://pediatrics.aappublications.org/cgi/content/abstract/114/3/729.
15. For Dr. Leo Gordon' description of approach, see Rediscovering the Power of the Surgical M&M Conference: The M+M Matrix at www.webmm.ahrq.gov/perspective.aspx?perspectiveID=48.
16. McLaughlin, C., and Kaluzny, A., 2006. *Continuous Quality Improvement in Health Care*. James and Bartlett, Sudbury, MA.

17. Nelson, E., et al., 2002. Microsystems in healthcare: Part 1. Learning fro high-performing front-line clinical units, *Joint Commission Journal on Quality Improvement*, 28(9): 472–493.
18. Institute for Health Improvement, 2010. Clinical Microsystem Assessment Tool, IHI.org, retrieved on May 26 from www.ihi.org/IHI/Topics/Improvement/ImprovementMethods/Tools/ClinicalMicrosystemAssessmentTool.htm.
19. Evans, J., and Lindsay, W.M., 2008. *Managing for Quality and Performance Excellence*, Seventh Edition, Thomson South-Western, Mason, OH.
20. Greider, K., 2009. Battling superbugs, *AARP Bulletin Today*, March 2.
21. Associated Press, 2009. Report: VA Hospital Botched Cancer Treatments, June 22, www.foxnews.com/story/0,2933,528024,00.html.
22. Bogdanich, W., 2009. Oncologist defends his work at a V.A. Hospital, *New York Times*, June 29, www.nytimes.com/2009/06/30/health/30veterans.html?_r=1.
23. The Joint Commission Sentinel Event Alert, 2008. Behaviors That Undermine a Culture of Safety, Issue 40, July 09.
24. Aleccia, J., 2008. Bad Behavior by Doctors Was from the Article "Hospital Bullies Take a Toll on Patient Safety," July 9, www.msnbc.msn.com/id/25594124.
25. ANSI/ASQC, 1978. *Quality Systems Terminology*, American Society for Quality, Milwaukee, WI. Document A#-1978.
26. Traynor, K., 2009. Latest Leapfrog survey finds hospitals lagging in quality goals, *American Society of Health-System Pharmacists* Web site, June 1. Founded in 2000 by the Business Roundtable, the Leapfrog Group is a voluntary member organization whose goal is to improve the quality and value of health care services funded by private employers. Leapfrog's supporters include its members, the Robert Wood Johnson Foundation, and the Agency for Healthcare Research and Quality, www.ashp.org/import/news/HealthSystemPharmacyNews/newsarticle.aspx?id=3089.

Chapter 4

Continuous Innovation Is Better Than Continuous Improvement

If you are not looking for a better idea, you are not going see one.

—**Malcolm Gladwell, author of**
What the Dog Saw: And Other Adventures

Introduction

Most incumbent organizations get saddled with making their existing products or services incrementally better versus making new innovations. They become wedded to their existing processes under the guise of best practices because the very means of improving makes it harder for organizations to make radical changes, particularly in the field of healthcare. Continuous innovation is what makes a quality healthcare organization do the right things at right time.

The usual focus is on making organizations run smoothly and efficiently. The most effective leaders, in contrast, are much more likely to ask: What if we try doing things in a new way, how will it change the world? This is the key difference between continuous improvement and continuous innovation. The innovators want to change the world *with ideas that have a high impact and produce a high return on investment (ROI).*

If we do not look for better ideas, we will never find them! This is one of the rules of innovation that has been defined as an idea that adds value for the customers and results in financial benefit for the innovator organization. It is an outcome-driven change to make a major improvement in efficacy and financial efficiency. For the purpose of this book, innovation is defined as an idea that usually eliminates a problem and results in a high ROI.

Even if an idea is overly simple, it qualifies as an innovation if it produces a high ROI. In one emergency department, the staff occasionally returned the unused drugs to the wrong pockets of the automated drug dispensing (ADD) equipment. This would sometimes cause irreparable harm to a patient. They considered two solutions. The first solution was to periodically inspect the ADD equipment. The second solution was to send the unused drugs back to the pharmacy department. Let us compare. The first solution is a "continuous improvement solution" because it only reduces the frequency of a mistake. It does not attempt to eliminate the problem. Inspection is not completely effective. It is at most 85% effective [1]. The second solution, "innovation," attempts to eliminate the problem permanently such that the wrong drug never goes into the wrong pocket. The ROI on the second is very high since the investment is only the cost of sending the unused drugs back to the pharmacy and the return is the cost saved by avoiding the liability.

This does not mean that continuous improvement is outdated. When a process needs a quick fix or it cannot be easily changed, then continuous improvement is the best choice.

Why Continuous Innovation?

Most of the continuous quality improvement and patient-safety programs aim at improving the current process. They are more about conforming to already set requirements that may be highly inadequate. They assume that the current process is either acceptable or they have no authority to change it, and it only needs to be tweaked. As a result, the improvements are marginal. The customers are not impressed! Especially for safety, the marginal improvements are very inappropriate and are subject to negligence charges in lawsuits. We may need to explore better and totally different processes, as well as systems, that aim at ultra-high quality and safety. Since the improvement issues are often complex and are in the hundreds, the innovations have to continue over a very long time. Therefore, continuous innovation should be the rule of all the rules for patient safety. Figure 4.1 shows that usually a major shift in improvement takes place from continuous innovation versus a minor shift in continuous improvement.

In my experience of more than 25 years of innovation, the ROI is usually at least 1,000%. In a large hospital, the drugs were delivered to various intensive care units by the pharmacy operations at a set time. Often the drugs arrived late because each delivery person used a different sequence for delivery or got stuck waiting for the slow elevator that almost stopped at each floor. To ensure that patients were getting the critical medications on time, some nurses often ordered extra drugs that resulted in wasting expensive drugs with a limited expiry time. The waste was eliminated by

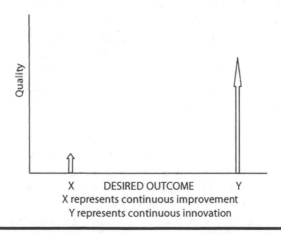

Figure 4.1 **Continuous improvement can be too slow to reach your goal.**

simply standardizing the delivery route so that drugs arrived at the predetermined time or earlier. The investment was hardly any, but the ROI was sky high. Innovation can be just as simple as this minor change. The major difference between an improvement and an innovation is that an innovation produces a high ROI to qualify as an innovation. We will discuss the types of innovations, the foundation for innovation, and the structure for implementing continuous innovation.

> Always look for a high return on investment, if you want elegant solutions.

Types of Innovations

There are at least eight types of innovations:

- Marginal innovation
- Incremental innovation
- Radical innovation
- Disruptive innovation
- Accidental innovation
- Strategic innovation
- Diffusion innovation
- Translocation innovation

Marginal Innovation

Marginal innovation is one in which there is enhancement of an existing process, such as using a checklist to prevent catheter-related bloodstream infections. A small idea in itself, when implemented in more than 100 Michigan hospitals, resulted in saving hundreds of lives and millions of dollars.

A physician slipped and fell on a wet floor in an ICU when a housekeeper finished mopping up about a 10-foot-wide hallway. I suggested that he fill an incident report form. The physician rejected the idea because he blamed himself for being careless. Later, a nurse slipped but did not fall. She also refused to fill out an incident report. A visiting mother of a patient mildly slipped also. No one seemed responsible for preventing the falls. I have learned over the years that employees who work day in and day out on the task already know the solution. He started soliciting solutions from the housekeepers. Sure enough, as an elderly housekeeper put it, the solution is simple. First mop up half the width on one side of the hallway so people can walk on the dry side. When the wet side becomes dry, then mop the other half. The solution worked. It did not cost anything. The ROI is obviously high since all the harm from falls is prevented with hardly any investment. This is a marginal innovation, but the savings are not marginal.

> Ask employees for the lowest-cost suggestions. They usually know the best and simplest solution!

Gruden [2] gives several examples of this type of innovation. In a Pittsburgh hospital, there was a rack that contained blank forms for various needs. Suddenly, a particular form location was empty. The hospital scrambled to find the form. To their surprise, they discovered that some healthcare givers were keeping the forms in their desks just in case there is an insufficient supply. There was absolutely no shortage of forms. The hospital instituted automatic ordering of the forms when a quantity was below a threshold. Then, there was no need for employees to stock up forms in their desks. A minor action like this can be an innovation. In another case, a hospital could not rely on staff to sanitize wheelchairs. The resulting infections were a major concern. They created a small facility like an automated car wash. Every wheelchair was accounted for going through the wash at a set frequency.

Gruden points out that sometimes the solutions are obvious. It was very difficult to locate items in one supply room because of clutter. When all the unneeded items were removed and assigned a unique location, it became very easy to find an item.

Incremental Innovation

Incremental innovations are significant improvements on existing technologies or practices. They involve extension of products such as for drugs that are already on the market. They are evolutionary in nature. Most incremental innovations are developed in response to customer needs. The European initiative IMI (Innovative Medicines Initiative) is such an effort to improve the competitive position of the European Union in the pharmaceutical research. It is aimed at removing research bottlenecks in the drug development process.

In a major hospital, the elevator made too many stops, opening its door at most of the ten floors. Continuous improvement programs would have assumed they had no choice of elevators and would have tried to reduce variation. Someone suggested a separate elevator for transporting patients. If this idea were implemented, it would be a good example of incremental innovation.

An incremental innovation can be as simple as using the "bundle" approach introduced by the Institute of Healthcare Improvement (IHI). It is known to have reduced mortality rates significantly with very little cost. A bundle is a series of interventions related to a care that, when implemented together, will achieve significantly better outcomes than when implemented individually.

The Wheaton Franciscan Healthcare–St. Joseph in Milwaukee, Wisconsin, used a bundle for preventing ventilator-associated pneumonia. This approach combines four interventions as a single process. The components of the bundle are as follows [3]:

■ Elevation of the head of the bed
■ Daily "sedation vacations" and assessment of readiness to extubate
■ Peptic ulcer disease prophylaxis
■ Deep venous thrombosis prophylaxis

According to Barbara Rogness, Director of Quality [4], "The numbers don't tell the whole story. The staff has learned to be such clear and critical thinkers and good communicators. How their confidence has grown! How they are continually learning and teaching each other about how to do even better!"

Radical Innovation

These are sometimes called the *breakthrough innovations*. They result in the creation of a totally new technology or a process that displaces the current way. An example is the Da Vinci surgical robot that has revolutionized the way a surgery is performed. It costs more than three million dollars, but its increasing use suggests that the benefits to hospitals and the patients are much higher. These innovations create new ways to satisfy customers. The technologies in the future may replace the need for a surgeon in many surgeries. A drug that cures diabetes would be an example of radical innovation.

> The best way to be outside the box is to be not inside the box.

Another example of a radical innovation is the introduction of an automated ability to hold the camera still during laparoscopic surgeries, eliminating the need for a person to hold the camera still and the inability to hold it still [5]. It improved productivity significantly for the surgeon in terms of workflow and reduces procedure time, both helping to lower the cost.

Disruptive Innovation

Clayton Christensen [6] introduced this term to describe an innovation in response to when an organization's own survival is threatened, but it is unable to prevent it from going out of business. It disrupts the market and takes away business from competitors. The resulting innovation rescues the organization. Apple computers probably would have gone out of the computer business if it was not for the introduction of the iPhone. It disrupted the market share of Motorola, Nokia, and several handheld device makers. Similarly, a hospital with a complete shift in services that other hospitals cannot easily provide, and be able to gain a market share, will be using a disruptive innovation. Gawande [7] gives an example of a hospital that attracts patients from far away because it has an assembly-line approach to surgery that rarely results in a mishap. This hospital was not threatened for survival, but the strategy offered a competitive advantage.

Accidental Innovation

This just happens when one is searching for something and notices something very strange that could be a revolutionary idea. Probably, the most famous innovation is Alexander Fleming's discovery of the antibiotic properties of penicillin described by Professor Austin [8]. Fleming accidentally left a dish of *Staphylococcus* bacteria uncovered for a few days and returned to find the dish dotted with bacterial growth, except in one area where a patch of mold (*Penicillium notatum*) was growing. Fleming himself said of this event, "I did not ask for a spore of *Penicillium notatum* to drop on my culture plate…. When I saw certain changes, I had not the slightest suspicion that I was at the beginning of something extraordinary…. That same mould might have dropped on [any one] of my culture plates, and there would have been no visible change to direct special attention to it."

Professor Austin gives several examples of the accidental innovations. They are anesthesia, cellophane, cholesterol-lowering drugs, cornflakes, dynamite, the ice cream soda, Ivory soap, NutraSweet (and several other artificial sweeteners), nylon, penicillin, photography, rayon, polyvinyl chloride (PVC), smallpox vaccine, stainless steel, Pfizer's viagra, and Teflon.

An interesting question is how do we train employees for accidental innovations? Austin offers an analogy of artists who cultivate an ability to discover value in interesting accidents. He says this is a nontrivial capability. Pasteur called it the "prepared mind."

Strategic Innovation

Strategic innovation is the creation of new product categories, services, or business models that changes the game. It generates new values for customers and the organization [9].

Strategic innovation is focused on generating ideas beyond incremental and breakthrough innovations. It is not characterized by mundane, incremental product extensions, the "me-too" business models of close followers, or band-aids for inefficient processes. It is not based on the extrapolation of the past in an attempt to predict the future. "It is perhaps the most devilishly difficult and most enigmatic management challenge, and surprises competitors by changing the rules of the game," according to a Harvard Business School publication [10]. A hospital giving a 30-day warranty on infections would be an example of this type of innovation.

Diffusion Innovation

Diffusion innovation is "the process by which an innovation is communicated through certain channels over time among the members of a social system" [11]. CPOE (computerized provider order entry) is such an innovation. It was innovated in response to reducing medication errors and improving patient safety as soon as the need for a prescription arises.

Like any innovation, new benefits come with new risks. Ditto with the CPOE. It allows different causes of errors, which can be more dangerous. It can give a false feeling of confidence with overdependence on technology. It can increase mortality rates such as in the Pediatric ICU of Children's Hospital of Pittsburgh where the mortality rate went up from 2.8% to 6.58% over a 5-month time span [12]. The following data from a MEDMARX study [13] shows the top seven types of errors. Some types of errors increased (risk) and other types of errors decreased the risk after the installation of the CPOE.

Types of Errors	Error % prior to CPOE	Error % after CPOE
Prescribing errors	22.4	73.5
Improper dose/quantity	22.5	40.5
Wrong dosage form	2.7	6.8
Extra dose	5.3	4.1
Omission errors	23.9	3.9
Unauthorized/wrong drug	10.4	3.6
Wrong patient	4.9	3.5

Translocation Innovation

This is simply importing an evidence-based idea from an unrelated industry to your industry. A very successful case of this is the use of Toyota Production Systems in U.S. hospitals. The former U.S. Secretary of Treasury Paul O'Neil brought this innovation to about 50 hospitals in Pennsylvania. Since then it has spread to more hospitals across the United States.

Allegheny General Hospital was one of the hospitals that embraced the Toyota system, called Perfecting Patient Care by the Pittsburgh Region Health Initiative (PRHI). Dr Richard Shannon, chairman of internal medicine, explains the basic system in three steps [14]:

- The standards for performing work activities (such as intravenous line placement and maintenance) should be highly specified (not simply assumed), based on best practices, so that problems and variations from standards are immediately apparent.
- When problems (such as nosocomial infections) are encountered, they should be solved in real time by people doing the work to determine root causes and employ countermeasures—or corrective actions—to prevent them.
- When workers cannot solve a problem, they invoke the "help chain" of expert support to solve the problem.

The results were astounding. After learning about the process, Dr Shannon challenged his hospital to eliminate the central-line-associated bloodstream (CLAB) infections in two ICUs within 90 days. The infections took a nose dive. The infection rate went down from 5.1 per 1,000 line days to 1.2 per 1,000 line days. Among the patients with CLABs, the number of deaths decreased by 95%. Of the six CLABs that occurred, four were from failure to follow the specified guidelines.

> The standards for performing work should be highly specified, so that problems and variations are immediately apparent.

The Foundation for the Innovation Culture

Making the choice of innovation, encouraging creativity, and providing the management structure for sustaining innovations are the foundation for the innovation culture. They all must be in place.

Choice of Innovation

The most important paradigm in innovation is: What gets measured is what gets done. A similar heuristic says, "If you don't know where you're going, any map will do." The point is that we must measure how effective we are at innovation. If there is no measurement in place, employees will perhaps not innovate. Management must choose one or more types of innovation described earlier to guide employees toward a common goal.

Encouraging Creativity

Creativity can be defined as the art of defining a problem and generating ideas to eliminate the problem. We all have the ability to create. Most of it is lost in the process of growing up under the pressures of parental discipline, society culture, limits imposed by the education system, and the work environment. A child born with more than 1,000 billion neurons has only around 1 billion active neurons left by the age four. But we can learn to create new ideas with thinking techniques such as the following [15]:

- Deny the current way. Assume that the current way has insufficient value. Ask the team to add significantly more value.
- Developing a wish list. Each team member should submit a wish list. Suddenly you may get 20 ideas. At least one of them will be worthy of implementing.

- Find future flaws. Brainstorm for what mishaps can occur in the future. That will give you ideas for innovating new solutions.
- Overstate the capabilities. Make a goal of increasing the throughput in the emergency department by 50% without increasing the staffing. You will be surprised by the number of ideas you receive.
- Develop "shall not" requirements such as "There shall be no wrong-site surgery." Ask for validation of this concept by criticizing the current procedures and protocols. Suddenly, you will find flaws in your system that need to be fixed.
- Link to unrelated ideas. You may link a car to the patient bed. The patient can have a small panel resembling the dashboard of a car. He/she can choose the television settings, call the nurse, choose the room temperature of a private room, change the fan speed, or change the radio station.
- Add or subtract options. You can take away options that create the opportunity for making mistakes. You can add options that safeguard against mistakes such as checking patient identification on the radio frequency interference (RFI) wristbands. A patient in the burn center was frequently dropping items such as a cell phone, eyewear, and silverware during meals. He fell several times trying to pick up these things. The hospital gave him an option of an expandable retraction cane capable of picking up things without getting out of bed. This was an inexpensive solution that prevented him from falling.
- Find out what the customers do not like. This is a proven tool. The most creative company in the world uses it (IDEO Corporation in Palo Alto, California). This company was hired by Xerox to find an easier way to use personal computers. This was before the invention of the mouse. The company asked the customers what they did not like. Most of them complained about too many commands to remember, and they did not like to read the instruction manuals. This is why the mouse was invented, by a company that knew very little about computers!
- Reward failures. The company IDEO always has about half the team from totally unrelated fields such as accounting, psychology, and biology. They encourage failures as long as it is a part of the learning process. They even have parties for the biggest failure of the month! Thomas Edison was once asked: You failed 2,000 times before you succeeded with the light bulb invention? His reply: There were 2,000 steps to the process! The same reasoning was used in naming a famous lubrication product as WD40. Why 40? Because it failed 39 times.
- Replace logic with intuitive thinking. Intuition is sometimes called thinking without thinking. There is no analysis involved. The only requirement is that we should be able to visualize the whole picture. Typically, most executives worry about the costs and fail to see the benefits. They are constantly analyzing partial data and shutting off their intuition. Intuition is not corrupted by past thinking. If we just calm down and wait for the solution, it just appears. It is like a new intelligence is eavesdropping on us. That is what Steve Jobs, the founder of Apple Computers, experienced when he decided to sell a personal computer (PC) to every household.
- Conduct scenario planning. Imagine future scenarios that require an innovative approach. A train accident in the city may result in more than 100 patients arriving by ambulances at the same time. What if there were an uncontrollable fire in the hospital? What if most doctors fell ill in an epidemic? Once we ask "what if" questions, we will see the need for innovation. We cannot wait till these mishaps happen.

- Use "blue ocean" strategy. Identify the unmet needs of the patients, doctors, and nurses and invent methods to satisfy the need. For example, patients may want more dialogue with the doctors, or a family member wants to stay with the patient 24 hours because the family does not trust the hospital care.

If none of these work, try this check list:

- Am I using old ways of thinking?
- Is this the best way?
- Am I certain this is the best way?
- If I did not know this method, what would be the solution?

Edward De Bono [16], who has written several books on creativity, suggests Six Hat Thinking to emphasize looking at a problem and the solution from at least six views. The six views can be from a physician's point of view, a nurse's point of view, a technician's point of view, a pharmacist's point of view, an anesthesiologist's point of view, and a patient's point of view. There should be a process for making a converging decision such that it is not dominated by a person with authority.

Using both sides of the brain is a very powerful technique for creativity. Neuropsychiatrist Richard Restak at George Washington University Medical Center recommends the following drill [17]: Stand erect, raise one leg such that the thigh is parallel to the ground while rest of the leg is hanging free, hold as long you can while the brain is doing the balancing only on one leg. Then repeat the drill using the other leg. Do it several times. He suggests 28 ways to improve mental fitness that enhance mental capacity and creativity. Leonardo da Vinci, an icon of innovation, used to write backward with his left hand even though he was right handed. His way is also very powerful, using both the sides of the brain. Microsoft acquired one of his original notebooks. You need a mirror to read his notes!

Some organizations create a sense of urgency to sow the seeds of creativity. They are given a seemingly unattainable goal and told to finish the work in ridiculously short time. Hewlett-Packard did this. Employees were told to develop new products in half the usual time and at half the usual cost. That is how they came up with the 3-in-1 printer. It is not just a printer, but it is a fax machine, and a copier also. If we buy these three machines separately, the cost will be double.

I usually set a goal of at least 500% ROI to create urgency. This strategy puts extra pressure on the team to think intuitively instead of sequentially as in logical thinking. Perhaps this example will help:

A client in Brazil made electrical control panels. The panels have a large lamp covered with a plastic cap. The team reported that they tried all kinds of plastics, and they all melted from heat generated by the lamp. The team was challenged to come with robust ideas and not to limit their thinking regardless of how much more it costs. It took less than 10 minutes to conclude that a glass cap will work. The only issue was that glass costs three times the amount of the plastic. They were reluctant to accept the solution. When they compared extra cost and the savings from new benefits, they discovered that benefits exceeded three times the cost (300% ROI). The team was very pleased with the outcome, until the author intervened "our goal is to get at least 500 percent ROI, not the 300 percent." They asked for hints. I suggested that all the team members take a long shower (Einstein used to do that) for next 3 weeks. They were told to think about the solution only during the shower

> Find out what the customers don't like. Replace it with what they like.

and not the root causes. Root-cause analysis limits creativity and blocks the power of intuition. Two weeks later I was the one taking a long shower. It suddenly occurred to me that the team gave shoddy conclusions on the kinds of plastics they tried. There are two kinds of plastics, those that melt with heat (thermoplastic) and those that become tougher with heat (thermoset). They obviously did not try the second kind. They totally missed the fundamental knowledge they already had. They tried the thermoset plastic. It worked. It never melted. They no longer needed to use the glass cap. With practically no investment, the ROI was over 10,000%.

Structure for Sustaining Innovation

David Parnas, one of our great software engineers, uses structure to mean both how a software system is divided into modules and also the assumptions that the various modules make about each other [18].

To make innovation sustainable for many years, an organization must choose the types of innovations they wish to pursue and create a management structure to sustain them. A management structure is a set of policies and processes that support the goals of interacting departments. When this author worked for GE Healthcare in the early seventies, the entire GE Company was involved in the strategic innovation structure. Every decentralized division was given the strategic goal "Business must be Number One or Number Two in the market share within an allocated time or liquidate the business!" Sure enough, one of the very profitable and growing businesses they liquidated was the information systems business. They sold it to Honeywell.

Even deciding to liquidate a business when it is very profitable is an innovation decision. It motivates the organization to be a leader, and stay as a leader for a long time. It provides an extra sense of accountability. This incidence happened about 35 years ago but the structure of innovation, being Number One or Number Two, is still there today.

There can be several forms of structures. Choose one of them. Usual structures are

Macrosystem Structure: where an innovation policy is implemented across the whole organization, such as in the above example of GE.

Microsystem Structure: where cross-functional teams are formed around a problem with a policy that supports innovation. It views a problem as a system that needs to be redesigned. Most Pittsburgh area hospitals use this Toyota Production System as a structure.

Blue Sky Structure: where employees can innovate anything they want, keeping in mind the future needs of the organization. Some corporations allow employees time to experiment with new ideas. Others allow employees to attend conferences of their choice even if it does not relate to their current job. IBM and 3M Company have this structure.

Structure of No-Structure: where employees are encouraged to think and act outside the box. This caption is given by this author because there is no name to it. Apple Computer and Google have this structure. That is why they keep reinventing themselves.

Summary

The Agency for Healthcare Research and Quality (AHRQ) has been a promoter for the need for innovation in hospitals. Industries such as automotive, medical devices, computers, and aerospace have been using innovation culture for over a century. Why not hospitals? Innovation culture gives hospitals a competitive edge, dramatically improves the quality of healthcare, and lowers costs significantly.

This chapter teaches us that continuous innovation is better than continuous improvement, although continuous improvement is necessary for processes that do not require radical changes. But to implement for high ROI, we must choose the types of innovations appropriate for our goals and provide sustainable management strategy. Innovation needs to be in every organizational DNA. This is true regardless of the size of an organization.

The remaining chapters in this book focus on applying innovation to create high value.

References

1. Raheja, D., and Allocco, M., 2006. *Assurance Technologies Principles and Practices*, John Wiley & Sons, Inc., Hoboken, NJ.
2. Grunden, N., 2007. *Pittsburgh Way to Efficient Healthcare: Applying Toyota-Based Improvements to Healthcare*, Productivity Press, Taylor & Francis, Boca Raton, FL.
3. Institute for Healthcare Improvement Web Site, 2010. Implement the Ventilator Bundle, retrieved on May 30 from www.ihi.org/IHI/Topics/CriticalCare/IntensiveCare/Changes/Implement theVentilatorBundle.htm.
4. Institute of Healthcare Improvement, 2007. Wheaton Franciscan Healthcare—St. Joseph Reduces Mortality Rate to 1.72 Percent, IHI.org, www.ihi.org/IHI/Topics/CriticalCare/IntensiveCare/ ImprovementStories/WheatonFranciscanReducesMortality.htm.
5. Daily Finance, 2010. CareFusion's New Camera Controller Improves Surgical Field Visibility during Minimally Invasive Procedures, April 12, http://srph.it/bnje90.
6. Christensen, C., 2003. *The Inventor's Dilemma: The Revolutionary Book That Will Change the Way You Do Business*, Collins Business Essentials, New York.
7. Gawande, A., 2002. *Complications: A Surgeon's Notes on an Imperfect Science*, Metropolitan Books, New York.
8. Gilbert, S., 2006. Q&A with Prof. Robert D. Austin, The Accidental Innovator, Working Knowledge (Harvard Business School weekly newsletter), July 5, http://hbswk.hbs.edu/item/5441.html.
9. Palmer, D., and Kaplan, S., 2007. A Framework for Strategic Innovation, a publication of Innovation Point, http://mail.google.com/mail/?zx=1aqzznwxvns90&shva=1#inbox/1261a612e7724f14.
10. Govindarajan, V., and Trimble, C., 2005. Not All Innovations Are Equal, Working Knowledge (Harvard Business School weekly newsletter), July 5, http://hbswk.hbs.edu/archive/5123.html.
11. Rogers, E., 2003. *Diffusion Innovation*, Fifth Edition, Free Press, New York.
12. Yong, Y., et al., 2005. Unexpected increased mortality after implementation of a commercially sold computerized physician order entry system, *Pediatrics*, 116(6): 1506–1512. http://pediatrics. aappublications.org/cgi/gca?submit.x=79&submit.y=13&submit=sendit&gca=116%2F6%2F1506.
13. Santell, J., 2004. Computer-Related Errors: What Every Pharmacist Should Know, USP Center for Advancement of Patient Safety, presentation based on MEDMARX 5th Anniversary Data Report, ASHP MCM, Orlando, FL, December 9, www.usp.org/pdf/EN/patientSafety/slideShows2004-12-09.pdf.
14. McCarthy, D., and Blumenthal, D., 2006. Committed to Safety: Ten Case Studies on Reducing Harm to Patients, The Commonwealth Fund Pub 923, April, available from www.cmwf.org, www.com-monwealthfund.org/~/media/Files/Publications/Fund%20Report/2006/Apr/Committed%20to%20 Safety%20%20Ten%20Case%20Studies%20on%20Reducing%20Harm%20to%20Patients/923_ McCarthy_committed_to_safety_10_case_studies%20pdf.pdf.
15. Takayama, Y., 2003. *Innovative Thinking System-Course Guide*, Business Consultant Network, Inc., South San Francisco, CA, 94080.
16. Bono, E., 1999. *Six Thinking Hats*, Little, Brown & Co., Boston, MA.
17. Restak, R., 2002. *Mozart's Brain and the Fighter Pilot: Unleashing Your Brain's Potential*, Three Rivers Press, New York.
18. Parnas, D., 1972. On the criteria to be used in decomposing systems into modules, *Communications of the ACM* (Programming Techniques Department), December.

Chapter 5

Innovations Should Start with Incidence Reports

Plans are only good intentions unless they immediately degenerate into hard work.

—**Peter Drucker**

Introduction

The return on investment (ROI) is high in any industry where mishaps are prevented before they become mishaps. Healthcare, in particular, should have the highest ROI. The investment is usually minuscule compared with the cost of defending a patient devastation. The strategy to nip the problems in the bud is to act decisively on incidence reports. They provide early warnings of mishaps that are on the way.

A *Wall Street Journal* article on May 27, 2010, reported that patient satisfaction has declined in hospitals, including a 12% plunge in the satisfaction with emergency room services [1], an indication that incidence reporting systems (IRSs) are not working well.

The sad state of medical incidence reporting is that most of the incidences are not reported and therefore preventing mishaps in such cases is out of question. A report issued in early March 2010 by the Inspector General of the U.S. Department of Health and Human Services [2] concluded that hospitals are not tracking their adverse events internally, never mind reporting them publicly. The inspector general investigated 278 hospitalizations in two undisclosed counties. It uncovered 120 problematic "events" in which patients were harmed either permanently or temporarily. Yet the hospitals had done incidents reports on only 8 of the 120 cases. They even missed two of three cases where patients were killed, the report said. Taylor et al. [3] arrived at similar conclusion at a survey of nurses and physicians in a pediatric hospital: Medical errors in pediatric patients are significantly underreported in incident report systems, particularly by physicians. Overall, 34.8% of respondents indicated that they had reported <20% of their perceived medical errors in the previous 12 months.

Even when the incidences are reported, the results are not pretty. The Agency for Healthcare Research and Quality (AHRQ), which has the highest collection of data on the quality and safety of care, gives a very low score to physicians for hardly reporting any incidence. According to an AHRQ study of two hospitals [4] and a review of 1,000 incidence reports, nurses fled 89% of the reports and physicians 1.9%. "As a result, few physician incidents involving high-risk procedures or prescribing errors get reported. Yet, these incidents are usually responsible for most adverse events. Nearly 60% of incidents were preventable."

This AHRQ study points to other studies which conclude that most adverse events occur in operating rooms, floor units, and intensive care units; only a handful of reports in this study involved high-risk procedures. We must find a way so that all incidences are reported.

The Purpose and Scope of Incidence Reports

The purpose of incident reports is to help identify potential and actual risks and, thus, mitigate hazards. Incident reports also alert risk managers to potential lawsuits. They are generated for at least four types of medical errors: near misses, adverse events, intentional unsafe acts, and sentinel events. These events may affect any person on the premises, including patients, employees, physicians, visitors, students, or volunteers. Incident reporting serves to describe incidences that are unexpected, unusual, or out of the ordinary routine of a healthcare facility's operations, whether or not they cause injury. The reports can include patients unable to tolerate side effects of medication, family members fail to use a caregiver's instructions, or when a family member is upset at the quality of healthcare.

According to the Patient Safety Manual published by the American College of Surgeons (ACS), the objective of an IRS is to identify 100% of adverse patient occurrences and potentially compensable events. According to the manual [5],

> Incidents should be reported and investigated immediately, regardless of whether the event resulted in an injury. This data then can be used in a quality management system to track trends, provide feedback, and educate, all of which allow for system improvements. In addition, the data protects an institution by minimizing future risk and reducing the institution's legal vulnerability. In essence, it serves to protect nurses, patients, and healthcare facilities. Proper controls and reporting between people needs to occur so that lessons are learned, education and training programs are reviewed and updated, and policies, procedures, and guidelines are revised to build on strengths and improve areas of weakness. With correct processes in place, clear lines of accountability for the quality and safety of clinical care result.

The manual includes an example of a positive change that occurred at St. Joseph's Wayne Hospital in New Jersey: Two nurses were part of the surgical team during a laparoscopic gynecological procedure. The nurses asked the surgeon if he wanted to send the retrieved fluid as a specimen to the laboratory. Both nurses understood that the surgeon had responded "no." The surgeon, however, dictated in his postoperative summary that the fluid had been sent to the laboratory. Upon questioning him after it was discovered that the specimen was missing, he agreed he was not sure what he actually said during surgery regarding the fluid. The incident report generated resulted in a change in policy and procedure. Surgeons now are included actively in the specimen collection process because they are required to sign the laboratory requisition slip that accompanies the specimen.

Healthcare today is a complex system comprised of numerous intricate parts that interact with multiple other parts in unexpected ways. Various levels of specialization and interdependencies exist in institutions. This places healthcare facilities at high risk for accidents.

Two large studies of adverse events show the extent of such medical errors [6]. In both studies, more than 50% of adverse events resulted from medical errors that could have been prevented. When near misses occur, instead of being thankful nothing negative happened, nurses should question what could be learned from the event to prevent future occurrences. This proactive stance is supported by the notion that to prevent is cheaper than to cure.

> The objective of an IRS is to identify 100% of adverse patient occurrences.

What to Do with Incidence Reports?

One of the goals is to determine whether an adverse event was preventable or unpreventable, and how preventive measures may be implemented.

Many incidents go unreported. The employees believe that the process does not result in constructive changes. Unfortunately, actions to improve processes often are not taken. Data should be used to develop interdisciplinary plans for improvement. In a complex system like healthcare, interdisciplinary teams must work together, and management must ensure timely actions and feedback to employees who took the time to submit incidence reports.

Some incidents go unreported because employees feel the incident will result in legal action against them. Management needs to ensure an environment that is conducive to identifying, analyzing, and reporting errors without the threat of litigation and without compromising patients' legal rights.

Incident reporting might increase if the reporting efforts are seen as important and productive. A more participatory approach is needed in which medical staff members help develop criteria for assessing adverse events and help implement changes. This would result in a more comprehensive and effective reporting system.

The goal of constructive IRSs is to achieve a better understanding of a facility's problems as they relate to patient safety. The approach needs to be without blame to foster process thinking and problem solving so that the system's errors can be corrected.

> Ensure an environment that is conducive to identifying, analyzing, and reporting errors with no punitive consequences.

A Sample Incidence Reporting Procedure

As a sample of an incidence reporting procedure, the procedure shown in Figure 5.1 is reproduced from Montana State Hospital [7]. This can be a good starting point, but the procedure can differ based on the risk management process of the hospital.

A Sample Incidence Report Form

The Great Ormond Street Children's Hospital in London seems to have an incident reporting form which includes all the essentials needed [8]. One can modify it to include the needs of the hospital. The copy of the form is shown in Figure 5.2.

MONTANA STATE HOSPITAL
POLICY AND PROCEDURE

INCIDENT RESPONSE
AND REPORTING

Effective Date: December 11, 2015   **Policy:** SF-04

Page 1of 6

I.   **PURPOSE:**

     A. To ensure prompt assessment and response to all incidents resulting in injury to patients, employees, or visitors. To accurately document threats or actions of violence, inappropriate sexual behavior, unsafe smoking, contraband, fires and environmental emergencies. To accurately document incidents of property damage.

     B. To accurately document events and to identify staff response to the events.

     C. To identify contributing factors/conditions that led to the incident and to identify steps taken to prevent the recurrence of a similar incident.

     D. To provide accurate, timely information for an ongoing incident report database.

II.   **POLICY:**

     A. Employees who witness or are aware of an incident are responsible for completing an Incident Report at the time they become aware of the incident.

     B. An Incident Report must be completed anytime there is an injury (regardless of severity) to patients, employees or visitors. An Incident Report must be completed in the event of damage to or loss of hospital and/or patient property. When possible, a photograph of the damaged property will be taken by Security and given to the Safety Officer.

     C. An Incident Report must be filled out when the transport blanket is used to move a patient.

     D. All Incident Reports must be filled out completely including patient's hospital number, patient's unit, date of injury, time of injury, etc. When completing an Incident Report that involves an injury (or property damage) to a patient or employee resulting from another patient, the hospital number of the patient who caused the injury must be provided in the "Description of Incident" portion of the report. The acting Supervisor's name will be stated on the report.

     E. The actual incident report will not be noted in the patient's chart.

Figure 5.1 Montana State Hospital, 2008. *Incidence Response and Reporting,* retrieved from https://dphhs.mt.gov/Portals/85/amdd/documents/MSH/volumeii/safety/ IncidentResponseAndReporting.pdf.

(Continued)

INCIDENT REPONSE AND REPORTING	Page 2 of 6

    F. Montana State Hospital (Safety Committee will monitor and evaluate data generated by the reporting process as part of the Hospital's performance improvement activities.

III. DEFINITIONS:

    A. *Incident* - Any unusual or unexpected occurrence that results in injury or potential injury to patients, staff, or visitors. Threats or actions of violence, inappropriate sexual behavior, unsafe smoking, contraband, fires and environmental emergencies. Any event that results in damage or potential damage to or loss of hospital property, patient property or specified employee property.

IV. RESPONSIBILITIES:

All employees are responsible for safety and reporting safety concerns to their immediate supervisor as addressed in the Hazardous Condition Reporting Policy.

    A. *Safety Officer* will maintain a database of all Incident Reports at Montana State Hospital. All Incident Reports will be assigned a severity rating and categorized according to type of injury by the Safety Officer. The Safety Officer will take appropriate action to decrease the potential for repeat incidents. The Safety Officer will coordinate with Montana State Fund to ensure appropriate management of worker's compensation claims.

    B. *Employees* must complete an Incident Report at the time they become aware of an incident. All Incident Reports must be completed prior to the end of the shift. Employees must notify their supervisor of all incidents before the end of the shift. An Incident Report must be completed for all patient, staff or visitor injuries, regardless of severity.

    C. *Licensed nurses* must assess the injury and administer first-aid as necessary. Injured employees can be referred to the Medical Clinic for medical emergency. Employees can also be referred to medical providers in the community. Nurse Supervisors must be notified of all incidents before the end of the injured employee's shift.

    D. *Nurse Supervisors/Immediate Supervisors* must take steps to ensure all injury reports submitted to them by employees are acted upon appropriately. This includes any immediate steps taken to prevent recurrence and the generation of work orders to maintenance to alleviate any hazardous conditions. Any Hazardous Condition reports generated from an incident must be forwarded to the Safety Officer after the supervisor completes their section of the report.

V. PROCEDURE:
An Incident Report must be completed anytime a patient, employee or visitor is injured – regardless of severity. An employee who witnesses an incident must complete the Incident Report. In the event of an unobserved injury, the employee who first becomes aware of the injury must complete an incident report.

Figure 5.1 (CONTINUED) Montana State Hospital, 2008. *Incidence Response and Reporting,* **retrieved from https://dphhs.mt.gov/Portals/85/amdd/documents/MSH/volumeii/safety/IncidentResponseAndReporting.pdf.**

(Continued)

Montana State Hospital Policy and Procedure

| INCIDENT REPONSE AND REPORTING | Page 3 of 6 |

A. **Patient Injury**:

   1. *Notification process and first response*:

      a. Regardless of severity, employees must immediately notify the licensed nurse assigned to the patient's treatment unit.

      b. A licensed nurse must assess the patient's injury and administer First Aid as indicated.

      c. A licensed nurse must notify the Nurse Supervisor who will determine the necessity for further intervention; i.e., notification of physician.

   2. *Documentation process*:

      a. An employee observing or responding to the incident must complete and sign an Incident Report Form (see attached form) and document information about the incident in the Progress Notes of the patient's medical record.

      b. The licensed nurse must document the following on the Incident Report Form *and* in the Progress Notes:

            - assessment
            - emergency care administered
            - persons notified and time this occurred
            - any needed follow-up

      c. Following assessment of the patient, the physician will document the following on the Incident Report Form and in the Progress Notes:

            - observations
            - treatment provided
            - plan for follow-up care

      d. The Safety Officer will review all Incident Reports and will assign severity rating and injury type. All incidents requiring hospital based services or result in death will be reported to the hospital administrator.

B. **Employee Injury**:

   1. *Notification and first response*:

      e. The employee's immediate supervisor must be notified of all employee injuries at the time of the injury – regardless of severity.

Figure 5.1 (CONTINUED) Montana State Hospital, 2008. *Incidence Response and Reporting*, **retrieved from https://dphhs.mt.gov/Portals/85/amdd/documents/MSH/volumeii/ safety/IncidentResponseAndReporting.pdf.**

(*Continued*)

Montana State Hospital Policy and Procedure

INCIDENT REPONSE AND REPORTING	Page 4 of 6

    f.   A licensed nurse or physician may provide care and treatment in response to an emergency condition or situation that is necessary to stabilize.

    g.   The employee's Program Manager must be notified as soon as possible.

  2. *Documentation process*:

    a.   Injured employees must complete and sign the Incident Report Form (see attached) at the time of the injury. If an electronic version of the form is used, this must be immediately emailed to the safety officer.

    b.   The immediate supervisor must complete the Incident Report if an injured employee is unable to do so.

    c.   When a registered nurse and/or physician assess the employee, they must document their findings on the Incident Report Form.

    d.   The completed Incident Report Form must be sent to the Safety Officer *immediately* and a copy will be sent to the supervisor stated on the report by the safety officer after the report is reviewed.

C. **Visitor Injury**:

  1. *Notification and first response*:

    a.   Regardless of severity staff must complete an Incident Report and notify a registered nurse or licensed practical nurse.

    b.   A licensed nurse will assess the visitor's injury and administer First-Aid as indicated.

    c.   The licensed nurse must notify the Nurse Supervisor who will determine the necessity for further intervention; i.e. notification of a physician.

    d.   The Hospital Administrator must be notified of all visitor injuries.

  2. *Documentation process*:

    a.   Employees who observe or respond to an incident involving a visitor must complete and sign an Incident Report Form.

    b.   A licensed nurse and/or physician must assess the visitor with their permission and document the following on the Incident Report Form:

        - observations
        - treatment given, and

Figure 5.1 (CONTINUED) Montana State Hospital, 2008. *Incidence Response and Reporting*, retrieved from https://dphhs.mt.gov/Portals/85/amdd/documents/MSH/volumeii/safety/IncidentResponseAndReporting.pdf.

(Continued)

Montana State Hospital Policy and Procedure

INCIDENT REPONSE AND REPORTING	Page 5 of 6

- any recommended follow-up care.

   c. Completed Incident Report Forms will be routed to the Safety Officer *immediately.*

D. **Emergency Care/Transportation:**

Emergency assessment and care will be the first priority for all patient, employee and visitor injuries. A licensed nurse and/or physician will be available to assess all injuries. If injuries require emergency transportation to an acute medical facility, arrangements will be made via the Nurse Supervisor or Staffing Services. The contracted ambulance service may be utilized to provide emergency transportation. In an emergency situation any MSH employee(s) may transport an employee, patient or visitor to a medical facility with the Nurse Supervisor's authorization.

E. **Damage/Loss of Personal Property**:

Instances of damage to or loss of personal property will be managed according to Montana State Hospital's policy HR-13 "Reimbursement for damage/destruction of Employee Owned Property."

F. **Data Collection and Analysis:**

  1. The Safety Officer will indicate the date when the Incident Report was received on the form and the Quality Improvement Department Administrative Assistant will enter information from each occurrence into a database. The database will include date, shift, time, location, severity and type of occurrence as well as information about patients and staff involved.

  2. Information contained in the database will be summarized and reviewed by the Safety Committee and a summary report will be given to the Quality Improvement Committee.

VI.   **REFERENCES:**

MSH Policy "Hazardous Condition Reporting Policy"
MSH Policy "Reimbursement for Damage/Destruction of Employee Owned Property"
MSH Policy "Personally Owned Articles Brought to Montana State Hospital by Hospital Personnel"
MSH Policy "Workers Compensation"

VII. **COLLABORATED WITH:** Hospital Administrator, Director of Nursing, Director of Quality Improvement & Public Relations, Safety Officer, and Staffing Services.

VIII. **RESCISSIONS:** SF-04, *Incident Response and Reporting* Policy dated December 9, 2011; SF-04, *Incident Response and Reporting* Policy dated November 1, 2008; SF-04,

Figure 5.1 (CONTINUED) Montana State Hospital, 2008. *Incidence Response and Reporting,* **retrieved from https://dphhs.mt.gov/Portals/85/amdd/documents/MSH/volumeii/ safety/IncidentResponseAndReporting.pdf.**

(Continued)

INCIDENT REPONSE AND REPORTING	Page 6 of 6

> *Incident Response and Reporting Policy* dated May 28, 2007; SF-04, *Incident Response and Reporting Policy* dated February 20, 2003; SF-04; *Incident Response and Reporting Policy* dated February 14, 2000; AD-05-01, *Incident Response and Reporting Policy*, dated July 10, 1995.

IX.   **DISTRIBUTION:** All hospital policy manuals

X.   **ANNUAL REVIEW AND AUTHORIZATION:** This policy is subject to annual review and authorization for use by either the Administrator or the Medical Director with written documentation of the review per ARM § 37-106-330.

XI.   **FOLLOW-UP RESPONSIBILITY:** Safety Officer

XII.   **ATTACHMENTS:** For internal use only.
                 A: Incident Report Form

Signatures:

John W. Glueckert   Connie Worl
Hospital Administrator   Director of QI and PR

Figure 5.1 (CONTINUED) Montana State Hospital, 2008. *Incidence Response and Reporting,* **retrieved from https://dphhs.mt.gov/Portals/85/amdd/documents/MSH/volumeii/safety/IncidentResponseAndReporting.pdf.**

Ideas for Innovative Solutions

Hospitals where incidence reports are religiously encouraged can get overwhelmed with the number of reports. In such cases, a different strategy may be needed without discouraging the act of submitting the reports. Robert Wachter, Chief of Medical Services at the University of California San Francisco Medical Center [9], says his hospital receives about 20,000 reports a year. "We don't report everything. If we really did, I'd estimate that my one hospital would receive at least five times as many reports: 100,000 yearly." His suggestions include the following:

■ Many incidents, even if important (e.g., common adverse drug events, patient falls, decubiti) do not warrant investigation as isolated incidents. In such cases, the IRS should simply capture the incident and the extent of injury to the patient, not barrage users with a series of root-cause analysis-style questions about the factors contributing to these events.
■ Limit reporting to only those errors that cause temporary or serious (1.5%) harm, along with a small number of reporting categories, such as the disruptive provider, that require complete data. For the remainder of the categories, switch to a monthly schedule: all medication errors get reported in January, all falls in February, all serious decubitus ulcers in March, and so on.
■ More importantly, free caregivers from the "report everything" mantra. They would be more enthusiastic about reporting, and hospital leaders and administrators would have the time to analyze the reports and develop meaningful action plans (as well as to focus on other methods of error detection such as Executive Walk Rounds and trigger tools).

Incident Form	Great Ormond Street
This form applies to ALL incidents and 'prevented incidents' including incidents involving patients, staff and visitors.	Hospital for Children NHS Trust

Manager to grade the incident according to the table below, by marking the box alongside the Grade with an X

X	Grade	Descriptor	Actual or potential impact
	5	Catastrophic	Unexpected death of one or more persons, national adverse publicity, potential litigation, major health and safety incident e.g. toxic gases, fire, bomb, catastrophic financial loss
	4	Major	Permanent injury, long term harm or sickness, involving one or more persons, potential litigation, extensive injuries, loss of production capability, health and safety incident, some toxic release, fire, major financial loss
	3	Moderate	Semi-permanent injury, one or more persons, possible litigation, medical treatment required, health and safety incident, moderate financial loss
	2	Minor	Short term injury following incident, first aid treatment required, on-site toxic release immediately contained, minor financial loss
	1	Insignificant	Incident occurred but resulted in no injury, and no treatment required; no financial loss
	0	Prevented Incident	Incident did not happen but could have, if an intervention had not taken place; no financial loss

Potentially Higher Grade?

If the incident was categorized as a prevented incident, or if the event was graded as a lower grade risk but had the potential to be more serious, please indicate the *potential* grade of the incident by filling in 1 to 5:

Re-Occurrence

What do you feel is the likelihood of a similar incident re-occurring?

Almost Certain ☐   Likely ☐   Possible ☐   Unlikely ☐   Rare ☐

Details of the Incident

Where?					
Division		Clinical Unit:		Ward / Dept:	
When?					
Date of incident		Time (24hr):			
Was this incident related to a research study?			☐ Yes ☐ No		

Figure 5.2   Great Ormond Street Hospital for Children, London (UK), 2009. *Incident Reporting.*
(Continued)

Details of Person Affected by Incident

Person is:	☐Patient ☐Visitor ☐Contractor ☐Staff ☐Agency		
Surname		Forename(s)	M / F
Date of Birth		Hospital Number (if applicable)	
Address		Job Title (if staff member/contractor)	

Description of Incident & Action Already Taken at Time

(Please state facts only, and not opinions. Continue on separate form if necessary, and staple to this form)

Sign name		Job title	
Print name		Contact Phone No/Ext.	

Documentation in Notes

Treatment / clinical summary documented in case-notes?	☐YES ☐ NO	Name of Doctor	
		Signature of Doctor	
First aid given to non-patients?	☐YES ☐NO		

Equipment

What type of equipment was involved in this incident?

☐None ☐Disposable ☐Non-Disposable/Electrical

What is the equipment?

NB if electrical equipment was used; please attach a photocopy of this form to the equipment. Ensure equipment is clearly labeled not for use. Do not clear the settings and inform Biomedical Engineering (5368).

For non-electrical equipment, please inform the Clinical Supplies Advisor (8676).

Please detail nature of fault and relevant details below.

Serial No. of equipment	Batch No.	Settings were at

Figure 5.2 (CONTINUED)   Great Ormond Street Hospital for Children, London (UK), 2009. *Incident Reporting.*

(*Continued*)

Why do you think that this incident occurred? (Contributing factors that led to this incident)

This section must be completed in conjunction with your manager and/or relevant dept. Examples of contributing factors can be found on GOS website.

Action or Recommendations Planned to Minimize/Prevent Repeat Incident(s)

This section must be completed, in conjunction with your manager, and must be completed even if "No Action" is stated.

Action	Person responsible for monitoring this action

Checklist	Yes/No	Date & Time
Parents Informed	Yes ☐ No ☐	
Incident Documented in patient's case-notes	Yes ☐ No ☐	
Staff member off sick >3 days (if yes, complete RIDDOR form)	Yes ☐ No ☐	

To be read by	Print Name	Date
Head of Dept. / Ward Sister / Charge Nurse		
Senior Nurse / Lead Clinician / Manager		
Member of Patient & Staff Safety Team		

Figure 5.2 (CONTINUED)   Great Ormond Street Hospital for Children, London (UK), 2009. *Incident Reporting.*

Nuckols et al. [10] studied 2,228 reports for 16,575 randomly selected patients discharged from an academic and a community hospital in the United States between January 1 and December 31, 2001. They suggest identifying contributing factors in the incidence

Identify contributing factors in the incidence reports. So that proactive actions can be taken immediately.

reports. Greater detail about contributing factors would make incident reports more useful for improving patient safety. In 80% of reports, at least one contributing factor was described. Patient factors were identifiable in 32% reports, most frequently illness (61% of these reports) and behavior (24%). System factors were identifiable in 32%, most commonly equipment malfunction or difficulty of use (38%), problems coordinating care among providers (31%), provider unavailability (24%), and tasks that were difficult to execute correctly (20%). Provider factors were evident in 46%, but half of these reports contained insufficient detail to determine which specific factor. When detail sufficed, slips (52%), exceptional violations (22%), lapses (15%), and applying incorrect rules (13%) were common.

Pugliese [11] suggests finding solutions to mislabeling of clinical laboratory and pathology specimens that result in repeating diagnostic procedures and delayed or unnecessary surgical procedures. Use of electronic patient identifiers is one key prevention strategy. A study of more than 200 root-cause analyses over an 8-year period in the veterans administration (VA) system identified vulnerabilities in specimen collection, processing, analysis, and reporting associated with patient misidentification involving the clinical laboratory, anatomic pathology, and blood transfusion services:

> Data were categorized by three stages of the laboratory test cycle. Patient misidentification accounted for nearly three quarters of 253 adverse events, and occurred in all three stages of the test cycle: pre-analysis, analysis, and post-analysis. Examples follow:
>
> **Preanalysis.** The largest percentage (73% of the 182 misidentification errors) occurred during collection at admission such as wristbands mislabeled or orders for the wrong patient due to similar names and Social Security numbers (SSN). This included two-source patient identification for clinical laboratory specimens and failure of two-person verification of patient identity for blood bank specimens.
>
> **Analysis.** Twenty of the errors included relabeling, as well as misidentified microscopic slides due to a failure of two-pathologist verification for cancer diagnosis as well as wrong patient transfusion due to mislabeled blood products or failure of two-person verification for blood products before release by the blood bank.
>
> **Postanalytic phase.** The smallest number (7%) included results being reported into the wrong patient medical record or incompatible blood transfusions associated with failed two-person verification of blood products.

Pugliese suggests the following solutions: One change includes (1) the use of the full SSN *and* (2) use of electronic means for at least two of three patient identifiers (name, birth date, or SSN).

Nolan et al. [12] points out some citations by a regulatory agency. Innovative solutions to address these issues should be mandatory. These issues were as follows: Three hospitals were cited for deficiencies in incidence reporting, including failure to report an incident. Six hospitals received cautionary feedback on timeliness of the follow-up reports.

I recommend a common vocabulary and approach to understanding and describing their incidents. Errors in the understanding of what an "incident" is may cause confusion and give an incentive to some to skip the incidence report. Another suggestion would be to simplify the report to increase efficiency and reduction in time for documenting and the follow-up.

The Progress System Wide

The government agencies have taken initiatives to develop good guidelines, defined near misses, never events, and sentinel events with good examples. According to Reference [13], the AHRQ, an effective event reporting system should have four key attributes.

1. The institution must have a supportive environment for event reporting that protects the privacy of staff who report occurrences.
2. Reports should be received from a broad range of personnel.
3. Summaries of reported events must be disseminated in a timely fashion.
4. A structured mechanism must be in place for reviewing reports and developing action plans.

While traditional event reporting systems have been paper based, this reference suggests web-based systems that can also receive information from electronic medical records (EMRs). Special systems have also been developed such as the *Intensive Care Unit Reporting System* and the *Surgical and Anesthesia-Related Errors*. The reference also states: "Voluntary event reporting systems are generally confidential, in that the identity of the reporter is known, but legal protection is provided unless professional misconduct or criminal acts took place. Some systems, such as *the ICU Safety Reporting System*, are entirely anonymous—neither the patient nor the reporter can be identified."

The reference points out a 2008 study of over 1,600 U.S. hospitals evaluated their event reporting systems using the criteria above and concluded that "according to these standards, most hospitals do not maintain effective event reporting systems. In addition to lack of physician reporting, most hospitals surveyed did not have robust processes for analyzing and acting upon aggregated event reports. Failure to receive feedback after reporting an event is a commonly cited barrier to event reporting by both physicians and allied health professionals."

A major limitation is that the reports supply the number of events of a particular type, but do not supply the number of patients vulnerable to such an event for calculating the percent of patients at risk. Therefore, the IRS has the following limitations, according to a National Institute of Health report [14]. They are as follows:

i. They cannot be used to measure safety (error rates).
ii. They cannot be used to compare organizations.
iii. They cannot be used to measure changes over time.
iv. They generate too many reports.
v. They often do not generate in-depth analyses or result in strong interventions to reduce risk.
vi. They are associated with costs.

IRSs do offer a significant value. The report points out that while they are relatively new in healthcare, similar systems in nuclear, railway, fire, and aviation industry have had tremendous success.

The Institute of Medicine (IOM) advocates for the development and use of IRSs [14]. The IOM recommended the following:

Recommendation 5.1: *a nationwide mandatory reporting system should be established that provides for the collection of standardized information by governments about adverse events that result in death or serious harm.*

Recommendation 5.2: *the development of voluntary reporting efforts should be encouraged.*

This reference contains the following needs also. The Joint Commission (TJC) now requires that all hospitals have and use IRS. In order to be a valid measure of the rate of adverse events, a measure requires three things. There should be a clear definition of the event (numerator); few adverse events in healthcare are well defined. There should be a clear definition of the population at risk (denominator); the population in healthcare is usually not defined. Finally, there should be a consistent surveillance system for detection of both the event and the population at risk. IRSs have a problem with all three of these.

The Office of Health and Human Services (HHS) reports more progress by the government agencies [15]. It provides procedures and examples of incidence reports in addition to the following updates:

- Hospitals must track and analyze instances of patient harm as a condition of participation in the Medicare program. In a 2010 report, the Office of Inspector General found that 13.5% of hospitalized Medicare beneficiaries experienced adverse events during their hospital stays that resulted in prolonged hospitalization, required life-sustaining intervention, caused permanent disability, or resulted in death. An additional 13.5% experienced temporary harm events that required treatment.
- Hospital staff did not report 86% of events to IRSs, partly because of staff misperceptions about what constitutes patient harm. We defined "adverse events" as significant harm experienced by patients as a result of medical care. We defined "temporary harm events" as harm that required medical intervention but did not cause lasting harm.
- Hospitals use IRSs to monitor adverse events and other patient-safety issues. Reports include adverse events, "near-misses," or situations with the potential to harm patients.
- Hospital administrators we interviewed explained that they rely heavily on IRSs to identify safety problems. Administrators from all 34 hospitals indicated that they rely on IRSs to capture much of the information used to conduct patient-safety improvement activities.

The AHRQ Primer includes so-called never events [16]. According to this primer, the term "Never Event" was first introduced in 2001 by Ken Kizer, MD, former CEO of the National Quality Forum (NQF), in reference to particularly shocking medical errors (such as wrong-site surgery) that should never occur. Over time, the list has been expanded to signify adverse events that are unambiguous (clearly identifiable and measurable), serious (resulting in death or significant disability), and usually preventable. Reference [17] contains the list in Figure 5.3.

TJC has included sentinel events requirement also in the incidence reports [18]. A sentinel event is defined by TJC as any unanticipated event in a healthcare setting resulting in death or serious physical or psychological injury to a patient or patients, not related to the natural course of the patient's illness.

Sentinel events include "unexpected occurrences involving death or serious physical or psychological injury, or the risk thereof" and all of the following, even if the outcome was not death or major permanent loss of function. Examples [18] are shown in Figure 5.4.

1. <u>Artificial insemination</u> with the wrong donor sperm or donor egg
2. <u>Unintended retention of a foreign body in a patient after surgery</u> or other procedure
3. Patient death or serious disability associated with patient elopement (disappearance)
4. Patient death or serious disability associated with a medication error (e.g., errors involving the wrong drug, dose, patient, time, rate, preparation or <u>route of administration</u>)
5. Patient death or serious disability associated with a hemolytic reaction due to the administration of <u>ABO</u>/<u>HLA</u>-incompatible blood or blood products
6. Patient death or serious disability associated with an <u>electric shock</u> or elective cardioversion while being cared for in a healthcare facility
7. Patient death or serious disability associated with a fall while being cared for in a healthcare facility
8. <u>Surgery</u> performed on the wrong body part
9. Surgery performed on the wrong patient
10. Wrong <u>surgical procedure</u> performed on a patient
11. Intraoperative or immediately postoperative death in an <u>ASA Class I</u> patient
12. Patient death or serious disability associated with the use of contaminated drugs, devices, or biologics provided by the healthcare facility
13. Patient death or serious disability associated with the use or function of a device in patient care, in which the device is used or functions other than as intended
14. Patient death or serious disability associated with intravascular <u>air embolism</u> that occurs while being cared for in a healthcare facility
15. <u>Infant discharged to the wrong person</u>
16. Patient suicide, or <u>attempted suicide</u> resulting in serious disability, while being cared for in a healthcare facility
17. <u>Maternal death</u> or serious disability associated with labor or delivery in a low-risk pregnancy while being cared for in a health care facility
18. Patient death or serious disability associated with hypoglycemia, the onset of which occurs while the patient is being cared for in a healthcare facility
19. Death or serious disability (<u>kernicterus</u>) associated with failure to identify and treat <u>hyperbilirubinemia</u> in neonates
20. Stage 3 or 4 <u>pressure ulcers</u> acquired after admission to a healthcare facility
21. Patient death or serious disability due to <u>spinal manipulative therapy</u>
22. Any incident in which a line designated for oxygen or other gas to be delivered to a patient contains the wrong gas or is contaminated by toxic substances
23. Patient death or serious disability associated with a burn incurred from any source while being cared for in a healthcare facility
24. Patient death or serious disability associated with the use of restraints or bedrails while being cared for in a healthcare facility
25. Any instance of care ordered by or provided by someone impersonating a physician, nurse, pharmacist, or other licensed healthcare provider
26. <u>Abduction</u> of a patient of any age

Figure 5.3 Wikipedia, 2018. *Never Event*, retrieved from https://en.wikipedia.org/wiki/Never_events.

(Continued)

27. Sexual assault on a patient within or on the grounds of the healthcare facility
28. Death or significant injury of a patient or staff member resulting from a physical assault (i.e., battery) that occurs within or on the grounds of the healthcare facility Artificial insemination with the wrong donor sperm or donor egg
29. Unintended retention of a foreign body in a patient after surgery or other procedure
30. Patient death or serious disability associated with patient elopement (disappearance)
31. Patient death or serious disability associated with a medication error (e.g., errors involving the wrong drug, dose, patient, time, rate, preparation or route of administration)

Figure 5.3 (CONTINUED) Wikipedia, 2018. *Never Event,* **retrieved from https://en.wikipedia.org/wiki/Never_events.**

• Infant abduction, or discharge to the wrong family.
• Unexpected death of a full-term infant.
• Severe neonatal jaundice (bilirubin over 30 milligrams/deciliter).
• Surgery on the wrong individual or wrong body part.
• Instrument or object left in a patient after surgery or another procedure.
• Rape in an acute-care setting.
• Suicide in an acute-care setting, or within 72 hours of discharge.
• Hemolytic transfusion reaction due to blood group incompatibilities.
• Radiation therapy to the wrong body region or 25% above the planned dose.

Figure 5.4 Wikipedia, 2018. *Sentinel Event,* **retrieved from en.wikipedia.org/wiki/Sentinel_event.**

Summary

Incident reports are the best tool to prevent adverse and sentinel events. The process should incentivize everyone to file incident reports, without any punitive intent. However, use it efficiently to reduce the valuable time of caregivers and make sure those who submit a report should also get feedback on preventive actions.

References

1. Morgan, S., 2010. Patient satisfaction declines at hospitals, *The Wall Street Journal*, May 27, www.smartmoney.com/Personal-Finance/Health-Care/patient-satisfaction-declines-at-hospitals/.
2. Nadler, E., et al., 2010. You Bet Your Life on Patient Safety, Timesunion.com, March 21, retrieved from www.timesunion.com/ASPStories/Story.asp?StoryID=913775.
3. Taylor, J., et al., 2004. Use of incident reports by physicians and nurses to document medical errors in pediatric patients, *Pediatrics*, 114(3): 729–735, http://pediatrics.aappublications.org/cgi/content/abstract/114/3/729.
4. Agency for Healthcare Research and Quality, 2008. Hospital Incident Reporting Systems Often Miss Physician High-Risk Procedure and Prescribing Errors, March, retrieved from www.ahrq.gov/research/mar08/0308RA2.htm.

5. American College of Surgeons, 2010. Performance Improvement and Patient Safety Manual, retrieved on May 28 from www.socialtext.net/acs-demo-wiki/index.cgi?performance_improvement_and_patient_safety_reference_manual.
6. Dunn, D., 2003. Incident reports, their purpose and scope, home study program, *AORN Journal (Association for OR Nurses)*, http://findarticles.com/p/articles/mi_m0FSL/is_1_78/ai_105439647/.
7. Montana State Hospital, 2008. Incidence Response and Reporting, retrieved from https://dphhs.mt.gov/Portals/85/amdd/documents/MSH/volumeii/safety/IncidentResponseAndReporting.pdf.
8. Great Ormond Street Hospital for Children, London (UK), 2009. Incident Reporting, May 19, retrieved from the hospital Web site www.ich.ucl.ac.uk/gosh/clinicalservices/Patient_and_staff_safety/CustomMenu_01/#H2_9857.
9. Wachter, R., 2009. Hospital Incident Reporting Systems: Time to Slay the Beast, Wachter's World, retrieved from http://community.the-hospitalist.org/blogs/wachters_world/archive/2009/09/20/hospital-incident-reporting-systems-time-to-slay-the-monster.aspx.
10. Nuckols, T., et al., 2008. Contributing factors identified by hospital incident report narratives, *Quality and Safety in Healthcare*, 17: 368–372, http://qshc.bmj.com/content/17/5/368.abstract.
11. Pugliese, G., 2010. Lab errors—Call for more automation to prevent mislabeling, misidentification and related harm to patients, Premier Inc., *SafetyShare Newsletter*, retrieved from www.premierinc.com/quality-safety/tools-services/safety/safety-share/05-10-full.jsp#Story-3-OIG-Study.
12. Nolan, P., et al., 2001. Hospital Surveys and Incident and Events Reporting, Final Report to the Rhode Island General Assembly, November, retrieved from www.health.ri.gov/hsr/facilities/hospitals/hospitals2001.pdf.
13. Patient Safety Primer, *Reporting Patient Safety Events*, Agency for Healthcare Research and Quality. June 2017, https://psnet.ahrq.gov/primers/primer/13/voluntary-patient-safety-event-reporting-incident-reporting.
14. National Institute of Health, What to do with healthcare incident reporting systems, *Journal of Public Health Research*, December 1, 2013 www.ncbi.nlm.nih.gov/pmc/articles/PMC4147750/.
15. Department of Health and Human services, *Hospital Incident Reporting Systems Do Not Capture Patient Harm*, Online primer downloaded on July 7, 2018 www.oig.hhs.gov/oei/reports/oei-06-09-00091.pdf.
16. Patient Safety Primer, *Never Events*, Agency for Healthcare Research and Quality. https://psnet.ahrq.gov/primers/primer/3.
17. Wikipedia, *Never Event*, Online description downloaded on October 15, 2018 https://en.wikipedia.org/wiki/Never_events.
18. Wikipedia, *Sentinel Event*, Online description downloaded on October 15, 2018 en.wikipedia.org/wiki/Sentinel_event.

Chapter 6

Doing More with Less Is Innovation

It is an advantage to be lean; it is a disadvantage to be mean.

—Theme of this chapter

Introduction

A kidney transplant appointment in a hospital required a 107-day elapsed time in a hospital [1] from the time a patient was selected to the time of actual approval for the transplant. This affected the hospital's ability to take more patients because some patients did not meet the qualifications for a transplant. In addition, many patients were frustrated because of almost 4 months of waiting. The two critical steps in the qualification were (1) the review process, which was done by a team, and (2) the clinical assessment process. They looked for solutions. They discovered that there were several redundant steps in the two processes. They combined the two processes and simplified the work. (The details are proprietary.) With some minor improvements, they reduced the appointment cycle time to about 57 days—a 47% reduction in the total time! This allowed them to process more patients with less staff.

As in the earlier examples, doing more with less is an opportunity for innovation, not an obstacle. Only those that innovate will be the leaders. Only the leaders will be motivated to provide the experience better than the expectations of the patients. Others will make excuses of costs and lack of time to avoid accountability. Some of them will close up the hospital because they no longer can keep paying for the inefficiency.

It is common to hear, especially in hospitals, how do you get more done with less staff? A good suggestion is: Do not just sit there! Do the right things to be lean. The question is what are the right things for a lean hospital? They are as follows:

- Be lean, do not be mean.
- Eliminate waste, do not eliminate value.

67

- Do it right the first time—excellence does matter.
- Add more right work to save time and money.
- Attack complacency.
- Create a sense of urgency.
- Establish evidence between lean and patient satisfaction to ensure payoff.

There are some examples in this chapter that are unpublished. Because of their proprietary nature, the names of the institutions are omitted.

Be Lean, Do not Be Mean

Most major airlines such as United and American cutout giving peanuts and pretzels to travelers to be lean. They cut pillows and blankets too. Cutting out a service to passenger sitting for 5 hours in a crowded plane is not lean. It is mean!

There is no evidence that these airlines made more profit compared with small carriers such as Southwest and Jet Blue that continued to be profitable. Probably the big carriers lost some customers to small ones. Similarly, making a patient wait too long for a doctor because a hospital wants to have a lean staff is mean. If the lean staff results in customer dissatisfaction, then it is not lean, because true lean is a win–win strategy for all stakeholders, including the patients. It is about cutting out the waste and not lowering the value to a customer. Waiting too long is a low value for the patient. Getting harmed is a negative value for the patients. A good team can find a way to reduce wait time even with the existing staff. With a true lean strategy, a hospital benefits by providing an exemplary service, and the patients are delighted by the speed and efficacy in care. The result is reputation for ultra-high quality for the hospital.

There is a strong tendency to take undesired actions when organizations cut staff in economic downturns. Cutting good employees is mean, which results in low employee morale and costs more in the long run to hire and train new employees. The right thing to do is to use such employees to innovate elegant solutions to minimize waste and to improve efficiency and efficacy.

Waste can also include waiting time experienced by the staff, delays in delivering medications to nurses, waiting too long for lab tests, wasting drugs not consumed by patients, keeping high inventory of drugs, buying drugs in larger packs requiring manual packing in smaller doses, transporting patients from one building to another, using slow elevators, and anything that is inefficient in terms of time, money, or efficacy. It also includes overuse, inadequate use, and misuse of staff services, poor quality work, input errors in electronic health records, errors in rework, bad followup, no follow-up, misuse of technology, downtime from equipment, mishaps from equipment such as overdose from CT scans [2], or poor record-keeping. Preventing such a tremendous variety of waste gives us an opportunity to give better care to patients with reduced resources.

Often the solution is very simple. A hospital had too many bins of drugs. The drug orders were processed in batches. It took too much "no value" time to walk over to bins in different locations and look for the right drug. Sometimes the wrong drugs were pulled because of the monotonous walking back and forth. They eliminated most of the walking by reorganizing the work that did not require walking back and forth. They partitioned the drugs with names from A through L, and the drugs names from M through Z. A separate technician was appointed for each section. The technician in the new process could pick out all the drugs without moving. The resources did not go up. For example, a technician worked 4 hours to do the job in the previous process. In the new process, there are two technicians each working for about 1.5 hours because each has half the workload and there is no walking. The total technician time is reduced 4 hours to about 3 hours even though there are more technicians working. The hospital did not hire more technicians. They just redistributed the work of the existing technicians.

Eliminate Waste, Do not Eliminate Value

Here is an example of how we can cut waste and not value. Eight employees at a hospital struggled to cut the 14 days it takes to send bills for certain surgeries to insurers. They mapped every step in the process, and saw an obvious bottleneck: A medical technician held onto patient billing records until making a call to the discharged patient to check on postsurgical health. Skipping that step would save 72 hours. So the team surveyed 40 patients and discovered more than half did value the call. The eventual compromise: upon discharge, patients are offered the option of a follow-up call. And the staffers who call get summary sheets instead of the billing record.

A special report from the Boston Consulting Group [3] claims: "If administrators could figure out how to cut the length of stay by 10%, the systems could add tens of millions of dollars to the operating budget." Reducing length of stay means safe and efficient care given to patients. It adds value. A longer stay is a symptom of inefficient care and therefore a waste. Patients are usually aware of the waste such as waiting for a medication to be delivered by the pharmacy, waiting hours for a doctor, waiting for days for lab tests, unnecessary tests, harm because of intervention errors, or potential harm from miscommunications and errors in handoffs. Many hospitals, therefore, work very hard to expedite discharges. In fact, one radiology unit put priority on reading studies that are labeled as "discharge pending." Some patients may view this as a negative and feel like they are pushed out the door before they are ready. But if rephrased to the patient, most would prefer to undergo routine recovery at home rather than in a hospital bed. Many providers do have some reservation about sending someone home until they are clearly safe to leave for multiple reasons, including the patient's safety, legal implications, and the cost/effort to readmit someone.

Example

A surgical pathology specimen defect rate at a hospital was 4.3 per 1,000, resulting in about 182 defects per year. The defects were due to incorrect labeling, incorrect patient identification, or missing label. This resulted in loss of value to the patients. The value was restored by including the correctness of the patient identification during the surgical briefing and debriefing required by the Joint Commission [1].

Eliminating waste is usually a marginal innovation, but it can be an incremental or radical. The staffers in the same hospital clinic were trying to cut a typical 61-minutes office visit, as well as staff overtime, by 50%. They produced a 25-foot wall map charting a pneumonia patient's typical office visit. They concluded that 17 steps are valuable and 51 are not. For instance, patients walk to a separate laboratory to get blood drawn was of no value to the patients. If they could eliminate the walking to a separate laboratory, this would qualify as a radical innovation, considering the time saved and providing timely diagnosis. The results can be obtained in minutes instead of days. In the Boston Consulting Group report cited above, a Wharton professor who went to talk to hospitals on lean practices has this to say "They thought I was evil." They told him we are doctors, not Toyota. He adds: Now these same institutions have chief medical officers saying, "We want to run this place like Toyota!"

Do It Right the First Time—Excellence Does Matter

The two most famous quality gurus of excellence, Dr Edward Deming and Philosopher Crosby, preached that high quality reduces costs. They both preached doing work right the first time to operate at lowest cost (the best definition of excellence). Crosby alleges that quality unto itself is free. He called his approach Quality Is Free [4]. Deming revolutionized the Japanese rise to the world leadership in quality. Such an excellence does matter to all the hospitals!

According to Crosby, there is no such thing as the economics of quality. The costs involved are the costs for doing the job right the first time, and doing it right the first time is always cheaper in the long run. Every other cost is the cost of waste, and the only performance standard is "zero defects." He believed that there is no such thing as a quality problem meaning that problems do not originate in a quality department *per se*. Rather, problems originate in a functional department. Deming [5] proposed a chain reaction theory as a workflow that outlines the processes of an efficient organization, which entails improving quality, reduces costs, improves productivity, improves market share, and leads to staying in business and reducing costs for the customers (an example of a better than expected service). In many ways, it is similar to Crosby's approach in that he suggests that less rework and fewer errors will result in decreased costs. In essence, both align reduced costs to fewer defects and fewer reworks.

Deming recognized the importance of viewing management processes statistically as well as the importance of top management leadership and viewed reduction in variation through advocacy in a never-ending cycle of product/service design.

He preached a system called 14 Points, which enables management practices to make critical business decisions and effectively manage business environments. Essentially, the 14 Points, also known as the "System of Profound Knowledge," consists of the following [6]:

1. "Create constancy of purpose towards improvement." Replace short-term reaction with long-term planning.
2. "Adopt the new philosophy." The implication is that management should actually adopt this philosophy, rather than merely expect the workforce to do so.
3. "Cease dependence on inspection." If variation is reduced, there is no need to inspect manufactured items for defects, because there would not be any defects. To be sure, the system can have alerts in case the variation is on the border line of acceptable limits.
4. "Move towards a single supplier for any one item." Multiple suppliers mean variation between feed stocks. Try to locate suppliers close to the hospital to prevent logistics delays. Have a backup plan for critical supplies just in case the supply cannot be trusted.
5. "Improve constantly and forever." Constantly strive to reduce variation.
6. "Institute training on the job." If people are inadequately trained, they will not all work the same way, and this will introduce variation.
7. "Institute leadership." Deming makes a distinction between leadership and mere supervision. The latter is quota and target-based.
8. "Drive out fear." Deming sees management by fear as counterproductive in the long term, because it prevents workers from acting in the organization's best interests.
9. "Break down barriers between departments." Another idea central to total quality management (TQM) is the concept of the "internal customer," that each department serves—not the management, but the other departments that use its outputs.
10. "Eliminate slogans." Another central TQM idea is that it is not people who make most mistakes—it is the process they are working within. Harassing the workforce without improving the processes they use is counterproductive.

11. "Eliminate management by objectives." Deming saw production targets as encouraging the delivery of poor-quality goods.
12. "Remove barriers to pride of workmanship." Many of the other problems outlined reduce worker satisfaction.
13. "Institute education and self-improvement."
14. "The transformation is everyone's job."

> Create constancy of purpose toward improvement.
> Replace short-term reaction with long-term planning.

Crosby had a simple five-point system on absolutes of quality:

1. Quality means conformance to requirements, not elegance.
2. There is no such thing as a quality problem.
3. There is no such thing as the economics of quality.
4. The only performance measurement is the cost of quality.
5. The only performance standard is "zero defects."

Seeing quality from a behavioral point of view, Crosby attributes high importance to the working people's attention and concentration when it comes to accomplishing their tasks. His "Zero Defect" principle for optimal performance relies on the employee's total focus with almost no tolerance to imperfection, which, if it occurs, puts the distracted worker to blame. Deming differs here. He puts the majority of the blame on system, which is the responsibility of the management.

Crosby sees quality as a mission that one is not expected to fail and sets the basic elements of improvement: determination puts management on the right way toward quality, education as to the absolutes goes hand-in-hand with the employee's compliance to a perfected job, and implementation makes management know how to apply the process.

Some follow Deming, and some follow Crosby. The best organizations follow both and add more strategies that result in a win–win strategy for all the stakeholders. The bottom line for this book is that excellence matters to all, especially the patients and their families. They pay for a safe and least painful service; they deserve to get the best.

Add More Right Work to Save Time and Money

The Boston Consulting Group report above makes a productive statement: "Lean is not about starving. It is about building muscle and trimming fat. The need is to view the business as a system, understanding how the things need to be connected, from activities to metrics. Hospitals are too fragmented to do this, unless the senior managers themselves actively practice the system, thinking." To connect people for integration, processes, and hundreds of interactions, additional procedures and tasks may be needed. Such efforts must be implemented with a vision of reducing the total cost, even though the cost of introducing an additional intervention is high. The added task must save more money and resources or generate more business, resulting in more operating income.

A very important metric for what to add is the reduction in total ownership cost (TOC). The reduction in the TOC is estimated over the expected number of years the task will be in place.

One can assume 10 years' duration if a task is going to be used for a long time. If you are not sure, use a 5-year time frame. The TOC model has to be decided first. I use the following model:

$$TOC = \text{Cost of introducing the task} + \text{cost of sustaining the task} + \text{estimated cost of mishaps}$$
$$+ \text{cost of legal liability} + \text{estimated cost of losing goodwill (business loss)}$$

The next step is to compare the TOC for the current method and the proposed method. The difference is the savings in the TOC. This is how the big business decisions are made in the government and in technology organizations. They call it life cycle costing:

Example

Assume that you are going to use the World Health Organization checklist to prevent surgery-related medical errors. Let us assume the following cost estimates (over 5 years) for the current method:

Cost of introducing the new method = $0, since there is no change
Cost of sustaining the current method = $50,000 (10,000 per year)
Estimated cost of mishaps in 5 years = $3,000,000
Liability costs (any cost other than mishaps such as negligence) = $1,000,000
Cost of lost business (5 years) = $500,000
The TOC = $4,550,000

Assume that the use of the checklist will reduce medical mistakes by 60% and implementing the checklists will cost $15,000. The cost of sustaining the method over 5 years will be $80,000. Then, the costs will be as follows:

Cost of introducing the new method = $15,000
Cost of sustaining the current method = $80,000 ($10,000 per year)
Estimated cost of mishaps in 5 years = 40% of $3,000,000 = $1,200,000
Liability costs = 40% of $1,000,000 = $400,000
Cost of lost business (5 years) = 40% of $500,000 = $200,000
The TOC = $1,895,000
The reduction in the TOC by adding the checklists is = $4,550,000–$1,895,000
= $2,665,000

The example shows there is a saving of $2,665,000 on an investment of $45,000 ($15,000 for introducing the method and a $30,000 increase for sustaining).

The potential return on investment (ROI) is savings/investment
= $2,665,000/$45,000 (assuming $15,000 is required each
year for 3 years)
= 5922%

Attack Complacency

Many organizations become complacent after a series of successes. They wind up ignoring the fundamentals of flawless execution. This even happened to Toyota, which operated almost flawlessly for more than 50 years—so much admired that more than 60 U.S. hospitals are following the Toyota style of very quick resolution and prevention of problems. In 2010, Toyota recalled more than nine million vehicles because most of them suddenly accelerated without any warning to the drivers. More than 50 people died. Toyota took months to investigate the problem and still did not know why it occurred at the time of this writing.

A reporter wrote the following to express the dismay of buyers [7]:

> One of the biggest mysteries is this: Why hasn't Toyota still not gotten to the bottom of what went wrong? The company is famous for inventing the practice of asking "the five whys." This was a rigorous methodology that permeated the company's culture: This practice for decades has allowed Toyota to respond to problems better and faster than General Motors and Ford.

The lesson we should learn from this example is that once you become a leader, you must never forget your mission to provide a service that always exceeds customer expectations at a lower cost than any other competitor! You cannot be the truly best unless this mission is owned by every employee. Hospitals should empower the employees to keep innovating. One of the criticisms against the Toyota recalls is that the company lost its focus on quality when it went for becoming bigger than General Motors. They did become bigger than General Motors but at the enormous cost of quality.

Some organizations are complacent because the buy-in from the healthcare professional is sporadic. Physician S. Jain and the CEO John Toussaint at ThedaCare, a four-hospital entity in Wisconsin, present their experience and suggestions after committing to Toyota methods [8]:

> The initiative encountered stiff resistance. While the select physicians who were chosen to lead the process-improvement efforts fully embraced the methodology and incorporated it into their work, the vast majority of physicians found the methods confusing or irrelevant and harshly questioned whether techniques pioneered in the auto industry were applicable in healthcare.
>
> The initiative decisively improved clinical and business performance. For example, improvements in management of postoperative extubation and bleeding resulted in a decline in cardiac surgery mortality from 4% in 2002 to 0.8% in 2009 with unchanged volume and case mix. Over a 30-month period, a redesigned inpatient care unit reduced medication reconciliation errors to zero, ensuring all medications a patient was taking upon admission were accounted for upon discharge. With no significant changes in its payer contracts, ThedaCare's operating margin grew from 2.5% in 2003 to 6% in 2009.

They suggest three steps to improve the buy-in from healthcare professionals:

> Physician leaders must anticipate and respond to questions about the appropriateness of applying concepts from outside healthcare to their organizations.
>
> Change efforts must use simplified language and, where possible, terms and concepts more familiar to physicians.
>
> Physicians using industrial metaphors should focus on the end goal—better healthcare—not the metaphor.

Create a Sense of Urgency

Adverse and "never" events must be prevented quickly and efficiently. Taking months and years can do very serious harm. When you allocate a short time for a project, teams become creative. An example of this method at Hewlett-Packard was covered in Chapter 4, where the goal was to develop mainstream products in half the time and at half the cost.

Another way to create a sense of urgency is to give seemingly impossible goals to teams or a tight deadline. It is not trying to make them work hard. It is to make them work smart. Sometimes hard work is required. Make sure it is not punitive in nature, and that there is a clear recognition of the team for high achievement. If they have a smart solution, it should be judged by the ROI. The smarter is the solution, the higher is the ROI. Always aim at very high goals to create positive urgency.

Such a success occurred at Ford Motor Company on their 1995 Lincoln model. The designers were given a goal of developing the automobile earlier and much cheaper than the competition. They were given a lower budget and significantly less time. The team saved $60 million in the budget and introduced the new car model 4 months ahead of schedule.

> People are capable of attaining tough goals most of the time.

An example of ThedaCare shows how smart solutions are invented [9]. "The goal is to eliminate the estimated 20% to 30% of medical spending that does nothing to improve patient care." Their strategy seems to be working. They claim they cut the costs by $22 million in 2005 and 2006 without layoffs, while reducing medical errors. They stopped tracking the savings when they saw the gains.

John Toussaint, CEO of ThedaCare hospitals, gives the following eight areas where waste needs to be eliminated at the hospital's own Center for Healthcare Value [10]:

1. Defect: making errors, correcting errors, inspecting work already done for error
2. Waiting: for test results to be delivered, for a bed, for an appointment, for release paperwork
3. Motion: searching for supplies, fetching drugs from another room, looking for proper forms
4. Transportation: taking patients through miles of corridors, from one test to the next unnecessarily, transferring patients to new rooms or units, carrying trays of tools between rooms
5. Overproduction: excessive diagnostic testing, unnecessary treatment
6. Overprocessing: a patient being asked the same question three times, unnecessary forms; nurses writing everything in a chart instead of noting exceptions
7. Inventory (too much or too little): overstocked drugs expiring on the shelf, understocked surgical supplies delaying procedures while staff goes in search of needed items
8. Talent: failing to listen to employee ideas for improvement, failure to train emergency technicians and doctors in new diagnostic techniques

Establish Evidence between Lean Strategies and Patient Satisfaction

If a hospital does not track why patients are not delighted by its service, it may never know the value of their service. Make sure to track the correlation between excellence in the quality of service and lower costs. The evidence on how we are doing on doing more with less can be gathered. There are skeptics who would not accept the conceptual arguments. The best way to convince everyone is to measure the results using the following metrics while implementing lean strategies:

■ Percent of customers delighted by the service
■ Percent of customers having bad experience at the hospital

- Percent families delighted with the service
- Total cost of service to patients, including the cost of waiting, downtime, and cost of harm. These costs should reduce as the service improves.
- Staff satisfaction with the service

The Emory Clinic in Atlanta and the Park Ridge Hospital [11] use the Ritz Carlton Hotels method for providing exceptional service. Using the Ritz-Carlton methods of "Daily Line Ups" and "Basics of the Day," the Emory Clinic has been able to handle the challenges of routinely devoting time to deliver key messages and cohesive communication in a nonstop workforce. It has seen unprecedented increases in patient satisfaction scores and has received national recognition as a Success Story winner through their patient satisfaction benchmarking group. The Park Ridge Hospital similarly adapted the Ritz-Carlton method of empowering employees to handle upset patients with exceptional service. They even trained employees to learn how to judge a patient's level of pain by using a chart with different faces that can be associated with the amount of pain a patient feels. Employees loved the program and felt that it made their jobs easier and helped them to show even more compassion than they had ever been able to show before. This is the true spirit of doing more with less: more customer satisfaction without adding more manpower.

Rosabeth Kantor, a Harvard Business School professor and the author of the book *Super Cop*, makes a point using Procter & Gamble, the world's largest consumer product company with a 171-year history of growth, as an example [12]. She remarks on their stunning strategy: It begins in a startling, almost counterintuitive way—with company values and sense of purpose. Invoke the heart and care about human needs, the strategy seems to say, and the money will follow.

Kantor quotes McDonald, the CEO:

> We will provide branded products of superior quality and value that improve the lives of the world's consumers, now and for generations to come. As a result, consumers will reward us with leadership sales, profit and value creations, allowing our people, our shareholders, and the communities in which we live and work to prosper.

Here are Kantor's lessons for everyone:

1. *Inspire employees to add their hearts to their heads.* An executive at another large company who describes herself as a mercenary plunged into a project to build an energy-saving technology ready to focus on just the financials but found herself a true believer when other team members talked about their desire to change the world. People cared more and worked harder because values were tapped.
2. *Use performance measurement based on potential for impact.* Measure how well you are doing not just by the past (better or worse than last year) or by peers (ahead or behind competition), but by potential. Which audiences, customers, clients, and recipients are not being reached? What are the unsolved problems and unmet needs? Seeing untapped potential raises aspirations.
3. *If purpose-inspired opportunities and commercial considerations seem to conflict, find another way.* Procter & Gamble struggled with finding a profitable market for a water purification powder but kept it alive by establishing a nonprofit organization with government and partners to take it on. The values were enhanced, not diluted.

Ideas for Lean Innovation

One example in which computer information systems help save money and increase quality is with electronic documentation systems. Computerized entry is faster and can be more precise than the written chart. In addition, barcode systems with medications can double-check patient identity and medication accuracy prior to the patient's receiving the medication, which can increase safety, which will contribute to quality.

Using robots can be an excellent source of cost reduction with a more productive use of humans. A robot named Mr. Gower now navigates the hallways of the R. Adams Cowley Shock Trauma Center, riding elevators and opening doors on its own [13]. Its mission is to deliver patient medications to nurses' stations. The robot has an onboard computer and advanced infrared "light whiskers" allowing it to steer around people and obstacles. The robot even speaks.

Similar robots Rosie and Roxy work at Henrico Doctors' Hospital [14]. "When the robots make deliveries, the pharmacy staff can spend more time preparing medications for patients and answering questions from doctors, nurses, and others on the patient care team," said Hayes. "The robots also decrease nurses' visits to the pharmacy to pick up medications, freeing up more of their time to focus on patients' needs."

Lola, Roxie, and Fenway, the team of robots in a VA hospital, deliver medication throughout the campus [15]. They are efficient and courteous, but if you try to be first on an elevator, you might get nudged out of the way.

Summary

Innovation in the healthcare environment must be an ongoing search for new effective ways to decrease cost and improve quality and safety of care. Some methods can be like installing special racks to cut down trips to the supply room for nursing employees, refining the process patients go through to get an x-ray, and organizing weekly meetings to talk with both staff and physicians about what they can do to make their healthcare setup more efficient and safe. This keeps everyone more interactive, and they are likely to offer ways to be competitive. Integrating more with less is a chore for everyone. If there is sufficient recognition of their efforts, they will do their best.

References

1. An unpublished Lean Six Sigma project in a Baltimore hospital witnessed by the author.
2. Zarembo, A., 2009. Cedars-Sinai radiation overdoses went unseen at several points, *The Los Angeles Times*, October 14, www.sott.net/articles/show/194885-Cedars-Sinai-radiation-overdoses-went-unseen-at-several-points.
3. Boston Consulting Group, Special report, Date unspecified, Rethinking Lean: Beyond the Shop Floor, retrieved on May 20 at http://knowledge.wharton.upenn.edu/papers/download/101109_SS_Rethinking_Lean.pdf.
4. Crosby, P., 1980. *Quality Is Free*, Signet Books, Charleston, SC.
5. Deming, E., 2000. *Out of Crisis*, The MIT Press, Cambridge, MA.
6. Evans, J., and Lindsay, W., 2008. *Managing for Quality and Performance Excellence*, Seventh Edition, Thomas-South Western, Mason, IA, 2008.
7. Holstein, W., 2010. How Toyota Manufactured Its Own Fall from Grace, BNET, February, www.bnet.com/2403-13056_23-391889.html?promo=713&tag=nl.e713.

8. Jain, S., and Toussaint, J., 2010. Getting physicians to buy in to lean health care, *Harvard Business Review*, March issue, http://blogs.hbr.org/cs/2010/03/getting_physicians_to_buy_in_t.html.

9. Boulton, G., 2008. Tending to improvements in health care, *The Journal Sentinel* (Milwaukee), March 31, www.jsonline.com/news/29572384.html.

10. Toussaint, J., 2010. More Organizational Transformation Topics: Gemba, ThedaCare Center for Healthcare Value, April 10, www.createhealthcare-value.com/blog/post/?bid=159.

11. Ritz-Carlton: Leadership Center, 2010. Case Studies, retrieved at http://corpo-rate.ritzcarlton.com/en/LeadershipCenter/CaseStudies.htm.

12. Rosabeth, M., 2010. Inside Procter and Gamble's New Values-Based Strategy, *Harvard Business Review*, March, http://blogs.hbr.org/kanter/2009/09/fall-like-a-lehman-rise-like-a.html.

13. Rivers, C., and Boston, M., 2004. Robot Delivers Medications at University of Maryland Shock Trauma Center, University of Maryland Medical Center, www.umm.edu/news/releases/robot.htm.

14. Henrico Doctors' Hospital, 2007. Courier Robots Deliver Medications at Henrico Doctors' Hospital, December, reported on hospital's Web site, www.henricodoctors.com/CustomPage.asp?guidCustom ContentID=%7B84FFC05B-01B3-4AFD-9964-6AC7E3DB0E29%7D.

15. Smith, J., 2008. Robots an Easy Pill to Swallow for VA Hospital, *West Roxbury News*, June 4, www.wickedlocal.com/west-roxbury/news/lifestyle/health/x396300674/Robots-an-easy-pill-to-swallow-for-VA-hospital.

Chapter 7

Reinvent Quality Management

You have your way. I have my way. As for the right way and the only way it does not exist.

—Friederich Nietzsche, German scholar and critic

Introduction

"What if you bought a used car and it broke down just a few days after you drove it home? That would be frustrating and costly at the very least. Now, imagine if just days after you were sent home after a hospital stay you ended up right back there. Unfortunately this situation happens more often than it should," says Carolyn Clancy, director of the U.S. Agency for Healthcare Quality and Research [1].

It is obvious we do not have best practices in place. Actually, there is no such thing as the best practice, *only the better practice*. Swensen et al. [2] at the Mayo Clinic have some suggestions. They say that developing highly reliable care for patients requires changes in some traditional beliefs of medical practice, an evolution toward a "system" of healthcare, the disciplined application of scientific principles, modifications in the way all future providers are trained, and a fundamental understanding by leadership that quality must become a business strategy and core work, not an expense or regulatory requirement. Quality at Mayo is defined as a composite of outcomes, safety, and service. With continuous innovation, we can reinvent quality to meet and exceed the criteria above.

> Quality is composite of outcome, safety, and service.

There are two powerful influences at work in healthcare today. One, an emphasis on cost containment, and the other is ongoing focus on quality improvement. Many people view these as competing forces since it seems intuitive that higher quality should cost more. In fact, there are ways to improve quality that do not result in higher costs, especially when viewed in the context of total expenditures over a multiyear time horizon. Such a value-based approach to healthcare is an attempt to move beyond the cost versus quality tension and focus on reinventing the value of quality.

Continuously innovating customer experience and eliminating adverse events by means of efficient quality management is the essence of a quality healthcare organization. In order for quality management to work, poor outcomes should never be viewed as unavoidable. Rather, healthcare professionals should proactively consider potential adverse events in order to ensure excellence in future results.

> High quality and lower costs are not the conflicting forces.
> They compliment each other if we understand the quality gurus.

A Recipe for Success

Charting errors, misspelled words, and poor handwriting should not be deadly weapons, yet in the hospital, such errors can be the difference between life and death. In the last decade, we have seen quality emerge as a central theme in healthcare with giant steps taken by the AHRQ (Agency for Healthcare Research and Quality), National Quality Forum (NQF), HealthGrades, LeapFrog Group, Consumers Union, Gallup organization, and others. In addition, the CMS (Center for Medicare and Medicaid Services) is refusing to reimburse in the event of a certain type of hospital error such as preventable falls with injuries. Hospitals are increasingly concerned about the skill competencies of employees. Not only are hospitals putting their best foot forward to make sure that improving quality is advancing in their area, but they are looking to the future as far as improving the increasing demands of the patients. Such external and internal pressures are creating challenges never handled before. It is time to reinvent the way we manage.

- Redefine quality to exceed customer expectations of care.
- Conduct negative requirements analysis.
- Develop strategic plan based on SWOT (strength, weaknesses, opportunities, threats) analysis.
- Consciously manage quality at all the levels of an organization.
- Architect a patient-centric quality system.
- Validate interactions and dependencies frequently.
- Incorporate feedback loops.

Redefine Quality

Innovation is the essential component of quality management that sets apart a quality healthcare organization. The continuous process of basing practices on evaluating effectiveness can never end. According to the American Society for Quality [3], in order to maintain a satisfactory level of quality a healthcare organization must utilize "a customer-focused systems approach by encouraging research, innovation, and the formation of learning partnerships to advance knowledge of healthcare quality."

The instant an organization becomes satisfied with its current level of functioning is the moment that organization's quality begins to decline.

I have seen several organizations file for bankruptcy because of poor quality and safety. Having hands-on experience as supervisor of quality assurance at GE Healthcare and experience as a quality management consultant to high-quality organizations, I emphasize the three most important priorities for breakthrough

> The three most important priorities for breakthrough quality are requirements analysis, requirements analysis, and requirements analysis!

quality in his book *Zen and the Art of Breakthrough Quality Management* [4]. They are requirements analysis, requirements analysis, and requirements analysis!

The requirements must have the character of wholesomeness. It implies that the requirements of various patients are assessed from different views such as patient view, patient's family view, nursing view, physician view, and a view of anyone involved in the care such as a surgeon, radiologist, or pharmacist, and indirect stakeholders such as housekeepers, janitors, and community members. In addition, the requirements must be a system integration view to prevent adverse events from system vulnerabilities such as inaccurate equipment, poor handoffs, poor interactions among caregivers, and oversights in care. It is extremely important that a hospital team understands its customers' requirements before starting a quality system design. If care does not meet the patients' subconscious requirements and expectations, it is of very little value. There may be a need for a different plan for each classification of service such as cardiology, oncology, pediatrics, and emergency medicine. Make sure patient safety is not confused with quality. It is the most important characteristic of quality, but there is a lot more to quality such as the quality of the food, quality of the response by the caregivers, and the quality of the room environment, including "green" features such as noise levels.

The wholesome quality requirements are then merely translating the customer needs into the hospital system requirements. A metric required should be the percent times a hospital exceeds the customer expectations. This single metric totally ties in with how competitive a hospital is. One of the best examples of exceeding customer expectations is the Best Buy electronics store chain. It does this by making sure they are always the best among competitors. Employees take regular tours of what the company calls its "retail hospital." About a dozen of them wear white lab coats, walk a row of real hospital beds, and scan charts describing the maladies afflicting each of their major competitors [5]. The retail hospital closed in the 2009 because all major competitors have "succumbed to terminal illness," the last one being Circuit City.

Since the focus should be on exceeding the customer's expectations, not just meeting them, a hospital may define quality as "the ability to exceed customer expectations with lower long-term costs." It implies that as the quality goes higher, the costs go lower. Deming, the world's most admired quality guru, was emphatic regarding his principles, noting that if quality was emphasized then profit would surely follow. Deming said to avoid slogans and catchphrases. Instead, teach by actions. He preached not only treating customers fairly and with great respect but also valuing the employee that did the work. And Japan has proved it: the higher the quality, the higher the profits [6]. The Korean manufacturer Hyundai, whose market share was declining, made more profits and dramatically increased its market share when it offered a 10-year warranty to its customers. If this paradigm does not happen, there is bound to be a flaw in managing quality.

Tracking the cost of quality is another metric that will ensure the quality of effectiveness of this paradigm. It is not the cost of the quality assurance department. There are four categories of costs. They spread over all functioning departments. The focus should be on the total of the four costs, not just the initial cost of investment. They are as follows:

- *Cost of prevention.* Cost of training, team development, robust communications, developing wholesome requirements, investment in new procedures or processes
- *Cost of appraisal.* Cost of data collection, daily checks, inspections, paperwork, audits, analysis, calibrations, testing of equipment
- *Cost of internal failures.* Cost of mistakes, disruptions from inadequate systems, waste, rework, the cost of hospital-acquired infections
- *Cost of external failures.* Litigations, negative publicity, loss of business

Conduct Negative Requirements Analysis

It is critical not to just identify what positive quality experience we provide to the patients but also to identify what should not happen to the patients. The system requirements should be such that these events do not take place. Relying on a person alone is a weak solution. *The system should have safeguards or barriers.* From my experience as a consultant and trainer to aerospace industry including NASA, the author has developed a technique that has worked in other industries. This book is the first publication of this technique. I call this technique the "Negative Requirements Analysis." An example readily familiar to most is the example of the Toyota recall of millions of vehicles that could accelerate suddenly and go out of control. If Toyota had included a negative requirements analysis in its design process such as "The car shall not accelerate suddenly," this recall of over eight million vehicles might have been prevented, saving Toyota billions of dollars. Someone can argue that all automobile designers know about this basic requirement, so it is unnecessary to add a new requirement. The lesson here is that you do not know how good a system is until you test it out for unwanted events. Obviously, Toyota did not test for sudden acceleration or did not develop a correct test because the requirement was not explicit.

They trusted their designers. A good quality system must demand proof of safety! Harm to a customer is the worst kind of quality defect.

The purpose of the negative requirements analysis is to identify only the hazards that lead to "never" events, adverse events, and sentinel events. This analysis is for the day-to-day level at the healthcare performer level. It is best to demonstrate through an example. Let us view a quality assurance procedure (Figure 7.1) for the OB/GYN surgeries [7]. Identify only those events that lead to adverse, sentinel, and never events. A requirement is "no alcohol prior to surgery." If violating this requirement can result in an adverse event, a requirement such as "the system shall not allow surgery if a patient has an unacceptable level of alcohol in the blood prior to the surgery." Such an emphasis on negativity surely gets more attention and makes us think more thoroughly on how to prevent the unwanted event than if we just say that "patients shall not have alcohol 24 hours prior to surgery." The latter would not be a robust requirement, because the patients can ignore the instructions and the surgeon may go ahead and perform the surgery to avoid downtime of the entire team. The idea of putting the responsibility on the system is to make sure in some redundant way, like checking with a family member a day in advance, that the chance of a patient arriving intoxicated is minimized. The surgeon should not be burdened at the last moment with choices such as accepting or rejecting the patient under the constraints of schedules and costs. This figure shows a protocol for hysterectomy surgery. The statement "antibiotic given on time" can be changed to "no skipping of antibiotics." If you do not like the negative words, you can turn the statements to a positive statement, "The system should ensure that antibiotics cannot be skipped."

Develop Strategic Plan Based on SWOT Analysis

SWOT analysis is a strategy planning process that stands for strengths, weaknesses, opportunities, and threats. The aim of any SWOT analysis is to identify the key internal and external factors that are important to achieving the objectives. The internal factors may be viewed as strengths or weaknesses, depending on their impact on the organization's objectives. The external factors may include competitive pressures, legal pressures, compliance pressures (such as through CMS and the Joint Commission), technological changes, or sociocultural changes.

I. Pre-Admittance Communication

- No smoking
- No alcohol
- No shaving of the surgical site
- Medication reconciliation (summary of medications, care record for transition of care)
- Explain risks and benefits to the patient

II. Pre-Admittance Hospital Preparation

- Bed rails, patient furniture, and hand-held devices sanitized with bleach or equivalent to eliminate bacteria and germs
- Bottom side of the bed also sanitized
- Drapes, ventilation, faucets, walls sanitized
- Stethoscopes, wheelchairs sanitized
- OR room supplies and staff ready

III. Patient Sign-In

- Confirm diagnosis, site of surgery, and procedure with the patient
- Explain risks and benefits
- Review blood laboratory evaluation such as enzymes, basic metabolic panel, and complete blood count (*phlebotomist available for blood draws, patient verification, laboratory available for emergent labs, timely communication of critical values to the physician)
- Confirm no smoking, no alcohol, no shaving of the surgical site
- Review patient history of medications, allergies, current illnesses, such as diabetes, high blood pressure, depression, mental instability, and prior surgeries.
- Ask if anything the patient would like to add
- Assess vital signs
- Assess risk of blood loss
- Anesthesiologist reviews the patient medication and allergy history with the patient
- Administer established protocol of medication (*redundant check required)
- Administer antibiotic and necessary meds at the predetermined time

IV. Perform Surgery

- Time out before incision: Surgeon, anesthesiologist, and nurse verbally call out the name of the patient, site and the procedure. Discuss critical events, unexpected events, anticipated blood loss, and the duration of surgery.
- Confirm the tools, supplies, and instruments (sponges, sutures, scalpels, etc.).
- Verify anesthesiology checklist: inspection of anesthetic equipment, availability of emergency medications, patient's anesthetic risks, breathing system, pulse oximeter functioning properly.
- Keep the patient warm
- Antibiotics given at a specified time prior to surgery if needed (*pharmacy has verified allergies and nursing staff check prior to administration)

Figure 7.1   Patient-safety processes for OB/GYN surgery.

(*Continued*)

- Verification that anesthesiology equipment is working accurately (*back-up equipment must be available)
- Sterility of equipment, surgical instruments, and surgical trays confirmed
- Periodic feedback from the anesthesiologist (to ensure complete the attention to monitoring)
- Someone responsible for everyone observing infection prevention protocols (scrubbing if anyone went out of the room or touched by someone external to the team, hand sanitizing before touching the patient)
- Count sponges, needles, and scalpel blades before, during, and after the surgery
- Sign out. Verify the specimen is labeled properly, including the name of the patient. Discuss equipment problems. Discuss improvements for safer care. Discuss key concerns for recovery and outcome management.
- Discuss what went right
- Discuss post-op care protocol

V. Postsurgical Care
- Antibiotic given on time
- Meds given on time
- Monitor vital signs, patient movements to avoid blood clots
- Controlled medications are administered using a reliable process
- Safeguards to prevent falls
- Monitor for signs of infection
- If symptoms of deterioration persist, the doctor must be available to the patient within 15 minutes(*)
- Postoperative care instructed (*Wound care instructions provided)
- Discharge instructions with medications for at least a week

VI. Post Discharge Follow-Up
- Postdischarge patient follow-up to ensure no infection
- Clinic follow-up as scheduled
- Survey family members to ensure that medications are administered appropriately
- Progress documented

Figure 7.1 (CONTINUED) Patient-safety processes for OB/GYN surgery.

It begins with management thoroughly understanding the system first. An organization can be much more successful if it starts with upper management and works its way down. With that said, it is also important that there is a partnership between management and employees for the quality improvement/performance to be successful. This method is widely used in competitive businesses. It has been occasionally used in healthcare. Queen Elizabeth Hospital in Bridgetown, Barbados, used it to improve the performance in the intensive care units [8] to identify projects to ensure achievement of desired quality and to prioritize the projects. They suggest performing the analysis with stakeholders, mainly clinicians.

The SWOT analysis is an extremely useful tool for understanding and decision-making for all situations requiring new or improved strategies. It provides a good framework for reviewing the strategy position, and direction an organization wishes to pursue.

Consciously Manage Quality at All the Levels of an Organization

McLaughlin and Kaluzny [9] discuss three levels of quality.

- Conformance quality level
- Requirements quality level
- Quality of kind level

Evans and Lindsay [10] call these levels Performer Level, Process Level, and Organization Level. There is a very little hope for excellence unless quality is thoroughly planned and is implemented passionately at all the levels.

Quality at Conformance Level

This level is also called the performer level. It ensures that a caregiver is following the given standards and specifications based on best practices, which may not be adequate. However, the caregiver is expected to question the validity of the specifications, suggest improvements, and assist in implementing a better specification. This does not always happen. The supervisors and managers must assist in determining the goodness of the standards and the specifications in meeting the needs of the internal as well as the external customers. Improvement should be a never-ending process.

While there are many activities at this first stage, such as the development of ethical work culture values, training to make to make sound decisions, adoption or development of a quality procedures, understanding of team management principles, and identification of assumptions and risks, focus must be on satisfying the internal customers who depend on the quality of the output as well as the external customers, the patients, and their families. A successful healthcare institution is one where the employees play an active role in the quality management process. Every performer must play an active role in suggesting and promoting improvements.

Quality at Process Level

A caregiver only implements a process specification. The specification has to be correct in the first place. Quality is a subjective term that means different things to different people. As such, no one approach can ensure that the needs of all impacted parties are met. However, the development of best practices can ensure that the level of quality is increased by marrying practical solutions that ensure the best possible outcome to the needs and wants of not only the population receiving care but also those delivering care. To accomplish such a task, the traditional hierarchy must be disbanded and a new partnership must be forged between all interested parties. From the physician to the facility, to the day-to-day caregivers, to the patient, all parties must have a say in the development of a care process, as the omission of any one group will result in an ineffective solution.

This level is sometimes called the process level because the specifications define the robustness of a process or a service. At this level, the objective is to meet or exceed requirements. The aim is to optimize the process such that it does not compromise the needs of the interacting functions. Unfortunately, many departments try to optimize their work at the cost of suboptimizing the process performance as a whole [11]. Sometimes suboptimization of the process results in the suboptimization of the macro system. Management must seek inputs to optimize the macro system performance.

Quality of Kind at Organization Level

At this level, the quality is so high, and it delights the customers. The caregivers are expected to go beyond the expectations of a patient. The specifications must make this goal clear and allow some flexibility in thinking outside the box in situations where conditions and situations change frequently, such as in ICUs and in surgeries. The concern here is with the external customer, the patient, and the families.

At organization level, the quality is an ever-changing concept, as not only do new advances dictate the level of care but also the needs and desires of all impacted parties. Therefore, *accountability* and *responsibility* become key concepts in understanding the impact an organization's actions have on quality. The term *accountability* "means being held answerable for actions taken and the subsequent success or failure of the program" [10] and works to govern the process as well as those involved. The term *responsibility* means "having the charge to ensure that things are done, and done within the specified parameters" and applies more to the implementation and facilitation of the process.

The key to overcoming these obstacles is an ability to create a unified effort. The success of this process is contingent upon understanding the motives of each of the impacted parties and looking for commonality among their varied agendas. It should not be a zero sum game where one gains and someone else loses. It should be a win-win situation for all the stakeholders.

Therefore, a quality healthcare organization is one that is willing to look at itself under a microscope and review not only what is causing issues but also refine what are perceived as best practices. This task is never easy, as it is human nature to continue following a path of what we believe works; however, the most effective organizations understand that no system is infallible and that improvement often requires a complete overhaul of current beliefs and practices. To achieve this task, the organization must periodically conduct a gap analysis, which finds the difference between what should be accomplished and the current measures. The

> A quality healthcare organization is one that is willing to look at itself under a microscope and refine what are perceived as best practices.

best data can be obtained from the individuals who perform these tasks every day, so it is imperative to create an environment of open communication, where retaliation for ideas outside of the norm is not tolerated. An organization's success in achieving the status of a high-quality facility lies in its ability to involve all impacted parties, communicate both the positive and negative findings, and work toward a mutually beneficial enhancement of these practices.

An organization must also seek customer inputs continually since no two customers are alike. The Centers for Medicare and Medicaid Services and hospitals across the United States have introduced public information about patient experiences during hospital stays on www.HospitalCompare.gov. This government-sponsored website allows consumers to access side-by-side comparisons of patient satisfaction scores at hospitals across the nation.

The survey, titled The Hospital Consumer Assessment of Hospitals and Health Systems (HCAHPS), captures opinions from patients on critical aspects of care, such as communication with caregivers and satisfaction ratings. The data from July 2008 to July 2009 show that the healthcare quality needs to be improved drastically. Here are two quality-related measures (out of a total of ten measures) with average score for all reporting hospitals in the United States:

How often did the staff explain about medicines before giving to patients—59%
Willing to recommend the hospital to friends and families—68%

When combined with the SWOT analysis and the balanced scorecard, the resulting actions could be astounding. When the going gets tough, the tough gets going.

Architect a Patient-Centric Quality System

The phrase "system architecting" was created by Eberhardt Rechtin [12], the former chief architect at NASA/JPL. As in civil structures, it means creating and building systems too complex to be treated by analysis alone. He used the term "architecting" to design a complex process. It mostly applies to nonquantitative situations such as diagnosis or making a trial-and-error in an intervention. It is based on practical lessons learned and on inductive reasoning. It is more art than science. Rechtin suggests four methodologies. Depending on the complexity, one may apply one or more of the methodologies; some systems require all the four methodologies. They are as follows:

Normative: Solution based. Example: Developing a standard to solve known problems.
Rational: Method based. Examples: Using the best practices from other hospitals and industries and using the Toyota production system architecture by the Pittsburgh Regional Health Initiative.
Participative: Stakeholder based. Example: Brainstorming for ideas in a cross-functional team involving all possible stakeholders including the families of the patients.
Heuristic: Lessons learned based. Example: A heuristic is a statement or words of wisdom based on past experiences. A common heuristic "Twenty percent of the problems are responsible for eighty percent of the dollars" is a very powerful tool. It defines priorities very clearly. Rechtin's favorite phrase is "Simplify, simplify, simplify." He used it as a heuristic.

A system can be a complex structure such as the NASA shuttle complex software, or a complex network as in a healthcare system. The logical analysis alone will not ensure the safety of patient care. In any system, an architecture starts with a goal. The goal for a healthcare system should be ultra-high quality because usually there is no room for error. Therefore, a hospital should discuss the current quality system and question its ability to deliver ultra-high quality. If not, keep using the architecting methodologies and keep innovating new ideas. Necessity is the mother of inventions.

Validate Interactions and Dependencies Frequently

Every part of the process is connected and can affect the other. Deming used the saying "It takes a whole village to raise a child" to illustrate that all the different parts of the system must work together. All parts of the system must be focused on one purpose. By working together as a whole instead of as individual departments the total

> Every part of the process is connected and can affect the other. "It takes a whole village to raise a child."

quality will be higher. Understanding the motivation behind why people do what they do and learning to use that as a way to get things done brings out the best in coworkers. As a manager if you can learn these and use them to your advantage, it will be easier to get the job done. Physicians can help ensure the success of a patient-safety program by creating an advisory panel that reviews the plan, and evaluates and reviews adverse events—both real and potential. This will in turn provide the best quality of product or service.

Ultra-high quality is viable by instituting evidence-based processes, ensuring that clinicians are well educated on these processes, regularly evaluating the processes, and implementing process innovations accordingly. Failure to comply with any of these four elements can compromise a customer's experience. According to McLaughlin and Kaluzny [9], attempting quality improvement efforts without understanding variations leads to the following mistakes: Acknowledging trends that do not exist, inaccurately blaming or giving credit, inducing fear, establishing barriers, decreasing morale, and lacking the ability to "fully understand past performance."

To feel the pulse of the quality system, one has to be like a doctor. If the heartbeat or any other vital sign does not indicate healthiness, then we must diagnose the illness. The symptoms of a healthy quality system are that the teams are frequently suggesting improvements, and they develop robust solutions. As mentioned in the beginning, there is no such thing as a best practice. Of course, as the system matures, the frequency of improvement reduces. But there is always room for improving quality or efficiency or efficacy.

To diagnose the illness of not making improvements, one can use verification and validation techniques that are evidence based in the software industry. The methodology is called Independent Verification and Validation (IV&V). Verification means verifying the way in which the work is done as a team to assess whether the work done is best under the current state of the art. Validation means testing to make sure there are no oversights and omissions. This includes oversights and dependencies in handoffs, verbal communications, and follow-ups.

Validation testing is a tricky part. If you need to know whether the staff will make a mistake in administering a medication, you need to throw in variables that you learned in the negative requirements analysis covered in this chapter. One of the negatives was "The medication shall not be delayed more than 30 minutes." To test for this condition, you may have to send in wrong dose, wrong medication, late medication, or put a wrong patient name on the drug. Make sure someone is monitoring the staff actions and that the patient is not given the defective sample (or better yet, have a mock patient). If the right medication is delivered within 30 minutes, then the process is validated.

Incorporate Feedback Loops

What makes a quality healthcare facility is teamwork, a positive attitude, and the staffs having a passion for their jobs. Townsend and Gebhardt [13] approach quality as an integration of two interdependent parts: quality in fact and quality in perception. Quality in fact consists of meeting your own specifications and quality in perception involves meeting your customer's expectations. Therefore, the feedback between the two must be of the ultimate goal of quality management. No matter what industry a business may consist of, the customers always want to feel welcomed, appreciated, and respected.

A quality healthcare organization is basically made up of a group of healthcare doctors, nurses, and the rest of the staff. In order for the healthcare facility itself to be considered a quality healthcare organization, many other kinds of feedback have to take place. The staff must first be able to get feedback on process variations and vulnerabilities. This means that every single thing that is given to the patient while under the hospital's care must be checked over thoroughly and deviations reported in incidence reports.

Another thing that makes a quality healthcare organization better is if they are able to understand what can be prevented and what is preventable. There should be an active feedback on what is preventable. Once it is agreed that an undesired intervention is preventable, there should be a closed loop system to get feedback on what is being done to prevent it.

When staff only see what is in front of them and close their eyes to the bigger picture, this results in oversights and omissions. Many hospitals are guilty of this because they turn patients away from the service, treatment, and proper care that they need because of being understaffed. This type of feedback should be taken seriously. It has a long-term effect on the hospital, because no one is ever going to consider returning to that particular healthcare facility or ever recommending to another individual to go there. If patients come to a hospital seeking treatment, then that is exactly what they should get, and in a timely manner. If a hospital is shorthanded, then it needs to think about hiring additional staff and rely on the benefits of good quality service, which should lower costs in the long run. They need to be prepared at all times to give the type of service needed, and the healthcare organization needs to make sure that their staff is properly trained to handle their job and the tasks presented in front of them.

Feedback from patients is just as critical. So many mistakes arise each and every day, and a lot of these mistakes are due to simple errors by staff. Before any procedures or treatments are done, someone should be assigned to get direct feedback from the patient to ensure that everything on the patient's record is accurate. The patient knows her or his own medical history, but may not volunteer everything at the time of entering an emergency room.

Feedback between pharmacy and the nursing units is a major area for reducing mistakes. Properly labeled medicine bottles and different types of bottles for various types of the same medications could ensure that two different versions of the same medication were not mixed up. If one staff member cannot understand the writing in the patient chart, then he or she should ask the person who wrote it exactly what it says. Many mistakes are made because people make assumptions. For instance, a patient comes in the hospital with an infection and writes on her medical history and allergy sheet that she is allergic to penicillin. The nurse may not understand her handwriting and instead of asking the patient, she puts down that the patient is allergic to pitocin. If the patient were given penicillin to clear up the infection, she could go into anaphylactic shock and possibly die. This could have been prevented had the clerk only asked the patient what she had written. The feedback must be turned into feedback on actions to prevent mishaps. Actions must be robust such as using certain bottles for topical medications and other types of bottles for medications that need to be injected.

Summary

Many quality management systems are based on past gurus and are over 30 years old. There is hardly any literature that questions how good they are. This is the key question in determining whether we have the process for preventing adverse, sentinel, and "never" events. This chapter and the earlier chapters suggest that we need to reinvent our quality management systems. The healthcare service industry is complex with multiple facets and levels of organization. Today there is a shift to an organization model in which the customer influences every function and managers must adapt to be instrumental in establishing a cultural change within the system to meet the new quality focus. Chapter 8 suggests we need to reinvent risk management too. Quality and risk management are interdependent on each other.

References

1. Clancy, C., 2009. Navigating the Health Care System, Agency for Healthcare Quality and Research, November 3, retrieved from www.ahrq.gov/consumer/cc/cc110309.htm.
2. Swensen, S., et al., 2009. Quality: The mayo clinic approach, *American Journal of Medical Quality*, 24: 428.
3. American Society for Quality, 2010. Healthcare Division, retrieved on May 20, from www.asq.org/health/.
4. Raheja, D., 2001. *Zen and the Art of Breakthrough Quality Management*, published by Design for competitiveness. Available at www.Amazon.com.
5. Edwards, C., 2009. Why tech bows to best buy, *Business Week*, December 10.
6. Raheja, D., and Allocco, M., 2006. *Assurance Technologies Principles and Practices*, John Wiley & Sons, Inc., Hoboken, NJ, 9.
7. The OB/GYN QA process was developed by Dev Raheja from discussions with two OB/GYN surgeons.
8. Dey, P., and Hariharan, S., 2008. Managing healthcare quality using combined SWOT and the analytic hierarchy process approach, *International Journal of Healthcare Technology and Management*, 9(4): 392–409, www.inderscience.com/search/index.php?action=record&rec_id=19675.
9. McLaughlin, C., and Kaluzny, A., 2006. *Continuous Quality Improvement in Healthcare*, James & Bartlett Publishers, Sudbury, MA.
10. Evans, J., and Lindsay, W., 2008. *Managing for Quality and Performance Excellence*, South-Western, Mason, OH.
11. Issel, L., 2008. *Health Program Planning and Evaluation: A Practical, Systematic Approach for Community Health*, Jones & Bartlett Publishers, Sudbury, MA.
12. Rechtin, E., and Maier, M., 1997. *The Art of Systems Architecting*, CRC Press, Boca Raton, FL.
13. Townsend, P., and Gebhardt, J., 1999. *Quality is Everybody's Business*, CRC Press, Boca Raton, FL.

Chapter 8

Reinvent Risk Management

Man can believe the impossible, but can never believe the improbable.

—Oscar Wilde, poet, novelist

Introduction

"Patient Safety Incidents at U.S. Hospitals Show No Decline, Cost $8.9 Billion."

This was the finding on Medicare patients by HealthGrades, an independent healthcare ratings organization [1]. This study concludes that nearly one million patient-safety incidents occurred over the years 2006–2008. One in ten patients—99,180 individuals—experiencing a patient-safety incident died as a result. Patients at hospitals in the top 5% hospitals experienced 43% fewer patient-safety incidents, on average, compared with poorly performing hospitals. The report says that if all hospitals performed at this level, 218,572 patient-safety incidents and 22,590 deaths could potentially have been avoided, saving $2.0 billion from 2006 to 2008.

Even the medication-adverse events for all the patients are not declining. They are on the rise, according to the Institute of Safe Medication Practice [2]. The third quarter 2009 summary report reveals that the U.S. Food and Drug Administration has seen steady increase in the number of serious, disabling, and fatal drug events during the previous 2 years. There were 29,065 case reports in the third quarter of 2009 versus 26,809 in the same quarter 1 year earlier.

These data suggest that the current risk management methodologies are marginally effective at many hospitals. Hubbard [3] suggests a major cause of such scenarios in industry in the following description:

> Ineffective risk management methods, often touted as "best practices," are passed from company to company like a bad virus with a long incubation period: there are no early indicators of ill effects until it's too late and catastrophe strikes.

The healthcare industry does not seem to be an exception to Hubbard's conclusion. His simple definition of risk "something bad could happen" is very appropriate for healthcare. This chapter is about risks in delivering safe healthcare.

> Ineffective risk management methods, often touted as "best practices," are like a bad virus with a long incubation period.

Whether healthcare risk management "best practices" are outdated or not, I see opportunities to fix the system. They are about looking outside the box to other industries. Even though the hospitals have imported Crew Resource Management from the aviation industry and the failure mode and effects analysis (FMEA) from the Department of Defense, there is a lot more to learn from the aerospace, nuclear, and chemical industry. Carl Sagan, the astronomer, said that it is far greater to grasp the universe as it really is than to persist in delusion, however satisfying and reassuring. We need to rethink risk management. The sound principles of risk management coupled with innovative solutions can ensure high return on investment (ROI). The principles are as follows:

- Identify risks.
- Assess risks.
- Mitigate risks.
- Orchestrate risk management.
- Aim at high ROI without compromising safety.

Identify Risks

Best practices must be built and doubted at the same time. We use them not because they are perfect, but because we feel secure in the company of peers. If you just ask a simple question at a morbidity and mortality (M&M) conference, "Can anything go wrong with the best practice?" there will be more unresolved issues offered than the number of people attending. Brainstorming with a diverse group and looking for what can possibly go wrong is one of the best ways to identify risks. Ask questions: What else can go wrong?

Fortunately, the formal and evidence-based risk identification techniques, called hazard analyses, are freely available from other industries, the pioneer being the aerospace industry. Reinventing risk management in healthcare becomes easier if we import such techniques and the mitigation methods from this industry. The veterans administration hospitals imported such a risk analysis technique called FMEA. It is now a required practice by the Joint Commission. This chapter contains an overview. This section will also give an overview of two other techniques (fault tree analysis (FTA) and the operations and support hazard analysis (OS&HA)), and point out references for some more techniques.

An advantage of using the aerospace hazard analysis methods is that most of them not only cover risk identification but also include the risk assessment, risk prioritization, and risk mitigation as shown in Section "FMEA".

Failure Mode and Effects Analysis

This technique is widely used at the VA hospitals. A training course is available to the public [4]. To speed up proactive use of this tool, the Joint Commission on Accreditation of Healthcare Organizations (JCAHO) introduced the standard LD.5.2 in 2001 to proactively identify high-risk processes, identify failure modes, redesign the processes, implement measures of effectiveness, and implement a strategy for maintaining the effectiveness.

The primary purpose of Healthcare FMEA is to deliver reliability of medical interventions for a standardized process, such as performing heart surgery, installing a pacemaker, replacing a failed heart with a mechanical implant, patient intubation, admitting patients, discharging patients, administering medication, and monitoring patient condition.

The Institute of Healthcare Improvement (IHI) defines *reliability* as failure-free performance over time. Since in healthcare each patient is different, there are often deviations. Standardization should also include rules on how to handle exceptions. The next step is to document the analysis in a matrix shown similar to the one in Table 8.1.

In this matrix, the following are documented during brainstorming:

1. Process steps
2. Potential failure modes (what can go wrong)
3. Causes of failure (root causes)
4. Effects of failure (on the patients and employees)
5. Risk (multiplication of three ratings on a scale of 1–10). S stands for the severity of the effect, F for frequency of the root cause, and D for how early the potential for harm is detected. Risk priority number (RPN) is the multiple of the three; the higher the number, the higher the risk. This method is mostly used in industry. Some organizations, such as the VA hospitals, use qualitative method described in the column "Recommended Action" of Table 8.1 of this chapter.
6. Recommended action (mitigation)
7. Revised risk (assuming the mitigation is implemented; this column is optional)

Fault Tree Analysis

This scenario-based technique is useful for preventing potential adverse events, sentinel events, and "never" events that can happen. The analysis starts with identifying scenarios of all the possible unwanted accidents. A separate analysis is done with each scenario. To do this analysis, one has to understand that accidents are never caused by a single factor such as a human error. Human error in combination with a latent hazard(s) causes an accident. James Reason [5] described this theory with the analogy of the holes in a Swiss cheese that lined up. The central thinking during FTA is to *identify the combination of events that can line up to produce harm*. The procedure is as follows [6]:

1. This tool uses graphical symbols developed for the Minuteman missile program with the goal of zero mishaps. These are shown in Figure 8.1 (see Figure 8.2 also to observe their use).
   The AND symbol and the OR symbol tell us how vulnerable we are. The AND symbol is used to show that an undesirable outcome will not happen until all the outcomes underneath it fail. This shows strength of the system. The OR gate shows the weakness. Any failed outcome under the OR gate can result in an undesired outcome.
2. Identify a scenario for harm. This is called the "top event." For example, the start of the tree of the hypoventilation of a patient from the ventilator can be seen in Figure 8.2. The figure contains an OR gate, which means hypoventilation can be caused by any of the five failed outcomes. These causes constitute level 1 of the analysis.

Table 8.1   FMEA Matrix for Documenting the Analysis and Actions

Process Step	Potential Failure Mode	Causes of Failure	Effects	Risk				Recommended Action	Revised Risk			
				S	F	D	RPN		S	F	D	RPN
Patient walks in for emergency care	Help not available immediately	Shortage of staff	Has to wait in line to see the triage nurse	10	6	6	360	Have a physician (who can delegate work to residents) fill in as a second triage nurse when required	3	4	3	36
		Overcrowding		10	6	2	120	Send less critical patients to register in intermediate care unit	4	3	2	24
Treat patient in the trauma room	Physician tied up with another patient	Shortage of staff	Risk of patient harm may increase	8	3	2	48	Have nurses/residents attend to less critical interventions freeing the trauma physician for critical needs	4	2	1	8
Transport patient to OR	Delay in reaching the OR	Elevator tied up by other users or not working	Potential death	10	4	8	320	Have OR on the same floor. Have portable vital signs monitored during transport	6	1	1	6
		OR too far from the emergency room (ER)	Potential death	10	2	4	80	Locate OR close to ER	5	2	1	10

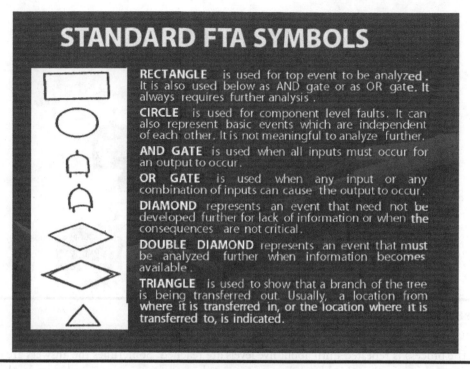

Figure 8.1   Fault tree symbols.

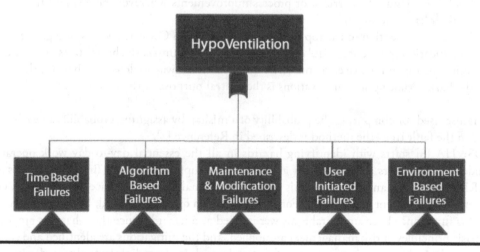

Figure 8.2   Level 1 of the ventilator fault tree.

3. Each level 1 outcome is then further broken down to its causes. These are called level 2 causes. Figure 8.3 shows the breakdown for one of the outcomes of level 1. This diagram shows the use of AND gates. This portion of the system is stronger. For example, the user programming error cannot cause harm until both the outcomes below go wrong at the same time (the user makes an error of choosing the volume control instead of respiration control and the alarms do not work).

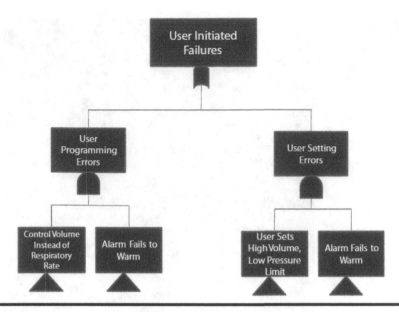

Figure 8.3   Partial level 2 of the ventilator fault tree.

4. The process is repeated until about five levels are reached. Sometimes the answers are obvious at the second or third level. For a very complex system, one may need more levels. It is easier if we use commercial software available on the Internet.
5. Look for safeguards, barriers, or process improvements wherever there is an OR gate, the weak links in the system.
6. Pay special attention to the top level. If it starts with an OR gate such as in Figure 8.2, it is an indication of lack of control on patient harm. For example, the harm starts because of the failure of any of the five elements; there should be some way to detect the harm early or limit the harm. Making such innovations is the central purpose of the fault trees.

FTA is also used for computing the probability of a mishap by assigning probability to each of the events in the fault tree. The method is described in Reference [7].

OS&HA [8] starts with identifying hazards in all the essential day-to-day work operations (includes human errors and equipment anomalies) and support functions (includes services such as MRI, wheelchairs, and lab tests). This is basically an analysis of workplace, environment, communication, and patient care hazards. For each function, a question is asked, "What can go wrong with this function?" Each undesirable answer is listed as a hazard. Once these hazards are identified, basic principles of risk management are applied, and the mitigations are identified and tracked as in an FMEA. An example of a support function hazard: in the radiology facility, radiation itself is a hazard but is an essential portion of an intervention. The mitigation risk may be accomplished by establishing the safe levels and monitoring the equipment for accuracy and precision.

Let us apply these principles to the operating room. The main task is the surgery itself, and although some tasks can vary, depending on the specific procedure, some tasks are routine for every case. Examples of these tasks include the following:

■ Patient identification
■ Verification of the correct side of the operation

- Medical reconciliation
- Identification of any allergies
- Time-out procedures, which include patient verification (three verifications can be performed by the surgeon, nurse, and anesthesiologist), procedure confirmation, giving medication such as pre-op antibiotics, and ensuring that all needed equipment was present.

The support functions in this process could include the following:

- To make sure that the stretcher was cleaned prior to use
- To ensure that all surgical instruments and trays are sanitized
- To verify that all equipment, such as vital sign monitors, are in working order
- All medications and supplies are available during surgery, including spare batteries if needed.

Table 8.2 shows the hazards and mitigation strategies for a sample of functions. To keep it simple, we have used a very simple classification of acuity or criticality (very high, high, moderate, and low). For a detailed review, see our previous article on preliminary hazard analysis [2]. These are the judgment of the team members. Make sure a cross-functional team is performing the analysis. A single person is sure to overlook many hazards. We have shown only a few causes of hazards to show the essentials. In practice, it is necessary to identify all the potential causes.

One can see that this analysis requires a significant amount of time and a qualified cross-functional team. It is easy for a decision maker to say we do not have resources and budget. But that is not acceptable since the high risks are not acceptable to any healthcare institution. To overcome this issue, we must look for efficiency, speed, and reduced manpower. Here are some suggestions: To gain speed, work on high risks first. If time permits, then work on moderate and low risks. To gain efficiency, assign a person who makes sure the team is discussing serious issues only, not spending much time on lower risks, and documenting high-risk issues only. These two approaches will automatically reduce the manpower required.

The benefits of this analysis is that with many safeguards, we can prevent many adverse and "never" events. Even if we prevent a single adverse event, the cost of the analysis is very easily justified.

More Safety Analysis Techniques

There are more techniques, but they are beyond the scope of this book. One can find these techniques in Reference [7]. The commonly used techniques are as follows:

- *Event Tree Analysis* is used for analyzing and mitigating potential disasters such as fires, accidents involving mass injuries, explosions, complete loss of power, earthquakes, or very severe weather consisting of several feet of snow. This analysis is especially of value to those in charge of emergency preparedness and disaster planning. It was developed in the nuclear industry.
- *Sneak Circuit Analysis* is used for predicting and mitigating unexpected harmful events or harmful events happening at a wrong time.
- *Preliminary Hazard Analysis* is used used for new systems and processes to predict hazards from lessons learned data and intuition, and using successful mitigations from lessons learned as well as from innovation.

Table 8.2   A Sampling of Operational and Support Functions with the Associated Hazards

Item #	System Functions	Potential Hazards	Criticality	Causes	Mitigation Strategy
1	Operational functions Perform three verifications	Wrong-site identified The patient speaks a foreign language and miscommunicates	Very high	Inappropriate identification and lack of verification There is no interpreter available	Encourage the patient to verify the correct site for surgery Interpreter must be arranged prior to surgery
2	Anesthesia	Delivery of wrong anesthetic Delayed anesthesia delivery Failure to properly monitor a patient Esophageal intubation	High	Drug improperly labeled IV errors, vaporizer leakage Malfunctioning equipment, alarm systems are not working Failure of tube verification	Labeling cross-checks Frequent equipment checks Equipment checks, close staff monitoring Visualization of endotracheal intubation, auscultation, capnography
3	Operation	Wrong-site surgery Retained foreign body	Very high	Failed verification Inappropriate sponge counts, oversight during surgery	Cross-checks Sponge counts, Surveying the appropriate body cavity prior to closure, obtaining x-rays if needed to check for any retained foreign body
4	Antibiotic delivery	Antibiotic is delivered too late Patient is administered the wrong antibiotic	High	Pharmacy delays IV infiltration Labeling errors	Having antibiotics available in the pre-op area Cross-checks prior to infusion
5	Support functions Pick up right patient for surgery	Multiple patients with same last name	Very high	Lack of proper patient identifiers	Using two or three identifiers, such as last name and first name, birth date, and medical record numbers
6	Surgical instruments and trays sanitized	Supplier supplies inadequately sanitized trays Sanitizing equipment in the OR malfunction	High	Autoclave thermostat malfunctioning Contamination during transport	Verification of equipment functions Appropriate sanitation packaging
7	Sanitized and functional equipment	Equipment may be infected with bacteria Equipment fails suddenly	High	Improperly sanitized equipment Equipment out of calibration	Appropriate labeling and timing of sanitation Equipment checks before and after every procedure Availability of backup equipment in case of failure

■ *Common Cause Analysis* is used for identifying events that can result in multiple failures, and designing safeguards into the system. For example, a failure of a switch can turn off several critical functions in a cardiac surgery. A redundant switch could be a safeguard.

Mitigate Risks

In most systems, the high risks exist is about 20% problems. About 80% problems are minor or acceptable. This is called the 80–20 rule. The minor problems should be delegated to junior employees who want to get some learning experiences. If they make a mistake, it is not a big thing. Since it does not require punitive action, it becomes a morale booster. This is an opportunity for employees to speak up freely without causing any mishap. The remaining 20% of major problems must be eliminated or their probability of occurrence should be less than one in a million. This is sometimes acceptable in aerospace. Mitigating these risks should be the responsibility of experienced and innovative teams. Make sure they are accountable also. If we identify a risk and do not mitigate it, then it becomes the subject of negligence in lawsuits.

The VA hospitals use a mitigation strategy similar in the form of a matrix shown in Figure 8.4. The matrix shows severity of harm on a scale of 1 through 4 and probability on a scale of A through E. They both are qualitative and their values are labeled. The robustness of mitigation depends on a combination of the severity and the frequency of harm known as the risk index. This matrix

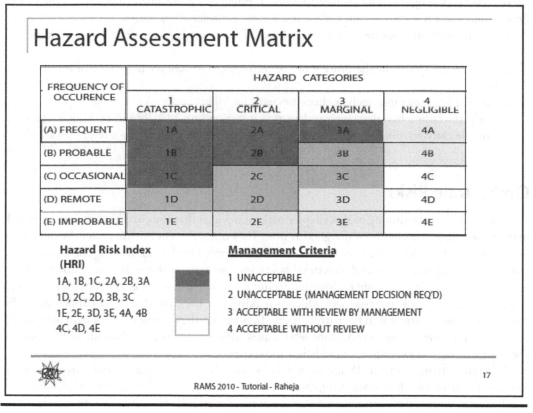

Figure 8.4   Hazard risk index versus management actions for safe outcome.

shows a guide for management and action needed for each combination of severity and frequency. For example, the most harmful combinations are shown in black. The bottom of the matrix shows that such high risks are unacceptable, which implies that the current system or a procedure is unacceptable. A drastic change is required. The proposed system must reduce either the severity or the frequency or both such that the corrected system reduces the risk to a much lower threshold.

Let us apply this matrix to the bacteria on patient's furniture. According to an *ABC News* broadcast on November 11, 2008, Grace Voros, 85, went to the hospital for an x-ray to check for broken bones. While there, she contracted *C. diff.* (*Colosterium difficile*; colitis) and died. The broadcast also claimed that about 7,718 patients are affected annually with this infection, and the death rate is 13 per 1,000. This is sufficient information to assign the rating "1" for severity. The frequency of patients getting infected depends on the hospital's system for preventing *C. diff.* infections. Case Western Reserve and Cleveland VA Medical Center have found that routine cleaning is not enough to protect you from *C. diff.* Bleach, they report, should be used [9]. After routine cleaning in a hospital, they found 78% of the surfaces were still contaminated. This kind of information is needed in deciding the probability of occurrence of a mishap.

Suppose you give a rating of "B" on frequency. The combination "1B" falls in the dark color zone, which means the current system of intervention is unacceptable. We must change our intervention strategy. The new strategy is one that requires disinfecting with a proven sanitizer.

There are instances when a viable solution for black-zone risks is not possible. In that case, senior management must either find a solution through research or accept the risk. The bottom line is that performing such analysis can prevent or reduce the risk of sentinel, adverse, and "never" events. Doing this prior to implementing a system or a procedure can produce a high ROI. Preventing mishaps is usually much cheaper when we consider all the costs.

Once the risks are prioritized, the order of precedence for mitigation actions is as follows:

1. Change the system or the process or the technology, whichever is capable of avoiding the harm.
2. Provide fault tolerance such as checklists with multiple checks.
3. Make the failure harmless, such as detecting infection immediately and making it harmless.
4. Provide early warning of the harm before it takes place by monitoring a relevant variable.

Orchestrate Risks

The statistics at the beginning of this chapter make it obvious that the current effectiveness of risk management functions has been marginal at best. They often prevent mishaps after the damage is done. It is not their fault since most of them are never exposed to the best techniques used in aerospace. They rarely use formal and structured safety analyses such as above. Nor are most managers familiar with the tried and tested mitigation techniques used in aerospace. But what is missing in risk management is risk orchestration, which is making sure the right things are happening at the right time, when a patient is in the path of harm. In other words, the role of a risk manager should be like a symphony orchestra conductor who makes sure every musician plays his or her piece at the right time and in synergy with the fellow musicians.

Take the situation of the 18-month-old baby Josie King in which all the caregivers were too engrossed doing their own things while she was dying from dehydration [10]. The staff administered wrong medication even when the mother protested. She told them that Josie needs fluids, not methadone, a narcotic pain medication. The nurses and doctors both ignored her requests. One thing led to another and Josie wound up with two infections and cardiac arrest. This happened in the nation's number one hospital. The question is who was making sure that the doctors and nurses did the right things at the right time to manage the risk? The risk manager was only involved later [11] when the parents decided to take legal action. In my opinion, the risk manager does not have to personally monitor all the risks, but the risk manager should delegate this responsibility to a staff member trained in risk management for every patient in critical care. This is one way the nurses, physicians, and support staff can orchestrate their work to play to the same music.

The orchestration process requires a structure for sound risk management that is sustainable. The structure should include the integration of the support staff. Once the structure is there, then rehearsals must be there as an evidence that the orchestra is prepared for the performance.

> The role of a risk manager should be similar to a symphony orchestra maestro who makes sure every musician plays at the right time, and in synergy with fellow musicians.

Create a Sound Structure

"A structure represents the basic characteristics of physicians, hospitals, other professionals, and other facilities," said Dr Carolyn Clancy, the head of Agency for Healthcare Research and Quality (AHRQ), in her testimony before the Subcommittee on Health Care, Committee on Finance, U.S. Senate [12]. "It describes whether there are well-educated health professionals, appropriate hospitals, nursing homes, and clinics, as well as well-maintained medical records and good mechanisms for communication between clinicians. For example, Is the mammography equipment up to date and maintained properly? Are the cardiologists well trained and board certified? If the structure is solid, we can concern ourselves with the process of medical care. Concern for process suggests that quality is determined not just by having the right people and facilities available, but also by having the right things getting done in the right way."

She defines healthcare quality as getting the right care to the right patient at the right time—every time. The implementation of this vision is a sound structure. In addition, there must be safeguards if an activity is not performed right. These are the core requirements.

A structure should also include a "thank you" system to employees who are fully engaged and willing to walk the extra mile. The Gallup organization measures what percentage of employees are engaged, the percentage of employees that are not engaged, and the percentage of employees that are disengaged who can harm the patient from carelessness. Most of the hospitals have less than 35% employees who are engaged. Reward teams for failure-free performance over time. Reward nurses who go out of their way to help families in grief. Seek peer opinions on decisions made with good understanding. Use this data also to improve the system.

Integrate the Support Staff

Make sure that the support functions are well integrated. If the support staff is not integrated with mainstream activities, the music cannot happen right. Imagine if a musician shows up but her piano does not show up because of a glitch in transporting. Ditto can happen when a device fails during surgery and nobody can locate the backup device, or the backup device also is not functioning. Someone needs to be in charge of making sure the support services are there when needed.

The support functions include the right medical technicians, supply of gowns, needles, sanitized wheelchairs, surgical instruments, and all emergency care providers. Make sure the housekeepers who disinfect patient rooms have a basic knowledge of infection control and knowledge of which chemical to use for which objects of the room. In a surprise visit by the Joint Commission, all the housekeepers were questioned about their knowledge of infection and chemicals. No housekeeper had satisfactory knowledge.

Conduct Risk Management Rehearsals

There is no way to trust the outcome of a symphony without a rehearsal. The same strategy applies to healthcare. In aerospace and aviation, the rehearsals are called "emergency drills." They can be used to verify that patient emergencies such as a cardiac arrest and strokes can be handled flawlessly. In healthcare, we need to take the extra step of rehearsing for the selected nonemergency situations also, such as listening to the patient's family, administering the right medication in a timely manner, and making sure the physicians are available in a reasonable amount of time, in spite of distractions and poor communications. Absence of these precautions are precursors to a real emergency.

Some ideas for emergency drills are as follows:

■ A person pretends to have a heart attack and suffers from methicillin-resistant Staphylococcus aureus MRSA infection at the same time; observe the events with a video that can be used as a training tool later.
■ Send about 100 patients to the emergency department (ED) as if they were being transported from a train accident in the city, and videotape the care.
■ Create an emergency where the surgeon is very busy and highly distracted.
■ Conduct emergency drills on day-to-day tasks such as taking a patient for an MRI from the emergency room.
■ Simulate a dummy fire in the ED and observe how the patients are protected from risks.

The ideas for nonemergency but relevant situations can be the following:

■ Send a wrong label on a medication to a designated staff member and observe how the defect is caught prior to administering.
■ Send a wrong dose such as heparin 5,000 instead of heparin 1,000 to a pediatric ICU.
■ Send a defective ventilator that gives more respiration than indicated. Observe whether this is noticed by the staff.
■ Follow a patient complaint with the patient. Same for a complaint from a family member.
■ Put an epidermal solution instead of injection solution in a surgery setup to verify whether the staff can reject the solution.
■ Follow the actions of the staff when a patient needs the doctor immediately but the doctor is not available.

A risk manager can choose to assign the risk management rehearsals to the quality assurance department or to the patient safety officer. The important thing is to make constant system improvements from this data. Occasionally, an independent outside team should audit how good the risk management strategy is and how well it is implemented. This process is a formal process in aerospace.

Another positive action is to take a look at adverse and "never" events. Find out the deficiencies in knowledge and execution. Then make system changes.

Aim at High ROI without Compromising Safety

Safety and high ROI are not opposite goals if you compare the cost of doing the right thing versus not doing the right thing. Sometimes, it is hard to put numbers on intangible benefits such as getting more customers, avoiding negligence claims, and avoiding patient harm. But a good manager can see them intuitively. I always aim at a minimum of 500% ROI even on safety. Usually someone in a team knows such an elegant solution. We just need to challenge them to think differently. Dr Pronovost's simple checklist for preventing the central-line-associated bloodstream infections in hundreds of hospitals mentioned in an earlier chapter produced over one million percent ROI.

Summary

Risk managers should compare their job to the job of a maestro in an orchestra. They will find many similarities and learn to seek flawless performance.

References

1. HealthGrades Study, 2010. Patient Safety Excellence Award, March 31, www.healthgrades.com/cms/ratings-and-awards/2010-Patient-Safety-Excellence-Award-Announcement.aspx.
2. Institute for Safe Medication Practices, 2010. QuarterWatch: 2009 Quarters 1–3, Report issued on February 25, www.ismp.org/QuarterWatch/2009Q3.pdf.
3. Hubbard, D., 2009. *The Failure of Risk Management: Why It's Broken and How to Fix It*, John Wiley & Sons, Inc., Hoboken, NJ.
4. VA National Center for Patient Safety, 2009. The Basics of Healthcare Failure Mode and Effects Analysis, Videoconference course, www4.va.gov/ncps/SafetyTopics/HFMEA/HFMEAIntro.doc.
5. Reason, J., 2000. Human error: models and management, *BMJ*, 320: 768–770, www.bmj.com/cgi/content/full/320/7237/768.
6. Raheja, D., and Escano, M.C., 2009. Reducing patient healthcare risks through fault tree analysis, *The Journal of System Safety*.
7. Raheja, D., and Allocco, M., 2006, *Assurance Technologies Principles and Practices*, John Wiley & Sons, Inc., Hoboken, NJ.
8. Raheja, D., and Escano, M.C., 2009. Patient safety through operations and support hazard analysis, *The Journal of System Safety*.
9. McCaughey, B., 2008. A Hospital Germ on the Warpath, *AARP Bulletin*, November 1, http://bulletin.aarp.org/opinions/othervoices/articles/a_hospital_germ_on_the_warpath_.html.
10. Pronovost, P., and Vohr, E., 2010. *Safe Patients, Smart Hospitals*, Hudson Street Press, New York.
11. King, S., 2009. *Josie's Story*, Atlantic Monthly Press, New York.
12. Dr. Carolyn Clancy's Testimony, 2009. What Is Health Care Quality and Who Decides? The Subcommittee on Health Care, Committee on Finance, U.S. Senate on March 18 can be found at www.ahrq.gov/news/test031809.htm.

Chapter 9

Human Errors May Be Unpreventable: Preventing Harm Is an Innovation

You can't cross the sea merely by standing and staring at the water.

—Rabindranath Tagore, Nobel Prize recipient for literature

Introduction

The quotation above is an inspirational reminder that people achieve nothing unless they take purposeful action that has measurable results. Taking action on potential human errors so that harm never reaches patients is a very productive innovation because its impact is significant.

Some errors can be prevented with safeguards, barriers, and forcing functions. Most are unpreventable without such barriers in place. Way et al. at the Department of Surgery, University of California–San Francisco [1], analyzed 252 laparoscopic bile duct injuries according to the principles of the cognitive science of visual perception, judgment, and human error. They found that the primary cause of error in 97% of cases was a visual perceptual illusion. Obviously, no one seems to be an exception to human errors. The author of the book with more than 30 years of experience in safety consulting still makes errors in judgment, as well as in actions, that can cause serious harm to others. Therefore, mitigation techniques using system improvements with innovative thinking must be implemented. This chapter covers the human factors engineering (HFE) principles and some techniques of preventing harm.

Principles of HFE

Some techniques for harm prevention are as follows:

- Crew Resource Management (CRM)
- Management Oversight and Risk Tree (MORT)

105

- Change Analysis
- Swiss Cheese Model for Error Trapping
- Mistake Proofing

At Tripler Army Medical Center, a newborn baby went into a coma with severe brain damage. They said medical personnel mistakenly gave him carbon dioxide immediately after birth instead of oxygen. Sources said the operating room may have been set up incorrectly [2]. This incidence is an example of the vulnerability of humans as well as the systems. Use of HFE can prevent or minimize the impact of such incidences and many more. "Human factors engineering is to patient safety as microbiology is to infection control," says Dr John Gosbee, VA National Center for Patient Safety, and the author of the previous source.

HFE focuses on how people interact with tasks, machines (or computers), and the environment with the consideration that humans have limitations and capabilities. Human factors engineers evaluate "human to human," "human to group," "human to organizational," and "human to machine (computers)" interactions to better understand these interactions and to develop a framework for evaluation [3]. But HFE in practice goes beyond this definition. It attempts to mitigate the mishaps after the evaluation, as will be seen in this chapter. This discipline is very appropriate for healthcare.

Errors are bound to occur. The most knowledgeable and experienced, such as the doctors who diagnose the illnesses, also make their share of mistakes. "The best evidence suggests that physicians are wrong 5%–10% of the time," according to Mark Graber, Chief of Medical Service at the Northport, New York, VA Medical Center [4]. Fortunately, as suggested by the quality gurus, that about 85% of the time, the system is improperly designed [5]. Therefore, improving the systems should be the focus for preventing harm. But first, we must understand the sources of human errors.

The major sources of human errors are as follows [6]:

- Errors of substitution—turning on hot water instead of cold during a shower.
- Errors of selection—such as selecting carbon dioxide for a patient instead of oxygen as in the beginning of this chapter.
- Errors of reading—a nurse may read 1.0 mg as 10 mg.
- Errors of oversight and omissions—a nurse may simply forget to give an antibiotic after a surgery.
- Errors of irritation—a caregiver may perform a task wrong when irritated with too many alarms and interruptions.
- Errors of warning—when warning signs are not clear or have too many steps in the instructions.
- Errors of alertness—the dangers of residents working on multiple shifts are obvious.
- Errors of interchangeability—such as connecting an oxygen hose to the nitrous oxide source in anesthesia equipment, because the fittings on both the sources are same.
- Errors of lack of understanding—an improperly trained staff is likely to make mistakes during emergencies.
- Errors of haste—a caregiver unable to perform the tasks in an allocated time is likely to skip seemingly minor tasks as hand sanitization prior to surgery; a surgeon leaving a sponge inside a patient.
- Errors of sequencing—a medical technician may not perform the work in the given sequence of a checklist and overlook an activity.

- Errors of overconfidence—this happens in diagnosis when a physician sees a very familiar symptom. Such an incidence was the motivation for the television show *Miami Medical*. The producer Jeffrey Lieber's wife went to an emergency room for a flu symptom. The doctor told her she has fu and sent her home. She soon went into coma at home. Luckily her mother was at home. She managed to get her to the emergency room again where she was confirmed with a different illness, and survived.
- Errors of reversal—a caregiver may increase the heart rate instead of decreasing it, not being aware of whether to turn the control clockwise or anti-clockwise.
- Errors of unintentional activation—a caregiver may inadvertently flip a life support switch to OFF instead of ON.
- Errors of mental overload—a pharmacy technician prepared a chemotherapy solution with a 20% sodium chloride concentration instead of 0.9% resulting in a fatality. Investigation revealed that she was distracted while working on her wedding plans [7]. Her supervising pharmacist had to serve 6 months of jail time. He overlooked her work because his own workload had increased due to the pharmacy's computer system being down.
- Errors of physical limitations—a short person may not be able to reach out to an object at an inconvenient height and cause an accident after climbing on a chair.
- Errors of casual behavior—sometimes a caregiver may not take a task seriously. A surgeon may not go through a scrub process when touched by another person. Or a surgeon may not mentally prepare a patient for a surgery.

Examples of system improvement are as follows:

- *To prevent a surgeon's leaving a sponge in a patient*, some hospitals use bar-coded sponges so they can be accounted for before and after each surgery.
- *In the case of the anesthesia equipment* in which the oxygen and nitrous oxide fittings are the same, many hospitals have equipment in which the fittings are unique for each supply. They cannot fit in a wrong place.

Harm Prevention Methodologies

There are many methods for preventing harm. The following are some that have been widely used and proven their effectiveness.

Crew Resource Management

This technique came from the commercial aviation industry for overcoming the barriers to poor communication, a leading cause of adverse events. It has recently found a home in healthcare, because of its quick ability to reduce patient-safety infection rates and other key measures in many hospitals by introducing checklists and other safety tools. Hospitals have found that a simple checklist, which a team can use to check each other such that no critical step is overlooked, makes CRM an easy-to-use solution. The World Health Organization is using a Surgical Checklist to save millions of lives.

David Marshall, the CEO of Safer Healthcare, and author of the book *Crew Resource Management*, defines CRM [8] as a flexible systemic method for optimizing human performance in general, and increasing safety in particular, by (1) recognizing the inherent human factors that cause errors and the reluctance to report them; (2) recognizing that in complex, high-risk endeavors, teams rather than individuals are the most effective fundamental operating units; and (3) cultivating and stilling customized, sustainable, and team-based tools and practices that effectively use all available resources to reduce the adverse impacts of those human factors. The Joint Commission has continuously monitored the path of CRM and has consistently reinforced its support, according to Marshall. He adds: *No matter how educated or careful healthcare professionals are, errors will occur. So, the natural question to ask is: "How do we prevent those errors from ever impacting a patient?"*

The essentials of CRM, according to Marshall [9], are to provide a concrete set of skills to the teams with the following goals:

■ Team building: How to conduct a briefing in 30–60 seconds with an overview of what is about to happen.
■ Team debriefing: Capture what went well, what did not go well, and how can they improve for the next time.
■ Assertiveness: How to speak up and when to speak up if anyone sees a problem.
■ Situational awareness: Being aware of what is going on and what is about to happen, and identifying red flags. If a team member falters, the team picks up the slack and brings it to the attention of the stakeholders.
■ How to use critical language: Using a couple of buzzwords that the entire team knows. The whole team stops and pauses.
■ Decision-making: How to work together and make effective decisions.

The CRM methodology is the biggest gift to healthcare from the aviation industry. It has worked beyond anyone's expectations in bringing the central line-associated bloodstream infections almost down to zero in many hospitals. It has saved millions of dollars and hundreds of lives [10]. As a result, healthcare has created the equivalent of the Commercial Aviation Safety Teams (CASTs), a public–private partnership intended to reduce hazards throughout aviation. At the time of this writing, Dr Peter Pronovost and his colleagues are exploring a healthcare version of CAST with an *ad hoc* group whose stakeholders include Agency for Healthcare Research and Quality (AHRQ), the Food and Drug Administration (FDA), the Joint Commission, ECRI Institute, and more than 15 large health systems. They call this approach the public–private partnership to promote patient safety (P5S) [11].

> The CRM has brought down the central line-associated bloodstream infections almost to zero in many hospitals.

Management Oversight and Risk Tree

This accident investigation tool was developed by the U.S. Department of Energy for high-risk industries. It can be very effective for exploring the cases of adverse events and to prevent harm to patients. It has been used in transportation, aviation, and nuclear systems. When the members of the National Transportation Safety Board broadcast updates on accidents, they usually use this tool. The top-down tree structure questions the adequacy of safeguards, barriers, safety analysis, policies, procedures, and the implementation of safety management. It questions the possible oversights in managing. The left side of the tree covers all variables that are relevant to the incident.

The right side lists deficiencies in management that allowed such an incidence. Almost all the major mishaps reveal some deficiency in management policies and execution.

Authors Nemeth et al. [12] from the Cognitive Technological Laboratory of the University of Chicago and other medical institutions recommend this methodology as one of the most powerful techniques. They point out the weaknesses in healthcare systems that keep such techniques at bay:

> Unlike the transportation sector, healthcare organizations have no objective national resource to rely on for investigation of their own adverse events. Instead, each healthcare institution is responsible for developing its own program. The safety that results in such an environment is designed to meet the approval of the hospital's accrediting organization. This amounts to a social contract that works well until an event occurs that draws the attention of the public and regulatory organizations.

The National Health System in the United Kingdom applied such techniques for an incidence in which the laboratory or radiology errors went undetected for long periods of time [13]. The analysis revealed communication breakdowns and organizational complications in their process.

If carried out completely, it is an extremely comprehensive technique examining an accident from several perspectives, according to a Woloshynowych et al. at Clinical Safety Research Unit, Imperial College London [14]. The report adds: the technique is also intended to support safety audits and to solve management problems. Detailed descriptions of the entire MORT tree structure and how to use it is available in the text *MORT Safety Assurance Systems* by William G. Johnson.

Figure 9.1 shows a portion of the left side of the tree that questions the factors relevant to an adverse event. They use standardized terminology such as LTA, which stands for "less than adequate."

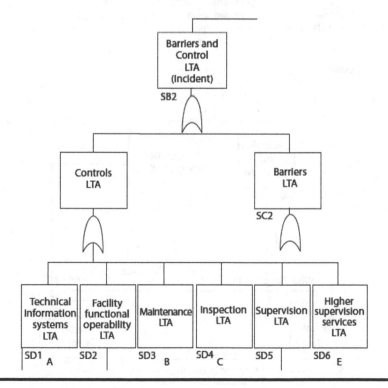

Figure 9.1   A portion of the left side of the tree questioning the process of preventing an adverse event.

The tree structure also uses standardized symbols similar to fault trees. It questions how adequate are the controls on an incidence. For example, when a nurse administers a wrong medication, the questions that need to be answered are: Were there barriers (safeguards) to prevent wrong medication from reaching a patient, such as a medication bar code matching the patient ID band? If there were barriers, then how effective were the controls on the process?

If the controls are less than adequate, then additional questions are raised, such as the adequacy of technical information, facility functional operability, maintenance, inspections, supervision, and higher supervision. The tree keeps expanding to lower levels of root causes. Similarly, Figure 9.2 shows a portion of the right side of the tree, the adequacy of management actions. It questions what future adverse events are possible. It identifies what kind of risks management has assumed and what are the management oversights and omissions.

An example of an assumed risk can be that management assumes that all HAIs (hospital-acquired infections) cannot be prevented. An example of an oversight can be that the patient-safety staff is busy firefighting the problems instead of preventing them, using a tool such as MORT, failure mode and effects analysis, and hazard analysis.

Figure 9.3 shows the expansion management system factors to the next lower level. It questions how adequate are the policies, implementation of the policies, and the hospital's risk assessment system. It shows two lower levels.

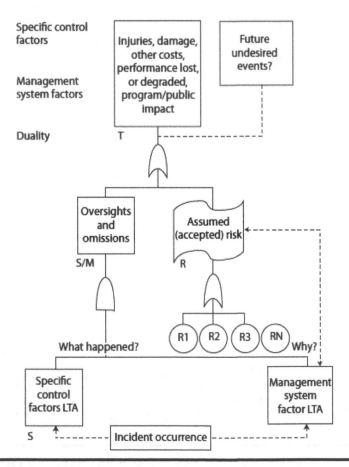

Figure 9.2 A portion of the right side of the tree questioning risks assumed by management.

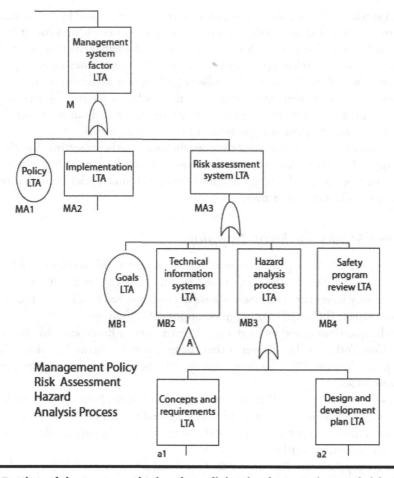

Figure 9.3   Portion of the tree questioning the policies, implementation, and risk assessment.

Even though MORT started as an investigation tool, the findings should be used for preventing future mishaps. MORT points to many mistakes, oversights, and weaknesses in execution of the procedures. Fix the system so the harm is intercepted before it reaches a patient. We can use MORT as a safety audit tool just as well. Develop questions from the MORT to design an audit.

Change Analysis

This analysis is very powerful in getting quickly to the bottom of the proximate cause of an adverse event. It compares the ideal procedure to the current procedure to discover the differences. One of these differences is usually the likely cause of the unfortunate event. I learned this method during MORT training through the Department of Energy about 20 years back. Two case histories (unpublished) bring up the vivid memories (sources not identified). *First case*: A mushroom factory had to recall mushroom cans because of botulism poisoning. Change analysis compared the old manual process that had proven to be very reliable and the new automated process. The only difference was that the mushroom slices were thinner in the automated process. The scientists concluded that the thinner slices got stuck together driving out oxygen between them resulting in botulism. A similar incidence of botulism in mushrooms is presented by Sugiyama [15]. *Second case*: Two women were killed by grizzly bears in separate incidents within Glacier National Park. The change analysis revealed that both the women were in their menstruation cycle. A theory emerged that, because of odor associated with menstruation, women may be more prone to attack by bears. A study was done to test the hypothesis [16]. When presented with a series of odors (including food scents and nonmenstrual blood), four polar bears elicited a strong behavioral response only to seal scents and used tampons. They ignored unused tampons and nonmenstrual blood. This finding was accepted as a proximate cause of the accidents.

The cases above are a demonstration of the concept. In a healthcare setting, the change analysis can easily be applied to uncovering why an adverse event took place in the first place. There has to be a difference between an ideal intervention and the actual intervention. One has to trace every step in the process to identify the differences.

Swiss Cheese Model for Error Trapping

A 32-year-old male with chest pain, low blood pressure, and rapid heartbeat died after 45 minutes of attempted resuscitation. The nurse failed to put the device in SYNC mode for a second shock (device silently leaves the sync mode, allows unsynchronized shock). Fire the nurse? Retrain emergency department (ED) staff? Forbid nurses from defibrillating?

These are the questions raised by Fairbanks, Department of Emergency Medicine, University of Rochester, New York [17]. The answer is that these actions by themselves alone will not work, according to James Reason [18], who developed the science of preventing adverse events through his Swiss Cheese Model.

This is how the model began [19]: One day in the late 1970s, James Reason was making tea, and the cat was clamoring to be fed. He efficiently opened the tin of cat food—and put it in his teapot. The two components got mixed up. Both the teapot and the cat's feeding dish afforded the same opportunity—putting stuff in.

As a cognitive psychologist, Reason suddenly realized a new research topic was literally under his nose. In tracing the causes of absentminded incidents, Reason began an exploration of human error. Three decades later, Reason has become a leading expert on error and one of the recognized architects of the tools used to improve patient safety.

Between absentmindedness and presentmindedness, what intrigued Reason most about absentmindedness was our ability to perform coherently in themselves one or more actions—opening a tin of cat food and putting it into a teapot—but, combined, totally divorced from our intentions. To investigate this conundrum, Reason interviewed hundreds of people about their absentminded errors. He found that although each incident was idiosyncratic, a pattern emerged. The errors had similar origins and characteristics.

According to him, it is not just about people; it is about the design of the system that includes equipment and procedures. The solution is to trap errors before they reach the point of harm. Reason explains that accidents happen from a combination of active errors (such as human errors) and latent errors that are dormant in the system. The more the safeguards on latent errors, the less likely is the impact of human errors. He uses the analogy of Swiss cheese. Assume there are system protections for four latent hazards in a hospital. Each protection is like a slice of Swiss cheese. A hole is an equivalent of a latent hazard sitting there until it is activated from the failure of the protection. There can be several other holes in the protection. Each hole is a path to an adverse event. For a human error to cause an adverse event, a hole in each of the four protections has to be activated to do the harm. In other words, a hole in each protection has to fail to interrupt the disruptive path of the error. As long as one of the holes does not line up with others, there is no possibility of harm. This is the essence of the Swiss cheese model. Appendix A contains the detailed description of this model.

Mistake Proofing

Do the nurses put medication in the drawer of a wrong patient? Do doctors forget to put information on the electronic health records (EHRs) when under pressure? Do caregivers make a mistake because of distractions? Do they forget something when discharging a patient? Yes, they all happen, and will keep happening unless there is system to mistake-proof such scenarios. We are all prone to such mistakes. Mistake proofing is a basic tool to catch problems and find a way to catch them through visual methods, before any harm is done.

Mistake proofing is also known as "poka-yoke" (avoiding inadvertent errors). Shigeo Shingo [20] formalized mistake proofing as a part of his contribution to the production system for Toyota automobiles. Allegheny General Hospital [21] is one of the many hospitals that have achieved significant benefits from it. The basic strategy is to prevent user error from occurring, alert users to possible dangers, and reduce the effect of user errors.

One of the methods of detecting mistakes in the work environment is the implementation of a Japanese visual system, also known as 5Ss. The goal is to detect the problem, work in teams to solve the problems immediately, and constantly improve the system. The five S designations are as follows:

- Seiri (organization) focuses on removing unneeded items from the workplace. Items that are actually used all the time are sorted from those that are superfluous. Unneeded items are tagged and removed to a holding area to await alternate allocation or disposal.
- Seiton (orderliness) involves arranging needed items so that they are easy to find, use, and put away.
- Seisou (cleanliness) involves making sure that the workplace is clean and stays clean. It is not about being clean. It includes an environment that can effectively contain and communicate information.
- Seiketsu (standardization) focuses on maintaining and institutionalizing organization, orderliness, and cleanliness (sanitization). It includes preventive steps that reduce the effort required to maintain the improvements already made.
- Shitsuke (discipline) involves avoiding a return to the comfortable behavior of the past. It focuses on aligning the culture and habits of the organization with its proactive approach to organizing work.

Gout gives many examples of mistakeproofing solutions in hospitals. Among them are

- Unintentionally exposing x-ray film to light destroys images that are vital to proper patient care. These images can usually be re-created, but they cost time and money. The darkroom door can be redesigned to prevent failing conditions that would damage film when normally opened.
- The fittings that connect medical gases from the tanks in the back room to the tubes leading to the patient needed extensive mistake proofing. Tanks now display a color-coding scheme.

The color coding serves as a "sensory alert" to ensure that the correct connections are made between the tanks and the valves in the patients' rooms. The tanks are also fitted with pin-indexed connectors to prevent incorrect connections.

■ Esophageal intubation is a common error that occurs when the intubation tube is inserted in the patient's esophagus instead of in the trachea. A low-tech approach was applied. After the patient is intubated, a staff member squeezes the bulb and places it over the end of the tube. If the bulb fails to reinflate to its original shape, the tube is in the esophagus. If it reinflates fully, the tube is placed correctly.

■ Birth control pills are sold packaged for use as a 1-month supply. The packaging indicates whether the patient has been taking her medication consistently. If clever packaging is not enough, a wristwatch can remind the user to take medications up to six times a day. Instead of an audible alarm, the watch vibrates discreetly.

■ The switch on an IV pump has a clear plastic cover that prevents inadvertent bumping of the switch.

■ Blood bank refrigerators are equipped with temperature monitors that sound as an alarm if and when the temperature is out of the safety range. The readout "Status OK" indicates that the refrigerators in this blood bank are operating properly. When the temperature or other operating parameters are not correct, a message scrolls across the display, indicating which refrigerator is out of specifications and which specification is violated.

Mistake proofing cannot eliminate all errors and failures, but often it is very cost effective in producing a high return on investment. Peters calls it goof-proofing [22]. He adds that even the best can goof. The remedies need only be reasonable under the circumstances, which are often quite complex. He suggests several techniques, such as the following:

Human Fault Tolerance: It means that a system will continue to operate safely despite human error or failure. In other words, the processes should be designed such that no serious harm is caused by any single error.

The Rule of Two: This is a process design rule that requires at least two independent errors or one error and an equipment malfunction must take place before any adverse event takes place. This is a solution for human fault tolerance. For example, the pharmacy protocols require that the pharmacist check the medications prepared by the pharmacy technicians. A wrong medication can reach a patient only when both of them made an error independently. A single error from either one cannot result in harm.

Automation: A scenario in which mistakes happen frequently should be automated when possible. In some operating rooms, the sterility check on surgical instruments, scalpels, and knives are automated.

Summary

Preventing harm is the top concern for hospitals. Using the techniques in this chapter can open up many possibilities. The most important requirement is that physicians, clinicians, caregivers, and service providers have to work as a team in which the system as a whole is considered, where fragmented parts come together.

References

1. Way, L.W., et al., 2003. Causes and prevention of laparoscopic bile duct injuries: analysis of 252 cases from a human factors and cognitive psychology perspective, *Annals of Surgery*, 237(4): 460–469, www.ncbi.nlm.nih.gov/pubmed/12677139.
2. Gosbee, J., 2004. VA National Center for Patient Safety, Human Factors Engineering and Patient Safety, Slide presentation at the Annual Conference of the Michigan Health & Safety Coalition.
3. Human Factors Engineering definition from Wikipedia.
4. Graber, M., 2009. Reducing diagnostic error in medicine-There is a job for everyone, *Focus on Patient Safety, A publication of the National Patient Safety Foundation*, 12(2): 6–7.
5. Evans, J., and Lindsay, W., 2008. *Managing for Quality and Performance Excellence*, Seventh Edition, Thomson South-Western, Mason, OH.
6. Raheja, D., and Escano, M.S., Human factors engineering applications in patient safety, *Journal of System Safety*, May–June issue.
7. Cohen, M., 2009. An Injustice Has Been Done: Jail Time for an Error, Patient Safety and Quality Healthcare, September–October, www.psqh.com/septemberoctober-2009/233-september-october-2009-viewpoint.html.
8. Marshall, D., 2009. *Crew Resource Management: From Patient Safety to High Reliability*, Safer Healthcare Partners, LLC, Denver, CO.
9. Marshall, D., 2010. Safer Healthcare, Video presentation by David Marshall, Youtube.com.
10. National Public Radio, 2007. Doctor Saved Michigan $100 Million, December 9, www.npr.org/templates/story/story.php?storyId=17060374.
11. Pronovost, P. J., et al., 2009. Reducing health care hazards: Lessons from the commercial aviation safety team, *Health Affairs*, 28(3): w479–w489.
12. Nemeth, C., et al., 2004. Afterwards: The Quality of Medical Investigations and Analyses, The article available at the Cognitive Technologies Laboratory, University of Chicago, at www.ctlab.org/documents/Afterwords.pdf.
13. Chozos, N., 2009. Focusing accident analysis on error handling activities: Three case studies in the NHS, *Risk Management*, 11, 159–178, www.palgrave-journals.com/rm/journal/v11/n3/full/rm20098a.html.
14. Woloshynowych, M., et al., 2005. The investigation and analysis of critical incidences and adverse events in healthcare, *Health Technology Assessment*, 9(19), www.hta.ac.uk/execsumm/summ919.shtml.
15. Sugiyama, H., 1975. Growth potential of *Clostridium botulinum* in fresh mushrooms packaged in semipermeable plastic film, *Applied Microbiology*, http://aem.asm.org/cgi/reprint/30/6/964.pdf.
16. Gunther, K., 2006. Bears and Menstruating Women, Bear Management Office, Information Paper BMO-7, Yellowstone National Park, March 2006, www.yellowstone-natl-park.com/bearsmen.pdf.
17. Fairbanks, R., 2007. Human Factors Engineering, Presentation at the Patient Safety Conference, University of Rochester, retrieved from www.health.state.ny.us/professionals/patients/patient_safety/conference/2007/docs/human_factors_engineering.pdf.
18. Reason, J., 1990. *Human Error*, Cambridge University Press, Cambridge, UK.
19. Zoominfo Web site, Dr. James T. Reason, profile was created using 128 online sources, retrieved on May 26, from www.zoominfo.com/people/PersonDetailLimited.aspx?PersonID=33945568&lastName=Reason&searchSource=page&firstName=James&id=33945568&page=1.
20. Shingo, S., 1986. *Zero Quality Control: Source Inspection and the Poka-Yoke System*, translated by A.P. Dillion, Productivity Press, New York.
21. The Commonwealth Fund, 2008. A private foundation for high performance healthcare, Case Study: Perfecting Patient Care at Allegheny General Hospital and the Pittsburgh Regional Healthcare Initiative, September 30, retrieved from www.commonwealthfund.org/Content/Innovations/Case-Studies/2008/Sep/Case-Study--Perfecting-Patient-Care-at-Allegheny-General-Hospital-and-the-Pittsburgh-Regional-Health.aspx.
22. Peters, G.A., and Peters, B.J., 2006. *Human Error Causes and Control*, Taylor & Francis, Boca Raton, FL.

Chapter 10

Managing Safety: Lessons from Aerospace

The problem is we need to generate new knowledge.

—**Dr Mark Chassin, President, The Joint Commission**

Introduction

According to Chassin, adverse events are different from routine process breakdowns because they represent unique sequences of errors that will never happen again the same way [1]. He further says:

> We have imperfect tools to assess exactly what happened in the course of an adverse event. If you consider Reason's Swiss cheese model (see Appendix A) and think about all the defenses that have to be breached before harm can be done, we have imperfect ways to figure out exactly which defenses failed in which way. Then, once we understand where the weak defenses are, we have imperfect analytic tools to tell us which one to fix first. Which one is going to be lethal tomorrow? Which one can we safely put on the back burner while the other high-priority project is underway? We lack a systematic way to learn across adverse events, to build knowledge about institutional vulnerability that benefits from seeing how the defenses fail in more than one adverse event. Our current tools do not encourage us to do that. They encourage us to do what we call *root cause analysis*, which I think is a misnomer since there is never a single cause. There aren't usually even two or three. Five, eight, or ten defenses fail in many of these adverse events, especially the more complicated ones. But knowing what happened in one is not enough information to understand what the vulnerabilities are in an institution. The analytic methods we have are from a different generation. We need to develop the next generation of those tools to achieve the goal of high reliability.

The aerospace industry has several tools that are based on the above hypothesis that a mishap is never a result of a single event. It is always a combination of at least two events and often multiple events. The tools are institutionalized under an umbrella called system safety. By no means is system safety science all-inclusive, but it does provide the structure and tools for preventing adverse events.

System safety processes can uncover many risks, depending on the quality of the team makeup, the variety of analyses performed, and how rigorously the analyses are done. The goal of system safety is to capture as many risks as possible proactively and mitigate them.

Where Does U.S. Healthcare Stand on System Safety?

The state of system safety in healthcare seems to be where the aviation industry was about 30 years ago, when engineers and managers did not question much regarding accidents. Engineers went to the reviews, just like in the morbidity and mortality conferences in hospitals. Active discussions were held, but there was practically no discussion of how to change the system to prevent many more accidents. Very few healthcare practitioners challenge one another and their superiors to bring out what is best for patient safety. The entire knowledge of system safety science is contained in Mil-Std-882, the military handbook on system safety requirements [2].

System Safety Theory of Accidents

System safety science is a system-based approach for identifying and mitigating systemwide sources of accident. These sources could be people, procedures, processes, the environment, electronic medical tracking systems, equipment such as patient monitoring systems and substandard MRIs, cell phones, and communications and information technology software. The analysis tools and the mitigation strategies have been standardized by the aviation industry. Since so much is at stake, system safety also requires proactive management of the programs.

The essence of system safety theory of accidents is that a mistake by a caregiver is only a trigger event in the presence of a combination of loaded hidden hazards (unsafe conditions) in the system. Accidents happen only when the combination of one or more latent hazards and a trigger event coexist. A loaded gun is a hazard, but it cannot kill until someone pulls the trigger. James Reason's Swiss Cheese Model (Appendix A) is similar to this theory used in aerospace for more than 50 years. It has been never challenged. The technique for identifying the combination of loaded guns, such as the pharmacist pulling a wrong medication for a patient and identifying the trigger event (the patient actually taking the wrong medication), is a part of the analysis called hazard analysis. Best practices on hazard analysis can be found in the book *Hazard Analysis Techniques for System Safety* by Clifton A. Ericson, or one can order *System Safety Analysis Handbook* from the System Safety Society [3]. Figure 10.1 shows the process of identifying and mitigating hazards.

Note that there are five options to mitigating mishaps in step 3. They are arranged in the order of precedence, which means the first action is the most significant of all. The guideline to use them is as follows:

■ Eliminate hazards or triggers. Since a mishap *cannot take place unless both (the hazards and the triggers) are there at the same time,* we do not have to prevent both. If we can prevent either the hazards or the triggers, we prevent the mishap altogether. For example, nurses used to prick themselves with the needles after they remove the injected needle from the patient. The hazard is the infected needle; the trigger is the nurse inadvertently pricks herself

| Step 1: | Identify hazards and trigger events. |

| Step 2: | Estimate the severity of mishap and the frequency of the mishap. |

Step 3:	Mitigate mishap in the following precedence:
	Eliminate hazards or triggers.
	Provide barriers/safeguards.
	Provide fail-safe system.
	Provide early warnings.
	Provide robust training.

Figure 10.1   Steps in hazard analysis.

| Hazard + Trigger Event = Mishap |

Figure 10.2   A single event cannot result in a mishap. At least a hazard and a trigger event must occur simultaneously.

or himself. We can prevent a hazard by using syringes with retractable needles. Or, we can prevent nurses from pricking themselves. Since the second choice is almost impossible, our best choice is to use retractable needles. This concept is shown in Figure 10.2.

▪ Provide barriers and safeguards. Barriers are usually physical, such as covering patients with lead aprons during x-rays. They can be nonphysical, such as an administrative procedure to block certain actions. Safeguards are usually additional steps or procedures to make it difficult to give a wrong intervention, such as a nurse observing the surgeon's actions during surgery and alerting when some protocol is violated. Let us explore the case of the twin babies of actor Dennis Quaid [4]. The 3-month-old twins were supposed to be given heparin, a blood thinner, to prevent coagulation of the blood. The first mistake happened when the hospital pharmacist picked out the adult dose instead of the baby dose. The adult dose makes the blood 1,000 times thinner. There was a safeguard: the nurse was supposed to verify the dose with the barcode embedded in the wristband of the baby. She trusted the pharmacist and did not verify. As a result, the baby got the wrong dose (the trigger). Since the blood of the baby was 1,000 times thinner, the baby started to leak blood through the navel and other life-support tube openings (access points). The hospital failed to notice because the babies were fully covered. It was the mother who came out to see the babies after midnight who found the babies leaking. If the mother had not shown up at the unusual hour, the babies could have died. Ironically, about 2 months later 16 babies got the wrong dose of heparin in a hospital in Texas. Two died.

This case shows that usually one safeguard is not enough. In Quaid's case more than one mistake was made. The adult heparin and child heparin were stocked on the same shelf next to each other, and they had identical labeling. If the adult medications were physically isolated from children's medicine, this would have been an additional barrier to selecting the wrong medication. In addition, the pharmaceutical company could have provided safeguards such as a different size for children, or bold lettering for child dose. Of course, if we put too many safeguards, caregivers start relying on others to safeguard, just as the nurse relied on the pharmacist in the Quaid case. Since safeguards are not as reliable as eliminating the hazards, hospitals must periodically audit to see how effective the safeguards are.

■ Providing a fail-safe system. Making the system fail-safe is not always easy. It means keeping the patient safe in spite of a medical mistake. For example, if a nurse forgot to give an antibiotic to a patient and if there is an automatic patient monitoring system designed to detect the absence of the antibiotic, the system can put out an immediate mayday alarm and avoid patient harm.

■ Early warnings. The purpose of early warning is to prevent harm by monitoring trends. They are the early indicators of future anomalies. They give us sufficient time to correct the situations well before something goes wrong. That is the purpose of the statistical control charts. They tell you whether the trend is within normal limits of variation or there is a tendency to go out of control.

■ Robust training. If all the above strategies fail, then we need to rely on training. Unfortunately, training on the average is about 80% effective. Not good enough. To make training more robust, we should have teams of those involved in the task to accept responsibility for detecting any loopholes in the training and constantly improve the process.

System Safety in Emergency Medicine

While formal system safety analysis may not be practical in emergency medicine because each situation is different, system safety thinking can lead to much better and structured decisions. To minimize risk in emergency medicine, hazard analysis can be performed on standardized processes. Examples of standardized processes include inserting a central line in the patient to pump fluid into the heart, admitting a patient, giving discharge instructions to a patient being transferred to a different hospital, or making patient rounds.

Aerospace Hazard Analysis Techniques

The analysis technique presented above is generic for any process. There are hazard analysis techniques for specific purposes also. The following is the listing of various analyses:

■ Preliminary hazard analysis for controlling hazards based on historical data. It is done for new systems and processes *before* implementing. See Reference [5].
■ Healthcare failure mode and effects analysis for predicting and controlling health care failures. This technique was covered in Chapter 8.
■ Fault tree analysis for solving complex problems. This is the world's best tool for root-cause analysis. This technique was covered in Chapter 8.

- Event tree analysis for constructing a mishap scenario in order to visualize what can go wrong in emergency situations. This analysis predicts events that can lead to a mishap if controls and barriers fail to perform their functions. See Reference [6] for the method.
- Subsystem hazard analysis for individual subsystems or processes at a department level, such as the care process in an ICU or the HIV treatment process. These processes affect the system functions that can result in mishaps. See Reference [6] for the method.
- System hazard analysis for the entire healthcare system or entire patient cycle, from admission to discharge. This analysis looks at system interactions and dependencies. See Reference [6] for details.
- Operations and support hazard analysis for prediction and mitigation of day-to-day caregiver errors. This analysis was covered in Chapter 8.
- Software hazard analysis for analyzing software in medical devices, electronic patient tracking systems, or electronic health record systems. This can be found in References [2,6].

> System hazard analysis is for the entire patient cycle, from admission through discharge. This analysis looks at system interactions, dependencies, handoffs, and communications.

Summary

As you have seen in this chapter, there is more to safety than safety as we know it. One prominent surgeon told me that this is like looking for a needle in a haystack. I told him there are thousands of needles in a haystack. If we go to the bottom of the haystack, we will find many!

References

1. Wachter, R., 2009. In Conversation with Mark Chassin, MD, MPP, MPH, April, 2009, issue of the AHRQ WebM&M, http://webmm.ahrq.gov/perspective.aspx?perspectiveID=73.
2. U.S. Department of Defense, 2000, *Military Handbook, Mil-Std-882, System Safety Program Requirements*, Department of Defense, Washington, DC, 20301.
3. *System Safety Handbook* can be purchased from System Safety Society, PO Box 70, Unionville, VA 22567. Tel: (800) 747–5744. Or see the text *Assurance Technologies Principles and Practices: A Product, Process and System Safety Perspective* by Dev G. Raheja and Michael Allocco, John Wiley & Sons, Inc. 2006.
4. Dillon, N., 2008. Dennis Quaid's baby nightmare, *New York Daily News*, March 15, www.nydailynews.com/gossip/2008/03/15/2008-03-15_dennis_quaids_baby_nightmare.html.
5. Raheja, D., 2009. System safety in healthcare: Preliminary hazard analysis for minimizing sentinel, adverse and never events, *Journal of System Safety*.
6. Raheja, D., and Allocco, M., 2006. *Assurance Technologies Principles and Practices*, John Wiley & Sons, Inc., Hoboken, NJ.

Chapter 11

The Paradigm Pioneers

You have your way. I have my way. As for the right way, the correct way, and the only way, it does not exist.

—Friedrich Nietzsche, German scholar

Introduction

Dr Lucian Leape, who cofounded the patient-safety movement more than a decade ago, is confident that healthcare is moving in the right direction but the progress to date is dismal. He is now pushing for reforming medical education. About 20% of hospitals still fail to conduct timeouts before surgery an effort known to be important in preventing the remarkably frequent wrong-site surgery [1].

We need a paradigm shift. In Chapter 1, we discussed paradigm followers who have nothing left when the environment is competitive. The paradigm pioneers on the other hand keep constantly innovating. And "bang!" they suddenly come up with simple and practical ideas, which are annoying even to peers who are very comfortable with the status quo. We will cover five paradigm pioneers that broke out and have risen to extraordinary heights.

Johns Hopkins Hospital

Dr Peter Pronovost, as medical director for Johns Hopkins' Center for Innovation in Quality Patient Care and professor of anesthesiology and critical care medicine at Johns Hopkins University School of Medicine, made history by creating an extremely simple checklist for preventing central-line-associated bloodstream infections, which brought the infection rate to zero not only at Johns Hopkins but also at hundreds of hospitals that used this checklist. The hospital institutionalized the miraculous accomplishment that has made Hopkins a world leader in the science and innovation of patient safety. "Our intensive care unit has not had a single bloodstream infection since linking up with a study developed by Johns Hopkins University," says Kathy Raethel, vice president of patient care services at Castle Medical Center in Hawaii [2]. Hospitals in Michigan alone reported in 2007 that over $100 million and more than 1,500 lives saved by using this checklist over 18 months [3].

This simple thinking comes from his creative way of attention to patient safety. When he goes through the patient handoff rounds in the cardiac surgery intensive care unit, he addresses the residents and nurses as "Grasshopper," a reference to a memorable incident from the David Carradine TV series *Kung Fu*. It is about a young pupil in the Shaolin monastery in China who told his blind master that to be blind must be the worst affliction. Master Po in response drew the attention of the young student to a grasshopper next to his foot that the Master could hear but of which the student was unaware. The point was to show the pupil how much he still had to learn about what is not obvious. Master Pronovost also uses the grasshopper as a symbol of awareness of the wholeness.

The question is: Why is such an approach out of the box? He feels the entire healthcare industry needs to step outside the box and be aware of the wholesomeness of patient safety. This is clear from *Hopkins Medical News*, the 2002 fall issue. It states that Peter Pronovost has his reasons for being a zealot about patient safety, and he is not shy about sharing them. When Pronovost was in his fourth year of medical school at Johns Hopkins, his father died as the result of an error made by a hospital in New England. It transformed everything—his choice of careers (critical care medicine) as well as his research interests (patient safety). He seems to have chosen the art of Kung Fu to make everyone around him aware that much more needs to be understood about safety.

The Kung Fu in Chinese medicine is used without any context to martial arts. Kung Fu simply refers to any individual accomplishment or cultivated skill obtained by long and hard experience from internal and external discipline and the internal experience of uniting the heart, spirit, and mind. This is all covered in the Chinese book on imperial medicine. The author of this book was the famous 19th-century Yellow Emperor who wrote it before he became China's king. The translation of the book is available at the UCLA library's rare books section under the name *Kung-Fu, or Taoist Medical Gymnastics* by John Dudgeon (1985).

Dr Pronovost and his team developed a five-step checklist to help reduce the number of infections caused when doctors put central-line catheters into a patient's body. The list requires doctors and nurses to monitor the following steps:

1. Wash their hands with soap.
2. Clean the patient's skin with chlorhexidine antiseptic.
3. Put sterile drapes over the patient's entire body.
4. Wear a sterile mask, hat, gown, and gloves.
5. Put a sterile dressing over the catheter site once the line is in.

Some peers were not impressed with the checklist and a requirement that nurses make sure the doctors complete each step on the list. When they saw the infection rate fall from 11% down to zero, they gave their blessing. Since 2003, use of the checklist has been required in all Michigan hospitals. At the time of this writing, ten hospital associations had committed to using the checklist with an Agency for Healthcare Research and Quality (AHRQ) funding. Many hospitals in this project have already brought down the infection rate to zero. Dr Pronovost says his system works because it is simple with very low number of steps. He has a good point. The more steps in the checklist, the more chances of errors.

This effort did not go unrewarded. Dr Pronovost was named a 2008 winner of the MacArthur Fellowship "genius grant"—for the second time in a row—and he appeared on the cover of *Time* magazine as one of the most influential people of 2008 [4].

Dr Pronovost chuckles: you can put part of his method to work the next time you or a loved one is in the hospital. "When a doctor walks into your room, you should absolutely say, 'Did you wash your hands?'," he says. "Likewise, when they are leaving, you can say, 'I hope you wash your hands on the way out.'"

Johns Hopkins has demonstrated that using a simple safeguard such as a short checklist can lower the infection rate to zero at practically no cost while preventing thousands of infections and saving millions of dollars to patients because they can avoid lengthy stays in the hospitals. That is innovation!

Allegheny General Hospital

Can a car company help a hospital become a leader in healthcare? That happened at 40 hospitals in the Pittsburgh region! The following illustration shows how Allegheny General brings efficiency and speed in patient safety [5].

A nurse brought the medical "production line" to a halt. Candice Bena thought a 76-year-old patient needed a new intravenous line but could not get the radiology department to install one immediately. Fearing the patient would develop an infection, the nurse phoned Dr Shannon, chairman of medicine.

That was the equivalent of pulling "the 'andon' cord," says Dr Shannon, using the Japanese word for "lantern." He immediately called the hospital's chairman of radiology, who within 2 hours installed the new IV line himself. "That's the Toyota production system. No problem should be left unsolved."

Yes, this safety and quality culture of resolving problems immediately came from the car company Toyota. There is more of Toyota at Allegheny, such as the following:

The culture emphasizes rapid flow of patients and staff, just like the rapid flow of cars on an assembly line.

Any time a quality problem develops, a self-organized team takes responsibility for examining errors immediately and develops countermeasures to avoid a repetition.

Workers identify nonvalue work constantly, aiming to eliminate steps that are not valuable to patients. For example, waiting in the emergency room for an hour or waiting a day to see the doctor has no value to the patient.

Similarly, getting an infection or wrong diagnosis from a hospital has a highly negative value to the patient.

The teams prove solutions in small steps first, before implementing. This is an insurance against implementing a system with many unknown errors.

Any nurse or a staff member who spots a serious problem can pull an "andon" cord and stop the error-prone work just like stopping an assembly line.

The driving force behind this new application was Paul O'Neill, the former Treasury secretary and ex-chairman of Alcoa Inc. He now heads a consortium of hospitals, insurers, and businesses devoted to improving healthcare while reducing costs. His Pittsburgh Regional Healthcare Initiative offers a 5-day training course based largely on the Toyota system. Dr Shannon is one of the graduates. The training is titled *Perfecting Patient Care*. After I took the course, I developed lot of respect for Toyota automobiles.

The progress did not stop here in 40 Pittsburgh area hospitals. Thirty executives of Seattle's Virginia Mason Medical Center spent 2 weeks in Japan visiting Toyota car factories and Hitachi Ltd. air-conditioning plants. After embracing the Toyota changes years ago, window and door maker Pella Corp. now has plans to loan employees for "hot teams" at a hospital in its hometown of Pella, Iowa, to scrutinize medical operations.

> Do not be blinded by the best practices in your own industry. Steal ideas from other industries. It is cheaper.

Geisinger Health System

You can think of Geisinger doctors as the Maytag repairmen of healthcare. When many hospitals depend on their revenue from more tests, more surgeries, more drugs, and this hospital wants to do less of them. Four years ago they decided that they could succeed by doing less, but doing it better [6].

Translocating the idea from an appliance company that advertised its products' reliability, they devised a 90-day warranty on elective heart surgery, promising to get it right the first time, for a fat fee. If complications arise or the patient returns, the hospital pays. The venture has paid off. Heart patients have fared measurably better, and the health system has cut its bypass surgery costs by 15%. Geisinger has extended the program to half a dozen other procedures.

Nearly 18% of hospitalized Medicare patients are readmitted within 30 days, an expense that experts argue can be reduced dramatically by doing things right the first time. Geisinger, a system of 41 clinics, 3 hospitals, and 650 staff physicians, achieves those goals through standardization. Science-based protocols are "hard-wired" into the process, in much the same way that high-end manufacturing works.

For heart bypass surgery, Geisinger guarantees that every patient will receive 40 action items it has identified as best practices. The list includes, for example, properly administering antibiotics within 30 minutes of the operation. The wrong dose increases the likelihood of infection, and infection can lead to a second surgery, prolonged hospitalization, and greater risk of death. At the start 3 years ago, only 59% of patients received all 40 critical elements. Within 3 months, the cardiac team hit the 100%. The in-hospital death rate on elective heart surgeries has dropped from 1.5% to 0%.

Surgeons can opt out of doing any element if they give a reason, and an operation is canceled if a single step is missed in the preparations. Electronic medical records contain built-in reminders for the surgical team and track the results. "No one thing on the list is magic," says Alfred Casale, a chief medical officer. "It's the reliability of knowing that every single one is going to get done on every single patient. That is the magic."

> Do less.
> Do it better.

A study of Medicare data for nearly 12 million Medicare patients discharged from hospitals in 2003 and 2004 found that one of five patients was readmitted within 30 days. The estimated cost of unplanned hospital readmissions in 2004 accounted for $17.4 billion of the $102.6 billion total hospital payments made by Medicare that same year [7]. If Geisinger can prevent 20% hospital readmissions, it is an innovation with a high ROI.

Veterans Affairs Hospitals

The Department of Veterans Affairs (VA) National Center for Patient Safety was established in 1999 to lead the VAs patient-safety efforts and to develop and nurture a culture of safety throughout the Veterans Health Administration. The program is unique in healthcare because it is focused on proactive mishap mitigation, not punishment. They drew ideas from high reliability organizations, such as aviation and nuclear power, to target and eliminate system vulnerabilities. One outcome of this effort was to institutionalize a proactive aviation tool called FMEA (the failure mode and effects analysis). They customized the tool to healthcare and called it healthcare failure mode and effects analysis or HFMEA [8]. It is used in all the 158 VA hospitals and has expanded to many other hospitals such as East Alabama Hospital, Northwestern University Medical Center, and Johns Hopkins Hospital. One can download the procedure from the VA website or from the Institute for Healthcare Improvement (IHI) website. The tool predicts future mishaps, helps in assessing the risk of each, and requires proactive actions to eliminate or reduce risk.

The Joint Commission also helped in institutionalizing the tool with the new standard LD.5.2 JCAHO (Joint Commission on Accreditation of Healthcare Organizations), which states: "Leaders ensure that an ongoing proactive program on identifying risks to patient safety and reducing medical/healthcare errors is defined and implemented."

The VA has created a protocol for risk avoidance instead of the usual costly firefighting. Through the Joint Commission efforts, it will be a permanent fixture in the hospitals.

Seattle Children's Hospital

In the late 1990s, the leadership of Seattle Children's Hospital (SCH) declared a bold vision to be the best children's hospital. To do so required them to make fundamental, long-lasting, and long-term changes to improve inefficiency and, at times, unsafe systems. Challenged to look outside the healthcare field, SCH learned from companies such as Boeing and Toyota, which focused on patients and removed waste that got in the way of their people and their customers. On a study trip to Boeing, hospital and clinical leaders discovered that Boeing is using the principles of the Toyota Production System and believed those principles could be applied in healthcare as well. This is the same system the Allegheny General Hospital system uses covered in this chapter. Highly impressed, the SCH adopted it and added an aggressive focus on lean principles and ultra-high quality of care into a program called continuous performance improvement (CPI). They have proved that as quality goes up, the costs go down. "Improving overall quality is the goal—reducing waste is the means," says Patrick Hagan, president and chief operating officer of SCH, in the *Washington Post* [9].

His paradigm is totally outside the box, but I agree. "Our healthcare problems will not be solved until we address the reality that, from the perspective of the patient, only 5% of what we do actually provides value. The other 95%? Waste. While this figure may seem absurdly high, waste includes everything in healthcare that does not directly address a patient's health. Some waste is necessary: registering patients, keeping records, moving a patient. However, most is unnecessary: errors, waiting time, unneeded complexity, and avoidable complications."

This author can attest to this paradigm. He avoided a major surgery in the lower back by reading Dr John Sarno's book *Mind over Back Pain* on the psychosomatic power of the mind. The entire surgery would have been a 100% waste. Similarly, the author avoided the 100% unnecessary knee surgery by using acupuncture treatment at a very low cost.

The children's hospital discovered that the largest waste was from the variations in the care processes (see Chapter 2 for examples). Standardizing and error-proofing the processes reduced the variation, resulting in improved quality of care and lower costs. The results speak for themselves:

- Patient days on ventilators reduced by 26% without compromising the possibility of infections, freeing up the specialists to focus on more patients
- Saved $2.5 million in the first year alone on medical supplies
- Decreased the bottlenecks in the patient discharge process, freeing up beds for other sick children
- Peripherally inserted central catheter insertion volumes decreased by 33.4%
- Reduced direct per-patient costs by 3.7%. Multiplied nationally, a similarly relative modest shift could have reduced the total cost of hospital stays nationally by more than $12.7 billion in 2007 alone.

Migita et al. [10] report more to this when it is applied to the computerized physician order entry system:

> From August 2006 to October 2006, 48% of peripherally inserted central catheters were placed on the same calendar day of order entry, 37% within 24 hours of order entry, and 15% within 48 to 72 hours. Overall, provider satisfaction with the ordering process improved according to a Likert scale. Scores increased from 2.68 of 5 to 3.55 of 5 over a 9-month period. This result was statistically significant at the 95th percentile level according to the t-test method. We conclude that properly constructed computerized order sets can be effective in altering physician ordering practices through standardization.

Another of Seattle Children's improvements is to shift the role for prescribing TPN (total parenteral nutrition, an intravenous feeding provided to patients who are unable to feed themselves) from physicians and residents to pharmacists to reduce errors [11]. It achieved "a reduction in errors from 9 to 3 per 1,000 TPN orders, less need for pharmacists to correct orders, a more efficient ordering and administration process, earlier delivery and administration of TPN, and increased staff satisfaction."

These are respectable innovations. Patrick Hagan is an innovator himself and has demonstrated that achieving this kind of change requires substantive and sustained leadership commitment. The hospital has taken a big leap in setting the direction for achieving its vision. First of all, the hospital needs engaged employees who are achievers and willing to be so at any time. The Gallup organization conducts surveys to determine the percent of employees who are engaged, percent not engaged, and percent actively disengaged (those who do not care). Nationally, these percentages are 29%, 51%, and 20%, respectively. The Seattle Children's numbers are 45%, 42%, and 13%, respectively [12].

"This is the real deal, one of the top Lean hospitals in the United States, if not the world," says Mark Graban [13], the author of the book *Lean Hospitals: Improving Quality, Patient Safety, and Employee Satisfaction.* Precisely, why Hagan believes the patients and families cared for at SCH deserve nothing less than the best.

Ideas for Future Paradigm Pioneers

There are unlimited opportunities for future pioneers. The ideas can be easily adopted from other industries. Below is such an idea from how Disney operates its amusement parks.

If you look at Disney resorts, you will find that the customers are more satisfied than anywhere else, but Disney's customer satisfaction score is much lower than other organizations [14]. What a contradiction?

It is actually an illusion, not a contradiction. The other organizations create an illusion of high customer satisfaction ratings so they can get away with shoddy work. Not Disney. It believes in avoiding shoddiness. Read on.

Most hospitals measure customer satisfaction in five classes:

Excellent
Good
Satisfied
Poor
Dissatisfied

To most hospitals, the customer satisfaction is the total of satisfied, good, and excellent ratings. Disney does not consider satisfied customers as loyal customers. They can find satisfaction somewhere else, also. They are easy to defect. The customers who give a "good" rating may come back. But if someone else gives better service, they will also fee. Only those who give an "excellent" rating are delighted and truly satisfied. They are unlikely to go anywhere else. Since only delighted customers are considered as satisfied customers, the percent of customers satisfied appears low on Disney surveys. But that keeps Mickey Mouse hopping all the time!

Disney is your real benchmark for freedom from shoddiness. Good luck to all.

Summary

The paradigm pioneers will exist for a long time because they think outside the box. They offer patients what others cannot or do not.

References

1. Lucian Leape Institute, 2010. Unmet Needs: Teaching Physicians to Provide Safe Patient Care, Report of the Lucian Leape Institute, www.npsf.org/download/LLI-Unmet-Needs-Report.pdf.
2. Altonn, H., 2009. Program at Castle Ends Bloodstream Infections, posted on StarBulletin.com on March 23, www.starbulletin.com/news/20090323_program_at_castle_ends_bloodstream_infections.html.
3. National Public Radio, 2007. Doctor Saved Michigan $100 Million, December 9, www.npr.org/templates/story/story.php?storyId=17060374.
4. Information on Dr. Peter Pronovost's work is available on the Johns Hopkins Web site www.safetyresearch.jhu.edu/qsr/.
5. The Commonwealth Fund, 2008. A private foundation for high performance healthcare, Case Study: Perfecting Patient Care at Allegheny General Hospital and the Pittsburgh Regional Healthcare Initiative, September 30, retrieved from www.commonwealthfund.org/Content/Innovations/Case-Studies/2008/Sep/Case-Study--Perfecting-Patient-Care-at-Allegheny-General-Hospital-and-the-Pittsburgh-Regional-Health.aspx.
6. Connolly, C., 2009. For this health system, less is more, *Washington Post*, March 30, www.washingtonpost.com/wp-dyn/content/arti-cle/2009/03/30/AR2009033003008.html.
7. Jencks, S., et al., 2009. Rehospitalizations among patients in the medicare fee-for-service program, *New England Journal of Medicine*, 360(14): 1418–1428, www.commonwealthfund.org/Content/Publications/In-the-Literature/2009/Apr/Rehospitalizations-Among-Patients-in-the-Medicare-Fee-for-Service.aspx.

8. VA National Center for Patient Safety, 2009. The Basics of Healthcare Failure Mode and Effects Analysis, Videoconference course, www4.va.gov/ncps/SafetyTopics/HFMEA/HFMEAIntro.doc.
9. Hagan, P., 2009. Waste not, want not: The key to reducing costs, *Washington Post*, October 8, www.washingtonpost.com/wp-dyn/content/article/2009/10/08/AR2009100802594.html.
10. Migita, D., et al., 2009. Governing peripherally inserted central venous catheters by combining continuous performance improvement and computerized physician order entry, *Pediatrics*, 123(4): 1155, http://pediatrics.aappublications.org/cgi/content/abstract/123/4/1155.
11. Hagan, P., and Axelrod, S., 2010. *Engaging Physicians in Continuous Performance Improvement*, Presentation at the World Health Care Congress, Washington, DC.
12. AHRQ Health Care Innovation Exchange, 2008. Total Parenteral Nutrition Reduces Errors in Children's Hospital, August 18, www.innovations.ahrq.gov/content.aspx?id=2323.
13. Graban, M., 2009. Exec from Seattle Children's on Lean Healthcare in the Washington Post, Lean Blog, October 13, www.leanblog.org/2009/10/executive-from-seattle-childrens-on/.
14. Lee, F., 2004. *If Disney Ran Your Hospital: 9½ Things You Would Do Differently*, Second River Healthcare Press, Bozeman, MT.

Chapter 12

Protect Patients from Dangers in Medical Devices

Introduction

Human errors may be unpreventable, but preventing mishaps is usually an option. Since humans decide on medical device functionality, clinical interfaces, manufacturing, testing, quality assurance, labeling, transporting, repairing, and maintenance, errors in medicine are inevitable. Errors often transform themselves into dangerous consequences. The 845 recalls of medical devices by the Food and Drug Administration (FDA) in 2008 were the highest ever [1]. This chapter presents two proactive approaches to minimizing patient harm, a closed-ended checklist approach for devices already in the hospitals and an open-ended "Usability Hazard Analysis" matrix approach for new devices or new technologies.

Hospital patient-safety teams can predict dangers. Hospitals must implement safeguards and barriers. Awareness of the need for barriers and safeguards is also needed prior to procuring newly introduced devices such as patient monitoring systems, surgical robots, ventilators, defibrillators, and dialysis equipment. Of major concern is the software in the devices. The FDA recalls between 1999 and 2005 show that one in three devices that use software was recalled due to software errors [2].

The Nature of Dangers

Inherent Dangers in Technology. Radiation from CT scans done in 2007 was estimated to have caused 29,000 cases of cancer and killed nearly 15,000 Americans, according to findings published in the *Archives of Internal Medicine* [3]. Rita Redberg, a cardiologist and an editor for the Archives has this to say: "What we learned is there is a significant amount of radiation with these CT scans, more than what we thought."

Software in the Equipment Dangers. In 2005, a Florida hospital disclosed that 77 brain cancer patients had received 50% more radiation than prescribed because one of the most powerful—and supposedly precise—linear accelerators had been programmed incorrectly for nearly a year [4]. A customer wearing a pacemaker failed when he tried to go through the cashier. The magnetic device that was supposed to detect stolen merchandise reacted with the software in the pacemaker, which resulted in the death of the customer at the cash register [5].

User Interface Dangers. The computerized physician order entry (CPOE) interface has resulted in the following errors: prescribing errors, improper dose/quantity wrong dosage form, extra dose, omission errors, unauthorized/wrong drug, and wrong patient [6]. In a color-coded screen in an emergency department, a color-blind nurse had problems in interpreting the priorities. About 5% of the population is color blind.

Device Reliability Dangers. Devices are designed by humans and assembled by humans. Because of human variability as well as variability in the manufacturing processes, the devices can fail at any time during normal use. In some portable VADs (ventricular assist device), the drivers have stopped due to earlier than expected wear-out of the compressor motor (much less than the expected 3,000 hours usage). The compressor motor can stop without warning. When the motor fails, there is a loss of VAD support for the patient. This results in inadequate blood flow to and from the heart [7].

Dangers from Defective Components. Some pacemakers caused serious injuries because of defective leads. They were recalled. In some catheters, pin holes and exposed wire braids were found that could result in a brain clot or a blood vessel puncture. They were also recalled.

Dangers from Sneak Conditions. Sometimes devices deliver unexpected behavior because of so-called sneak circuits. This is especially true of electronic devices because of uncontrolled interactions among circuits, software, and the components. The devices can fail to deliver required functions, deliver wrong functions, deliver unexpected outputs, not deliver a function when it should, deliver too much treatment, or deliver too little treatment. There are many instances of such incidences in ventilator, defibrillators, and infusion pumps. A hospital reported a fatal central venous air embolism caused by the separation of a specific manufacturer's side port/hemostasis valve catheter-to-sheath adapter from the same manufacturer's percutaneous sheath hub. The accident occurred when the standard Luer-lock fitting disconnected as a patient was moved from a bed to a chair. The hospital could have bought a one-piece device interface instead of two-piece interface from the same manufacturer to avoid the mishap by giving up minor inconveniences of a two-piece design [8].

Dangers from Expired Sterility. Surgical devices with an expired sterility date can result in infections. They may also come in unsterilized or improperly sanitized bags.

Dangers in Accessories. An FDA warning includes the intravenous (IV) tubes used in cardiac surgeries. The plastic material in the tubes may contain a chemical, bisphenol A (BPA), which is highly toxic. It can combine with the warm blood in the tubes.

Dangers from Incorrect Labeling Information and Instructions. In a video-guided catheter, the label insert contained inappropriate information on use with energy-delivering instrumentation. The *Instructions for Use* for an IVAD (implantable ventricular assist device) stated that it may be implanted or placed in the external position. If the IVAD is placed in the external position, air leaks may develop in the pneumatic driveline [9].

Dangers from False Positive and False Negatives. Bankhead [10] reports that cardiac positron emission tomography-computerized tomography (PET-CT) reveals 40% remedial false-positive rate. Fortunately, he adds that most of the errors can be identified and corrected before inappropriate treatment.

Dangers from Incorrect Servicing. Accidents from inaccurate settings of MRIs or improper calibrations of other devices are not uncommon (FDA Recall Number Z-0586–2008).

There are many other dangers in medical devices. One can look up the list of medical device recalls on the FDA.gov website.

Hazard Mitigation for Existing Devices

The current law preempts medical device companies from failure-to-warn and design-defect lawsuits on defects designed into a device if it was approved by the FDA. It would be prudent for hospitals to use one or all of these choices.

Use FDA recall information to strengthen the current device use procedures and develop safeguards and checklists. Manufacturer and user facility device experience (MAUDE) data are available on the FDA site. www.fda.gov/MedicalDevices/DeviceRegulationandGuidance/PostmarketRequirements/ReportingAdverseEvents/ucm127891.htm. For Medical Device Reporting (MDR) data, see www.accessdata.fda.gov/scripts/cdrh/cfdocs/cfMDR/Search.cfm. Enter a single word (e.g., catheter), an exact phrase (e.g., catheter line) or multiple words connected by *and* (e.g., catheter *and* tubing). A list of Device Recalls is available at www.fda.gov/MedicalDevices/Safety/RecallsCorrectionsRemovals/ListofRecalls/default.htm.

Other methods of mitigation can include the following:

■ Inquire about unsafe incidences at other hospitals through professional contacts or surveys.
■ Conduct a hazard analysis such as the failure mode and effects analysis for new dangers on new technologies and new devices. Some hazards will not be on the FDA recall list since the dangers have not shown up yet.
■ Discuss the results of the hazard analysis with the suppliers so they can design the equipment to include safeguards, alerts, monitoring software for inaccurate performance, and built-in self-checks. An example of a built-in check is your car. Every time you turn the ignition key, the built in software makes sure the air bag is in good working condition.
■ Create the equivalent of the Commercial Aviation Safety Teams (CASTs), a public–private partnership intended to reduce hazards throughout aviation in healthcare. Dr Peter Pronovost and his colleagues at Johns Hopkins School of Medicine are exploring a healthcare version of the CAST with an *ad hoc* group whose stakeholders include Agency for Healthcare Research and Quality (AHRQ), the FDA, the Joint Commission, ECRI Institute, and more than 15 large health systems. This method has worked well in over 200 U.S. hospitals [11].
■ Use this knowledge in bedside intelligence systems. The physicians and nurses will directly benefit from the alerts related to an intervention.

We can call this approach a closed-ended approach because we are seeking specific answers. One can achieve a high return on investment just by seeking information from the FDA data or inquiring about improvements from other hospitals, and implementing barriers and safeguards.

Potential Dangers in New Devices and Technologies

How does a physician know the potential dangers of a newly designed device? One of the most desirable ways is to organize a divergent brainstorming in a structured way. We can call this approach an open-ended approach and a usability hazard analysis. It requires a team with diverse functions such as surgery anesthesiology emergency medicine, nursing, patient safety, and risk management, as well as anyone affected by the device under consideration.

One reason for having a divergent group is to combine both the experience and the diverse opinions. It is good to have at least one creative person in the team with no experience at all. In fact, the world's most admired innovative company, IDEO Corporation, started by Stanford graduates, requires about 50% of the team to have unrelated experience. This company developed the mouse for personal computers with hardly any knowledge of computers.

The word usability analysis originated with the computer graphical user interfaces to evaluate the user friendliness of what is on the screen. It includes interactive needs. We can expand the idea to safety analysis.

A part of this proactive technique aims at preventing user errors. Preventing them minimizes the need for reporting user errors to FDA, which is mandated by the MDR requirements (21CFR803). Under these requirements, hospitals are required to report user errors in which there has been a death or serious injury or illness. FDA also requires reporting of maintenance user errors such as failure to service according to manufacturer recommendation, or failure to follow the instructions, or reusing device beyond label specifications [12].

The analysis requires brainstorming on the following structured way to get a comprehensive vision:

- **What can go wrong in normal use?** Includes unexpected behavior of the device, user errors, and sudden failures. Make sure to include software anomalies.
- **What can go wrong in abnormal situations such as loss of electric power, fire, or an epidemic?** This is part of disaster planning and emergency management.
- **How can anyone in the system misuse the product?** Includes misuse by caregivers, patients, visitors, maintenance technicians, and support staff.
- **How can the product experience abuse?** Includes someone ignoring procedures or a housekeeper spraying water near the electrical devices while washing the floor. In one hospital, a patient died because the housekeeper unplugged the life support system in order to plug the vacuum cleaner in the outlet.

Below is an example of a usability hazard analysis (Table 12.1) on an automated ventilator used in a battle environment. The list is partial and excludes mitigation actions because of their proprietary nature. The mitigation strategies are included in the illustration. These are based on the radical approach developed by the aerospace industry.

This technique is widely used at NASA and in the Department of Defense [13]. It has been tried and tested for more than 50 years. It is called the system safety approach. It was covered in Chapter 8 and is worth repeating. This must be memorized because it is used in all safety analyses. It suggests actions in the following order of precedence:

- **Eliminate the hazard entirely.** In an analysis on neuraxial analgesia at Washington Hospital Center, the team discovered that a major potential cause of error was an additional port on the line that would allow for a medication to be administered into the epidural

Table 12.1   An Example of Usability Analysis

USABILITY HAZARD ANALYSIS	
Product: *Automated ventilator*	
Mitigation strategies: *(a) eliminate risk, (b) fault tolerance, (c) fail safely, (d) early warning, (e) robust training*	
Use Profile	*Mitigation, Safeguards, Barriers*
What Can Go Wrong in Normal Use? (Including Software)	
Battery runs out	
Pump stops working	
Patient circuit unhooked	
Blockage to the circuit	
Pressure delivered too high or too low	
Pressure sensors failed	
User interface failure	
Loss of ground affecting other equipment	
What Can Go Wrong in Abnormal Situations?	
Prolonged high temperature in desert environment	
Malfunction in prolonged freezing temperatures	
Unusual power surges (Africa)	
High supplemental oxygen depriving right breathing	
Water intrusion in the device	
How Can the Device be Misused?	
Someone turns off alarms	
Someone turns off LEDs	
Device stored in extreme environment	
How Can the Product be Abused?	
Circuit not changed for new patients	
Filter not changed for new patients	
Product carelessly dropped	
Gets thrown with extra force in transportation handling	
Heavy goods on top of the device in transportation	
Fine sand intrusion in a desert environment	

space. They asked the manufacturer of the equipment to eliminate the additional port. The cost was nothing. The errors disappeared forever! [14]

- **Implement fault tolerance.** In a blood analyzer device, the analysis revealed that the blood test results can be false if the device temperature is above a threshold temperature. The supplier added a fan to keep the device cooler. Someone in the team questioned, what if the fan failed? The team added another fan in such a way that the fans took turns. This alerted the device technician to know when either of the fans failed. The result is: the device worked fine even if a fan failed. This is the concept of fault tolerance. We can have two procedures such that if one procedure failed, the other procedure will safeguard the patient safety. At Johns Hopkins, the surgeon prevents central-line bloodstream infections by having a nurse monitor his/her steps in the process. This is still the fault tolerance.
- **Fail safely.** If the above strategies are not practical, design intelligence in the system (inside or outside the device) to shut down the system before any harm is done.
- **Build-in early warning of potential harm.** Usually statistical control charts are used for monitoring trends of patient's vital signs or the device's abnormal behavior with an alarm.

Hazard Mitigation for New Devices and Technologies

On existing devices, we can hypothesize solutions once the risks are discovered through checklists. We have choices. We can implement safeguards. Or, we can replace an existing device with a new one if the return on investment is justified. We only need to compare the cost of ownership for the existing device, including lawsuits, with a new dependable device.

For new devices entering the market and new technologies, there are at least three approaches as follows:

- **Wait for about 2 years.** This duration allows the dangers to show up in hospitals and allows manufacturers to correct the design or recall the device.
- **Use the results of the usability hazard analysis and develop new requirements for procurement.** Often suppliers will not charge for minor changes because we are helping them to improve their design. Intel, a high-technology company, paid $400,000 for making 70 design improvements to a supplier of high-speed robots, which saved them over $2 million on downtime alone. Hospitals can take the same path. Downtime for a medical device can be life threatening for a patient. Changes in procurement requirements have resulted in significant improvements in patient safety. A report on patient-controlled analgesia pumps concluded that an improvement in a human interface resulted in a 55% reduction in user errors [15]. In another study of operating room alarms, the proportion of the time the alarm was correctly identified was below 50%. The rate of correct detection shot up to 93% with a better design [16].
- **Require usability testing by the manufacturer.** The test profile can be developed from the usability hazard analysis to make sure all the scenarios are tested for safety. For example, try misusing the product during the test and look for evidence of serious consequences. Or have an untrained employee perform all the functions of the device. Create distractions while the employee is trying to use the device. The Mayo Clinic uses its own simulations to test the usability of medical software before purchasing [16].

Can We Use This Knowledge in Bedside Intelligence?

Mitigation knowledge should definitely go into the supply chain procurement process. Some knowledge should be in the hospital equipment maintenance procedures such as when to replace components and the devices themselves *before* they fail. This can be built into bedside intelligence. Bedside intelligence can also include what precautions a patient should take to use the device properly and what to do in case of a failure. More research is needed to determine how it can be useful to physicians at the bedside.

Summary

Those who are not involved directly in preventing hazards may feel that we are opening a Pandora's box when we are looking for signs of danger. Our experience shows that this is neccessary in order to identify hazards and prevent harm.

References

1. F-D-C Reports, Inc., 2009. *The Silver Sheet*, Vol. 13, No. 2, February.
2. Anderson, P., 2009. Standards reduce medical risks, *Medical Design Technology*, February/March.
3. http://injury-law.freeadvice.com/defective_products/medical-device-recalls.htm.
4. Bogdanich, W., 2010. Radiation offers new cures, and ways to do harm, *The New York Times*, January 23, www.nytimes.com/2010/01/24/health/24radiation.html.
5. Raheja, D., and Allocco, M., 2006. *Assurance Technologies Principles and Practices*, John Wiley & Sons, Inc., Hoboken, NJ.
6. Santell, J., 2004. Computer-Related Errors: What Every Pharmacist Should Know, USP Center for Advancement of Patient Safety, presentation based on MEDMARX 5th Anniversary Data Report, ASHP MCM, Orlando, FL, December 9, www.usp.org/pdf/EN/patientSafety/slideShows2004-12-09.pdf.
7. Thoratec® TLC-II® Portable Ventricular Assist Device (VAD) Driver, Class 1 Recall, www.fda.gov/MedicalDevices/Safety/RecallsCorrectionsRemovals/ListofRecalls/ucm062465.htm.
8. The ECRI Institute, 1995. Air Embolism and Exsanguination from Separation of Two-Piece Side Port/Hemostasis Valve Cardiac Catheter Introducers, www.mdsr.ecri.org/summary/detail.aspx?doc_id=8098&q=%22Air+Embolism%22+and+Exsanguination.
9. Thoratec Corporation Implantable Ventricular Assist Devices (IVAD) Class 1 Recall, A FDA alert: www.fda.gov/MedicalDevices/Safety/RecallsCorrectionsRemovals/ListofRecalls/ucm062374.htm.
10. Bankhead, C., 2007. Cardiac PET-CT Reveals 40% Remedial False-Positive Rate, Reviewed by Zalman S. Agus, MD; Emeritus Professor at the University of Pennsylvania School of Medicine. | July 5. ConsultantLive.com www.consultantlive.com/display/article/10162/23489.
11. Pronovost, P., 2009. et al., Reducing health care hazards: Lessons from the commercial aviation safety team, *Health Affairs*, 28(3): w479–w489.
12. Bogner, M. (Ed.), 1994. *Human Error in Medicine*, Lawrence Erlbaum Associates, Mahwah, NJ.
13. MIL-STD-882D, 2000. *Standard Practice for System Safety*, U.S. Department of Defense, Washington, DC.
14. Source for Washington Hospital Center FMEA was the *Directory of Solutions*, Fifth Annual Maryland Patient Safety Conference, 2009.
15. Murff, H., et al., 2001. *Human Factors and Medical Devices*, Technology Assessment No. 43, Making Healthcare Safer: A Critical Analysis of Patient Safety practices, US Department of Health and Human Services, www.ncbi.nlm.nih.gov/bookshelf/br.ficgi?book=hsertasum&part=A86569.
16. Peters, G., and Peters, B., 2006. *Human Error Causes and Control*, Taylor & Francis, Boca Raton, FL.

Chapter 13

Heuristics for Continuous Innovation

Experience is the name everyone gives to their mistakes.

—Oscar Wilde

Introduction

Medicine has avoided facing a harsh reality. Although we assume that medical decisions are driven by established scientific facts, even a cursory review of practice patterns shows that they are not. Angioplasty became a multibillion-dollar industry long before a single randomized trial or epidemiologic study had shown its benefits (http://www.annals.org/content/124/1_Part_1/56.full-ref-1). Large numbers of MRI units were purchased during the first 5 years of their clinical availability before any data were available to show that MRI was preferable to the diagnostic alternatives.

These are the findings of a joint study by the Regenstrief Institute for Health Care and the Indiana University School of Medicine, summarized by Clement McDonald [1]. He says that robust scientific conclusions are too sparse to inform fully most of the choices for treatments. Instead, *ad hoc* rules of thumb, or "heuristics," must guide them. Since heuristics are inherently context driven, they "should be discussed, criticized, refined, and then taught. More uniform use of explicit and better heuristics could lead to less practice variation and more efficient medical care."

Heuristics can be short statements of lessons learned. They can be the words of wisdom from experience or educated guesses. They are often shortcuts in complex situations, and can lead to smarter and efficient work. They work most of the time. Over the span of 30 years, I have developed some heuristics as a consultant. Some are included in this chapter.

The readers can develop such heuristics from their own experience. This chapter will cover the following:

- Heuristics for medicine
- Heuristics for frontline processes
- Heuristics for management

Heuristics for Medicine

Unfortunately, the heuristics used by physicians are poorly understood and rarely discussed, according to McDonald [1]. "It may be that we physicians are reluctant to admit that 'nonscientific' mechanisms may guide much of medical care. But admitting the role of heuristics confers no shame. Mathematics—described by many as the queen of the sciences—has profitably explored the heuristics that underlie mathematical insight." He gives three examples of heuristics that can be used in diagnosis: *Occam's razor* is one borrowed from general science. Interpreted simply, Occam's razor advises choosing the simplest hypothesis that explains a set of observations; this heuristic can be directly applied to the diagnostic process. He describes the second heuristic as follows:

> As a resident I was often chided to "treat the patient, not the numbers." I still hear this dictum used to discourage treatment of asymptomatic or mildly asymptomatic patients with abnormal results or findings. Since my house staff years, most of the arguments about "treating numbers" in the case of asymptomatic patients have been won by the "numbers treaters." In 1970, a Veterans Administration study settled the argument about treatment for mild-to-moderate hypertension in favor of treating patients with diastolic blood pressures greater than 90 mm Hg. The arguments about maintaining glucose levels tightly near normal in patients with diabetes have now been settled as well. The better the control of glycemia, the better the long-term outcomes.

His third heuristic is very appropriate: "Never use a new drug when an old drug will do."

Dr William Oetgen [2] of George Washington University offers a corollary to Occam's razor: the Zebra Rule, which states, when you hear hoof beats, think of horses, not zebras. Dr McDonald, in the same publication, recasts the Zebra Rule as a rule of prevalence. For example, "Work up the diseases in the differential with prevalences of greater than 1:100 before you work on prevalences of less than 1:1000." Dr Oetgen offers another heuristic on the futility of end-of-life cardiac pulmonary resuscitation: "If you can't keep them while they are alive, you can't keep them when they are dead."

The Agency for Healthcare Quality and Research (AHRQ) is also concerned about significant errors in diagnosis [3]. It cited a Harvard Medical Practice Study in which diagnostic error accounted for 17% of preventable errors in hospitalized patients, and a systematic review of autopsy studies covering four decades found that approximately 9% of patients experienced a major diagnostic error that went undetected while the patient was alive. Taken together, these studies imply that thousands of hospitalized patients die every year due to diagnostic errors. It concludes, "As applied to healthcare, we have learned that clinicians frequently use heuristics (cognitive shortcuts) in the face of complex situations, and thus they serve an important purpose in coming up with a provisional diagnosis, especially when faced with a patient with common symptoms. It also highlights the negative side": While heuristics are ubiquitous and useful, researchers have used categories developed in cognitive psychology to classify several types of errors that clinicians commonly make due to incorrect applications of heuristics (Table 13.1).

Table 13.1   Cognitive Heuristics for Medicine

Cognitive Bias	Definition	Example
Availability heuristic	Diagnosis of current patient biased by experience with past cases	A patient with *crushing chest pain* was incorrectly treated for a myocardial infarction, despite indications that an aortic dissection was present.
Anchoring heuristic (premature closure)	Relying on initial diagnostic impression, despite subsequent information to the contrary	Repeated *positive blood cultures* with *Corynebacterium* were dismissed as contaminants; the patient was eventually diagnosed with *Corynebacterium endocarditis*.
Framing effects	Diagnostic decision-making unduly biased by subtle cues and collateral information	A heroin-addicted patient with *abdominal pain* was treated for opiate withdrawal, but proved to have a bowel perforation.
Blind obedience	Placing undue reliance on test results or "expert" opinion	A false-negative *rapid test* for *Streptococcus pharyngitis* resulted in a delay in diagnosis.

Other Heuristics for Medicine

Primum non nocere: It is Latin for "First, do no harm." Wikipedia adds that another way to state it is that, "given an existing problem, it may be better to do nothing than to do something that risks causing more harm than good. Since at least 1860, the phrase has been for physicians a hallowed expression of hope, intention, humility, and recognition that human acts with good intentions may have unwanted consequences."

Heuristics for Frontline Processes

Some heuristics are presented here from my experience. These are thought-starters. Feel free to modify for your application.

Stop Working on Wrong Things, and You Will Automatically Work on Right Things

Dr Edward Deming (the father of Japanese quality control) and I taught short courses at George Washington University. He once said: "Working hard won't help if they are working on wrong things." How true! He tried to teach this to the U.S. automotive industry. Unfortunately, the industry looked the other way. The hospitals can use this as a heuristic—a very powerful one. The author has saved millions of dollars for clients using this heuristic. For example, buying a standard CPOE (computerized physician ordering entry) system is usually a wrong thing to do. If you ask the question "What is the right thing to do?" you are likely to add a "Why?" If you do not know why, you will probably ask people having experience with the CPOE systems. They will tell you that there are hundreds of problems in the standard systems. They may tell you that the right thing to do is to develop a list of problems at other hospitals and tell the supplier you want them removed from the software!

A study from the University of Pittsburgh Children's Hospital reported a 3.3-fold increase in the mortality rate for children transferred in for special care when it initially implemented a commercial CPOE application [4]. The Cedars-Sinai experience is often cited; its implementation of CPOE 6 failed for a variety of reasons, and the application had to be withdrawn even though it was working [5]. A 722-page report compiled by Kaiser Permanente's IT department details hundreds of problems with an EMR (electronic medical records) system [6].

The best way to stop working on wrong things is to form a cross-functional team. Encourage everyone to identify wrong things. I ask every team member to identify at least five wrong things. They always do. With a good leader this can be done. Then create a plan to stop working on wrong things and replace them with right things. In one case, employees came up with 22 solutions for a single problem. About five of them had over 600% return on investment. Almost always, the right things just appear by themselves! You just have to ask, and you shall get it.

Learn to Say "No" to Yes Men

In a previous chapter, we discussed how undesirable it is to accept a consensus without challenges from team members. If all say yes-yes, your answer should be a no-no.

> Working hard would not help if you are working on wrong things

We may not be able to make a good decision on complex interactions until we see the situation from different points of view. If we introduce a new process, we need to see potential problems and potential harm from experience of nurses, doctors, psychologists, support staff, risk managers, quality assurance staff, and safety officers. Each will have a different concern. Let them challenge the oversights and omissions based on their experiences. Dr Edward De Bono, the author of *Six Thinking Hats*, suggests at least six members to a team, each assigned to look from a specific point of view. This method makes sure that the different challenges are always welcome and are indeed expected.

It is important to avoid group speak, agreeing to agree on everything. All decisions must be made from a position of knowledge and credible information; otherwise, decisions have little integrity and grow difficult to defend. Nonverbal communication is important and tells a story even when a person will not or cannot. It is said to also reveal a person's true feelings when they are not willing to reveal them.

"No Action" Is an Action

Often caregivers make no decision. It may be out of denial, or because of an inability to take action, or they cannot upset the superiors. An example of a "no action" is not to submit an incidence report on a serious harm. Sometimes the action is passive in the form of a suggestion only without any action taken to prevent harm. In all these situations, it is an action of *not to action*. The patient is usually the victim. The following is a case reported in the *Boston Globe* in which passive actions amounted to no meaningful action [7]. The names are left out to protect their privacy.

When Dr X began his first case at about 8 a.m., an operating room nurse noticed he looked tired and wobbly. She was so concerned, according to one account, on that Friday last June, that she suggested Dr X postpone his next patient.

Dr X said he had been up all night working on a book, but he kept operating, starting a second case during which he briefly fell asleep, according to a report from state investigators. The nurse again called him aside and suggested "Maybe he should take a break," according to her interviews with investigators, but he continued the surgery.

These findings are part of a report in which state Department of Public Health investigators found that hospital Y provided poor care to Dr X's second patient that day. They also faulted the hospital's response to Dr X's apparent impairment.

The patient, Mr. Z, has said he suffered complications after liposuction surgery and repair of a scar on his chest, and in July he sued the hospital, six doctors including Dr X, and two nurses. He has settled his case; the terms are confidential.

The operating room nurse called the plastic surgery department twice to report Dr X's behavior that morning and early afternoon, the report said, and the office nurse told her to "keep an eye on him." But no senior surgeon or administrator ordered Dr X to stop operating—even though there was widespread awareness of his history of drug and alcohol abuse, according to investigators.

He didn't stop working until 1:30 p.m., when a resident—a doctor in training—who was assisting him had to leave to see patients. The resident called another plastic surgeon for help because Dr X wasn't on his "A game," the resident told investigators. The plastic surgeon sent another fellow, a more senior doctor in training, to assist Dr X. About 10 minutes after he arrived, Dr X left for unexplained reasons.

State investigators said the hospital did not treat the patient appropriately after his surgery, either. The patient was not assessed by a physician before he was discharged that night, and hospital administrators did not tell the patient that Dr X had to abandon his operation, and why, until 10 days after the surgery. The operation lasted 7 hours, rather than the estimated 90 minutes.

The hospital fired Dr X, and the state temporarily suspended his license.

"How common is it that nurses and other personnel don't speak up? I can't think of any [hospital] in the world where this isn't an issue," said Dr Allan Frankel, former director of patient safety at Partners HealthCare and founder of a patient safety consulting company based in Washington, D.C.

This case shows that the staff tried to take action, but they were the equivalent of inactions or passive actions from the point of view of the patient. Dr Frankel suggests in the above report that "the hospitals should designate a specific manager who will come and make the final decision. Nurses do not have the power over surgeons. It is not their job to confront surgeons."

No Control Is the Best Control

We need to view this in the right context. The central thinking is that we should design the process in such a way that it does not require day-to-day control or frequent monitoring. A periodic audit or a spot check should be done to assure the process is working right. Take the example of inventory control of gowns, gloves, syringes, needles, and pharmacy medicines. Often these items suddenly get used up completely and are not there when needed. The only solution seems to be to overstock, which becomes an inefficient use of money. We can use the Walmart technique to reduce inventory and assure adequate supplies all the time. In this method, as soon as an item is removed from the shelf, the supplier is notified through the information systems. It is the supplier's responsibility to automatically replace the inventory after a few items are removed, instead of shipping a large number of units less frequently. This assures there is never a large amount of inventory not being used. As far as Walmart is concerned, they do not need to control or monitor inventory at all. The supplier does.

Heuristics for Management

If You Do not Know Where You Are Going, Any Road Will Get You There

Hospitals where many incidences are not reported do not know when a major lawsuit or a "never" event will strike. An incident today is a "never" or adverse event tomorrow. Incidence reporting should include reporting on peers but must be nonpunitive. Hardly any doctor or nurse reports on their own mistakes in the incidence report. They rarely report on the mistakes of peers. When a patient walks away in frustration from the emergency room (ER) because she could not see the triage nurse in a reasonable amount of time; it may not go on the incidence report. Ditto when a medication is given to the wrong patient. Even misdiagnosis sometimes does not go on an incidence report. But these incidences, when ignored, often turn into adverse and "never" events.

Some worry that more the incidence reports, the more a hospital knows about when a major lawsuit will be filed. These documented reports can favor the plaintiff. Actually they work more in favor of hospitals if they can show that incidence reports have been used to prevent or minimize patient harm. The jury understands that some accidents cannot be easily prevented; therefore, they reduce punitive penalties to those who have a record of honestly preventing the patient harm. Many incidence reports and proactive actions on them is a very good defense against the plaintiff's charges of negligence and criminal liability. Also, knowing in advance when a major lawsuit can be an advantage. It allows time for the hospitals to investigate the root causes and prepare to defend themselves. Once the harm has occurred, the lawsuit is likely regardless of whether an incidence report is filed on not. Not fling an incidence report in such cases is more damaging to hospitals in the eyes of a jury. Such an inaction proves that the hospital does not have a good process to prevent harm.

Each incidence should produce a new solution to make certain a hospital has a good process to prevent harm. The solutions can be very simple and very cheap if a hospital uses the innovation methods covered in Chapter 4. One area where this heuristic is true is the use of standard EHRs (electronic health records) by hospitals. Many hospitals have very little idea about very serious hazards in these systems. They spend millions of dollars buying systems they do not understand. A hospital must know if the EHR system is free of very obvious hazards such as residents able to override alerts or shut them because there are too many alerts, records going to the wrong patient's file, physicians not entering the data on time, confusion between old records and new records, incomplete medication histories, unfriendly user interfaces that make life complicated for clinicians, patient weights not consistently reported in pounds or kilograms (babies can get overdosed because of this error), poorly scanned reports, and images that can result in misdiagnosis, and test results fled improperly in the EHRs.

Convert Bad News into Good News

Hospital care statistics are painful not only for patients but also for hospitals that are working hard to prevent harm. Patient-safety incidents in Medicare patients still account for nearly 100,000 preventable deaths and nearly $7 billion in excess costs yearly. Only 7% of hospitals meet medication error prevention standards. About 75% do not meet the standards for evidence-based safety practices (AHRQ Discharge). The solution is to not to take this news negatively but to recognize it as an evidence for a need to change. But, to convert bad news into good, the process improvement must be rapid to create good news. Allegheny General has a policy to solve serious problems immediately. You saw an example in the chapter on paradigm pioneers.

As Quality Goes up, the Costs Go down

This is a well-known heuristic preached by all the gurus covered in earlier chapters. But there must be a discussion on this heuristic, too on how to prove it. There are still some hospitals that complain about costs going up to improve quality. They need to be aware that the cost may go up for a short time. But the savings go on for years.

That Which Gets Measured, Is What Gets Done

This heuristic is a very powerful tool for getting problems solved faster. It is representation of the Hawthorne Effect, a study in which the employee productivity was increased dramatically because the management was tracking it. Any time the management tracks the progress on anything, the progress takes place almost all the time. To track, the management needs measurements. Wherever there is no measurement, there is hardly any progress.

20% of Causes Are Responsible for 80% of Effects

Almost everyone knows this rule of thumb. About 20% of problems are responsive for 80% losses in revenues. Managers must constantly encourage innovation for these 20% of the problems.

Summary

Each organization should develop intelligence in the form of heuristics so that the chosen knowledge gets transferred from a generation to generation. It should be in the training curriculum including the pitfalls, the context, and the assumptions. Heuristics are right to the point and easy to remember. They are a good tool for friendly challenging. If we do not challenge, we create harm continuously and hurt the reputation of the hospital.

Peter Drucker, the best-known business guru, used to say: "If you want to start doing something new, stop doing something old."

References

1. McDonald, C., 2010. Medical heuristics: The silent adjudicators of clinical practice, *Annals of Internal Medicine*, 152(8), www.annals.org/content/124/1_Part_1/56.full.
2. Oetgen, W., 1996. Letters (to the Editor), *Annals of Internal Medicine*, 125(1), www.annals.org/content/125/1/77.1.full.pdf.
3. Patient Safety Network PSNET, 2010. Patient Safety Primer: Diagnosis Errors, retrieved on May 26, AHRQ, http://psnet.ahrq.gov/primer.aspx?primerID=12.
4. Han, Y., et al., 2005. Unexpected increased mortality after implementation of a commercially sold computerized physician order entry system, *Pediatrics*, 116(6): 1506–1512.
5. Ornstein, C., 2003. Hospital heeds doctors, suspends use of software: Cedars-sinai physicians entered prescriptions and other orders in it, but called it unsafe, *Los Angeles Times*, January 22.
6. Emrupdate.com, 2006. Kaiser Permanente Financial Troubles and EPIC EMR, posted on November 23, retrieved from www.emrupdate.com/forums/p/7756/59296.aspx.
7. Kowalczyk, L., 2009. Doctor dozed during surgery, report says beth israel faulted in case, *Boston Globe*, March 25.

Chapter 14

Aequanimitas—The Best-Known Strategy for Safe Care

He who studies medicine without books sails an uncharted sea, but he who studies medicine without patients does not go to sea at all.

—Sir William Osler

Introduction

Emblazoned on the shield of The Johns Hopkins Department of Medicine is the word *Aequanimitas*. The term means "imperturbability," and was regarded by Dr William Osler as the premier quality of a good physician. In his essay *Aequanimitas*, Dr Osler further defines this concept as coolness and presence of mind under all circumstances, calmness amid storm, and clearness of judgment in moments of grave peril. In full development, as we see it in some of our older colleagues, it has the nature of a divine gift, a blessing to the possessor, a comfort to all who come in contact with him. At the beginning of their Osler residency, interns are given a copy of this essay—both to bolster their spirit and to refresh their memories during the trial of the following year.

This paragraph was downloaded from the Johns Hopkins School of Medicine website [1]. *Aequanimitas* was the subject of Osler's address at the graduation ceremony at the University of Pennsylvania School of Medicine in 1889, just before he moved to Johns Hopkins as its first chief of medicine. He was 39 years old, but his legacy continues even today after 120 years.

"What more can be said about Sir William Osler? He is, for all intents and purposes, already canonized by the medical profession as its most current saint and the epitome of the ideal physician for the twentieth century" says J. Shedlock in the *Journal of the American Library*

Association [2]. He adds that Osler has retained his strength as a spokesperson for medicine. In an age of advancing technology applied to the diagnosis and treatment of disease, physicians can still point to one physician who articulates the values of the profession even in the face of daunting and difficult decisions regarding ethical choices.

Aequanimitas Explained

Anders [3] in his paper *Aequanimitas Centennial* (100th Anniversary of Osler's address) has this comment. Osler noted that while there are many things that could contribute to a physician's success, his discussion would cover only two: imperturbability and equanimity. New York University School of Medicine websites [4] offer these simple definitions: "Imperturbability" means the outward expression of calmness and coolness, even under difficult circumstances. This virtue suggests that physicians should be relatively "insensible" to the slings and arrows of patient care. "Equanimity" is the complementary "mental" virtue, which is the personal quality of calmly accepting whatever comes in life. These virtues, however, should not lead to "hardness" in dealing with patients. The website clarifies further: Osler believes that some distance is necessary in order for the physician to develop what we would call "empathy," the ability to understand the patient's problem accurately and to convey that understanding back to the patient. The virtue of aequanimitas also suggests a general attitude of acceptance that is crucial to good medical practice.

Why Aequanimitas Is the Best-Known Strategy for Safe Care?

A recent study shows the need for aequanimitas very loudly. A Harris poll conducted for the *Wall Street Journal* [5] found that patients judged their physicians' interpersonal skills and listening as more important than good medical judgment! Fry of the Institute for Health and Human Potential [6] says that 84% of healthcare personnel in hospital settings have witnessed

> Patients judge their physicians' interpersonal skills and listening as more important than good medical judgment!

coworkers taking shortcuts that could be dangerous to patients, yet fewer than 10% of physicians or nurses directly confront their colleagues about their concerns. He reports this finding is from a white paper *Vital Smarts, Silence Kills* from the American Association of Critical-Care Nurses. He includes an example of incompetence that goes unreported. *A group of eight anesthesiologists agree a peer is dangerously incompetent, but they do not confront him. Instead, they go to great efforts to schedule surgeries for the sickest babies at times when he is not on duty.*

Pauline Chen, a liver transplant/liver cancer surgeon and author of the book *Final Exam: a Surgeon's Reflections on Mortality,* heard this comment at a summer potluck. "I don't rely on the doctor anymore. These days, you have to look out for yourself [7]." Needless to say, she felt a great sadness for her profession and patients.

She says, "More and more Americans feel disconnected from their doctors, especially compared to a generation ago. And they certainly have less confidence in the profession as a whole. In

1966, a Harris Poll found that almost three-quarters of Americans had 'a great deal' of confidence in their healthcare leaders. That number has steadily dropped over the last four decades, so that today only slightly more than a third feel the same way, the same poll shows. I know there's a problem with the way medicine works these days, but as a surgeon, I've also stood on the other side. I have felt my heart drop when a patient whose new liver I struggled to sew into place decides without telling me to stop taking immunosuppressive medications. There is a tragic irony in the growing divide between us. We all want the same thing: the best care possible. But we have lost the ability to converse thoughtfully with one another. And because of that loss, we can no longer discuss the meaning of illness, care, health, and policy in a way that is relevant to all of us."

A study on frequent interruptions of care supports Chen's assessment. This study in the emergency department of a 400-bed teaching hospital, observing 40 doctors, found that interruptions led doctors to spend less time on the tasks they were working on and, in nearly a fifth of cases, to give up on the task altogether [8]. The study also found that physicians spent less time on interrupted tasks than on uninterrupted tasks. In addition, doctors were multitasking 12.8% of the time.

Chen also brings attention to the role of electronic medical records (EMRs) in creating a southward trend in patient–doctor relationships [9]. EMRs have many big benefits in efficiency and ease of getting real-time information but have created a negative situation for physicians as well as patients. "In order to use the computer, I had to turn my back to the patient as I spoke to him. I tried to compensate by sitting on a rolling stool but soon found myself spending more time spinning and wheeling back and forth between patient and computer than I did sitting still and listening. And when my patient did talk, his story came only in spurts because every time I turned my back to him to type, the room fell silent."

Chen quotes a study on the effects of EMR on physician communication by the Center for Studying Health System Change involving 26 medical facilities: All the physicians expressed concerns that EMR had less than salutary effects on the patient–doctor relationship, including difficulties replicating the narrative aspect of a patient's illness and the constant interruptions from alerts and instant messaging. This makes a good case for aequanimitas practice.

If such is the state-of-the art between a patient and a doctor that definitely affects safe care, the most needed solution seems to be the aequanimitas. Shedlock, cited above, noted Osler's following advice: He told the graduates of the University of Pennsylvania that *imperturbability* is necessary for physicians to maintain their self-control so as to aid their patients confidently from their scientific knowledge and the ways to apply it in individual cases, and *equanimity* is necessary for physicians to maintain presence of mind by being patient and persistent in working with patients, and others. In 1913, he urged the Yale students to "Shut off the future as tightly as the past. No dreams, no visions, no delicious fantasies, no castles in the air." In other words, fully concentrate on the patient care. Obviously, patient safety is the primary concern.

The Practice of Aequanimitas

Assuming that many current practices are counterproductive for physician–patient synergy, aequanimitas is a good way to start new thinking. Some call it "thinking without thinking." It means empty your mind of the past practices. Let the ideas and solutions flow freely through you. This often leads to an "aha! moment" experienced by the innovators.

Dr C. Bryan [10], University of South Carolina School of Medicine, gives the account of Osler's powerful style. A medical student said of Osler that his motto seemed to be to "Do the kind thing and do it first." Another student wrote his mother, "He seems to be the least sentimental and the most helpful man I've ever seen."

Bryan gives examples of Osler's compassion, how he resolved this tension between technical competence and detachment on the one hand and caring on the other. The first example is about a young Englishman visiting Montreal on business.

Osler met him at the Metropolitan Club in Montreal, where Osler, being a bachelor, frequently took his meals. One day the young Englishman did not look very well, and Osler asked him what was wrong, attended to him, and diagnosed smallpox. It became obvious that his case was going to be severe, and Osler arranged for him to be seen by the leading internist in Montreal, his mentor, Palmer Howard. Osler got him into the hospital, but the young man went downhill and died. Thereafter, Osler wrote a factual and detailed letter to the young man's parents. Osler described exactly what had happened and what had been done, stated that the young man had gotten the best care, and explained that during his last hours he had frequently spoken of home, had asked Osler to read him a passage from Isaiah that was his mother's favorite, had talked about his mother, and had died peacefully. Osler did not hear anything further for about 30 years. Then at Oxford at a reception, a woman came up and said, "Would you happen to be the same Dr Osler who took care of my brother?" And he said, "Yes, I remember." The woman said, "I can't tell you what your letter meant to my mother. She cherished that letter for the rest of her life." Osler then arranged for a picture of the boy's grave to be sent to the family.

The second example concerns a small boy with whooping cough. One day as Osler was going to graduation ceremonies at Oxford in his full academic regalia, he was stopped by a friend whose son had whooping cough, which then was untreatable. Osler saw that the boy had a more severe bronchitis than usual. Although he was running late, Osler examined the boy and sat at his bedside. The boy's problem was that he would not eat. Osler carefully peeled an orange, broke it into segments, and coated each one with a little bit of sugar. He told the boy that it was magical fruit and that if he would just eat it one piece at a time he would get well. Osler went outside the door then and told the dad, "I'm sorry, Ernest, but when they're this bad off, they seldom make a full recovery." Osler was told that the little boy thought he was a magical figure in his academic gown. Thereafter, for the next 40 days, Osler went to the infirmary carrying his academic gown, put it on outside the boy's door, and then went in. And the little boy made a steady recovery, regaining his health.

Modern Variations of Aequanimitas

Emotional Intelligence

Daniel Goleman, the inventor of this model at MIT and author of the book *Emotional Intelligence,* explains how typically if you go into the doctor's surgery with, say, three questions, you may be lucky to get one or two questions answered in a way which you properly understand.

"If you don't know what the term *emotional intelligence* means, you will soon. It's being used with more regularity in healthcare professions and touted as an essential element for leaders and teams," says Rouston [11] in her article *Emotional Intelligence: An Essential Skill for Nurses.* She elaborates: It is your emotional smarts. It is an ability that has four main components:

The ability to identify emotions
The ability to use emotions in one's thought process more intelligently
The ability to understand emotions in transitional situations, such as anger leading to rage
The ability to manage one's emotions and those of others to achieve your goals

She writes about May Taylor Moss, vice president of operations at Accordant Health Services, who saw many departures out of the executive suite. She wondered, "I said to myself, 'These people are so smart, how come they fail?' I learned that they were not looking at the emotional side of the workplace. They were losing jobs because they were going about them the wrong way." Moss wound up writing a book, *The Emotionally Intelligent Nurse.*

Emotional Intelligence (EI) is getting to be a popular voice in healthcare as shown by the following findings:

■ In a study of 550 nurses, Güleryüz et al. [12] found that EI was significantly and positively related to job satisfaction and organizational commitment.
■ Another study by Deshpande and Joseph [13] on 103 nurses concluded that the level of EI and ethical behavior of peers had a significant impact on the ethical behavior of nurses.
■ Girdharwal's [14] study on EI in the healthcare industry says that research in a variety of industries and job levels reveals EI was two times more important in contributing to excellence than intellect and expertise alone. Healthcare is no exception.
■ Kravvariti et al. [15] examined the relation between coronary heart disease and EI on groups of patients who had the disease and those who did not. The results indicated that facets of EI such as decreased ability to use and regulate emotions, as well as frequency of negative expressiveness are associated with incidence of coronary heart disease.
■ In the *Journal of the American Medical Association* [16], Grewal et al. proposed including EI in the graduate medical education. "We propose that the scientific concept of emotional intelligence (EI) has the potential to deepen understanding of the competency: *interpersonal and communication skills.*"
■ Gewertz [17], at the Department of Surgery, University of Chicago, points out that the increased interest in EI is supported by a growing compilation of data that demonstrates that enhanced social interactions improve personal performance in a wide range of settings.

At Ohio State College of Nursing, EI is one of the resources for nursing [18]. It emphasizes how you work with others and how you incorporate self-awareness into your role may play an even larger part than the nursing skills.

It offers the following guidelines (Figure 14.1) on developing competence in the EI.

Training the staff in EI can improve quality and safety very significantly, but using the process of EI is an innovation by itself. As pointed in this section, nurses are also equal partners in serving the emotional needs of patients as well as coworkers. EI should not be limited physicians.

The Beginner's Mind

Steve Jobs, chairman and founder of Apple Computers, gave a remarkably personal and frank commencement address at Stanford University in June, 2005 [19] on a concept similar to aequanimitas. He talked about how failure led him back to success, and also referred to "Beginner's Mind," a Zen idea made famous in America during the 1960s through the published lectures of the late San Francisco-based Zen Master Shunryu Suzuki. The concept refers to the openness

PERSONAL COMPETENCE

Self-Awareness

EMOTIONAL AWARENESS: Recognizing one's emotions and their effects. People with this competence:

- Know which emotions they are feeling and why
- Realize the links between their feelings and what they think, do, and say
- Recognize how their feelings affect their performance
- Have a guiding awareness of their values and goals

ACCURATE SELF-ASSESSMENT: Knowing one's strengths and limits. People with this competence are:

- Aware of their strengths and weaknesses
- Reflective, learning from experience
- Open to candid feedback, new perspectives, continuous learning, and self-development
- Able to show a sense of humor and perspective about themselves

SELF-CONFIDENCE: Sureness about one's self-worth and capabilities. People with this competence:

- Present themselves with self-assurance; have "presence"
- Can voice views that are unpopular and go out on a limb for what is right
- Are decisive, able to make sound decisions despite uncertainties and pressures

Self-Regulation

SELF-CONTROL: Managing disruptive emotions and impulses. People with this competence:

- Manage their impulsive feelings and distressing emotions well
- Stay composed, positive, and unflappable even in trying moments
- Think clearly and stay focused under pressure

TRUSTWORTHINESS: Maintaining standards of honesty and integrity. People with this competence:

- Act ethically and are above reproach
- Build trust through their reliability and authenticity
- Admit their own mistakes and confront unethical actions in others
- Take tough, principled stands even if they are unpopular

CONSCIENTIOUSNESS: Taking responsibility for personal performance. People with this competence:

- Meet commitments and keep promises
- Hold themselves accountable for meeting their objectives
- Are organized and careful in their work

ADAPTABILITY: Flexibility in handling change. People with this competence:

- Smoothly handle multiple demands, shifting priorities, and rapid change
- Adapt their responses and tactics to fit fluid circumstances
- Are flexible in how they see events

INNOVATIVENESS: Being comfortable with and open to novel ideas and new information. People with this competence:

- Seek out fresh ideas from a wide variety of sources
- Entertain original solutions to problems
- Generate new ideas
- Take fresh perspectives and risks in their thinking

Figure 14.1 Guidelines for EI.

(*Continued*)

Self-Motivation

ACHIEVEMENT DRIVE: Striving to improve or meet a standard of excellence. People with this competence:

- Are results-oriented, with a high drive to meet their objectives and standards
- Set challenging goals and take calculated risks
- Pursue information to reduce uncertainty and find ways to do better
- Learn how to improve their performance

COMMITMENT: Aligning with the goals of the group or organization. People with this competence:

- Readily make personal or group sacrifices to meet a larger organizational goal
- Find a sense of purpose in the larger mission
- Use the group's core values in making decisions and clarifying choices
- Actively seek out opportunities to fulfill the group's mission

INITIATIVE: Readiness to act on opportunities. People with this competence:

- Are ready to seize opportunities
- Pursue goals beyond what's required or expected of them
- Cut through red tape and bend the rules when necessary to get the job done
- Mobilize others through unusual, enterprising efforts

OPTIMISM: Persistence in pursuing goals despite obstacles and setbacks. People with this competence:

- Persist in seeking goals despite obstacles and setbacks
- Operate from hope of success rather than fear of failure
- See setbacks as due to manageable circumstance rather than a personal flaw

SOCIAL COMPETENCE

Social Awareness

EMPATHY: Sensing others' feelings and perspective, and taking an active interest in their concerns. People with this competence:

- Are attentive to emotional cues and listen well
- Show sensitivity and understand others' perspectives
- Help out based on understanding other people's needs and feelings

SERVICE ORIENTATION: Anticipating, recognizing, and meeting customers' needs. People with this competence:

- Understand customers' needs and match them to services or products
- Seek ways to increase customers' satisfaction and loyalty
- Gladly offer appropriate assistance
- Grasp a customer's perspective, acting as a trusted advisor

DEVELOPING OTHERS: Sensing what others need in order to develop, and bolstering their abilities. People with this competence:

- Acknowledge and reward people's strengths, accomplishments, and development
- Offer useful feedback and identify people's needs for development
- Mentor, give timely coaching, and offer assignments that challenge and grow a person's skill

Figure 14.1 (CONTINUED)   Guidelines for EI.

(Continued)

LEVERAGING DIVERSITY: Cultivating opportunities through diverse people. People with this competence:

- Respect and relate well to people from varied backgrounds
- Understand diverse worldviews and are sensitive to group differences
- See diversity as opportunity, creating an environment where diverse people can thrive
- Challenge bias and intolerance

POLITICAL AWARENESS: Reading a group's emotional currents and power relationships. People with this competence:

- Accurately read key power relationships
- Detect crucial social networks
- Understand the forces that shape views and actions of clients, customers, or competitors
- Accurately read situations and organizational and external realities

Social Skills

INFLUENCE: Wielding effective tactics for persuasion. People with this competence:

- Are skilled at persuasion
- Fine-tune presentations to appeal to the listener
- Use complex strategies like indirect influence to build consensus and support
- Orchestrate dramatic events to effectively make a point

COMMUNICATION: Sending clear and convincing messages. People with this competence:

- Are effective in give-and-take, registering emotional cues in attuning their message
- Deal with difficult issues straightforwardly
- Listen well, seek mutual understanding, and welcome sharing of information fully
- Foster open communication and stay receptive to bad news as well as good

LEADERSHIP: Inspiring and guiding groups and people. People with this competence:

- Articulate and arouse enthusiasm for a shared vision and mission
- Step forward to lead as needed, regardless of position
- Guide the performance of others while holding them accountable
- Lead by example

CHANGE CATALYST: Initiating or managing change. People with this competence:

- Recognize the need for change and remove barriers
- Challenge the status quo to acknowledge the need for change
- Champion the change and enlist others in its pursuit
- Model the change expected of others

CONFLICT MANAGEMENT: Negotiating and resolving disagreements. People with this competence:

- Handle difficult people and tense situations with diplomacy and tact
- Spot potential conflict, bring disagreements into the open, and help deescalate
- Encourage debate and open discussion
- Orchestrate win-win solutions

BUILDING BONDS: Nurturing instrumental relationships. People with this competence:

- Cultivate and maintain extensive informal networks
- Seek out relationships that are mutually beneficial
- Build rapport and keep others in the loop
- Make and maintain personal friendships among work associates

Figure 14.1 (CONTINUED) Guidelines for EI.

(*Continued*)

COLLABORATION AND COOPERATION: Working with others toward shared goals. People with this competence:

- Balance a focus on task with attention to relationships
- Collaborate, sharing plans, information, and resources
- Promote a friendly, cooperative climate
- Spot and nurture opportunities for collaboration

TEAM CAPABILITIES: Creating group synergy in pursuing collective goals. People with this competence:

- Model team qualities like respect, helpfulness, and cooperation
- Draw all members into active and enthusiastic participation
- Build team identity, esprit de corps, and commitment
- Protect the group and its reputation; share credit

Figure 14.1 (CONTINUED)   Guidelines for EI.

and eagerness of a learner. Suzuki said, "In the beginner's mind there are many possibilities, in the expert's there are few." Jobs told the graduating class, "The heaviness of being successful was replaced by the lightness of being a beginner again, less sure about everything."

Steve gives us a way of achieving the aequanimitas mind by using no preconceived notions. Larry Ellison, the CEO of Oracle Corporation, uses this method to enhance creativity, since a beginner's mind has no limitations.

Beth Israel Medical Center in New York City [20] is teaching their caregivers and patients how to go Zen. Darcy O Sullivan, R.N says "People really appreciate these options." Elaine Meszaros, R.N., says, "It helps people get through treatment and to fight."

Andrews [21] quotes the *Britannica Concise Encyclopedia* to define Zen philosophy as one that believes "enlightenment is inherent in everyone but lies dormant because of ignorance. It is best awakened by breaking through the boundaries of mundane logical thought." He also discusses how Steven Berger teaches a Zen Budgeting class for the Healthcare Financial Management Association. Says Berger, "Almost everyone, from the CEO down to the operating manager, believes that budgeting is a grind that each hospital has to go through year after year. I propose that budgeting does not have to be a grind. The way we develop budgets is not natural or effective. Simplicity could and would work—hence, the Zen theme."

A beginner's mind is in line with several examples Osler gave, such as the following:

- The three steps of patient care are: diagnose, diagnose, diagnose. Because action often preceded thought in Osler's day, this edict was probably needed to counterbalance thoughtless empiricism [22].

> In the beginner's mind, there are many possibilities, in the expert's, there are few.

- "The student tries to learn too much, and we teachers try to teach him too much—neither, perhaps with great success [23]."

Ray Brown's 31 Senses

Ray Brown et al. [24] was a healthcare administrator and a great teacher with experience at Chicago, Duke, Harvard, and Northwestern. He served as the professor of administration and director of the graduate program in hospital administration at Duke University. He also was the chief elected officer of the American Hospital Association and the American College of Healthcare Executives. There are now awards by both organizations given in his name.

Similar to Osler, he believed that an administrator was not bound by personality, but must rather develop a second personality. "A purpose of professional education is to enable the individual to develop this second personality, and failure to do so means the individual will not be fully able to see things according to the demands of the profession. The administrator must be able to develop a way of acting that is beyond the self." He clarifies by saying that good judgment occurs when you have the ability to see the values of the people around you. These principles seem to apply to all caregivers and are not just limited to administrators and physicians.

Ray developed a list of 31 senses that determine the attitude of the administrators, but the list is more generic than specific. So, it should apply to all caregivers.

- Sense of restlessness (versus complacency)
- Sense of incompleteness
- Sense of innovation
- Sense of personal adequacy
- Sense of accountability
- Sense of purposefulness
- Sense of detachment
- Sense of skepticism
- Sense of the significant (putting first things first)
- Sense of tentativeness
- Sense of appropriateness
- Sense of propriety (how thing ought to be done)
- Sense of discrimination (the difference between things that appear similar)
- Sense of perplexity (inquiring mind)
- Sense of fatalism (not devastated by loss)
- Sense of urbanity (broad-mindedness or adaptability)
- Sense of foresight (predicts state of events)
- Sense of timing (knowing when something is important as to what and how)
- Sense of relevance (distinguishes what is important)
- Sense of newness
- Sense of system (ability to see the forest *and* the trees)
- Sense of history (recognizes what he/she needs to know)
- Sense of direction (handle many highly varied activities)
- Sense of compatible (recognizing what will fit rather than what is fitting)
- Sense of feasibility (the art of the accomplishable)
- Sense of competitiveness (against others and against self)
- Sense of wariness (takes risks but also takes precautions)
- Sense of balance (balances many different activities without going to pieces)
- Sense of professional attitude (follows the script written for his/her role)
- Sense of organizational rhythm (senses a developing problem or weakness in the organization)
- Sense of probing (making inductive leaps)

This list makes up a good checklist for an aequanimitas practitioner. It is a part of the graduate medical education at Duke University School of Medicine.

Summary

While aequanimitas practices can differ, the essence does not. The essence is developing Osler's outer self, which has to be compassionate for everyone around a caregiver. "Although certain degree of analytical and technical skill is a minimum requirement for success, emotional intelligence may be the key attribute that distinguishes outstanding performers from those who are merely adequate" according to Goleman's *Harvard Business Review* article [25]. Bryan [10] and Wilcox [26] summarize the value of aequanimitas for healthcare today. According to Bryan, if we understand his philosophy and methods, we will be better prepared to use and pass on something of greater value: the ability to make wise choices that are in society's best interest. The extent that we live up to the Osler hero-myth, our profession will prosper. Wilcox in his article *The Symbol of Modern Medicine* quotes Osler: "The practice of medicine is an art, not a trade; a calling, not a business; a calling in which your heart will be exercised equally with your head." This quote is timeless!

References

1. Johns Hopkins Web site, 2010. www.hopkinsmedicine.org/Medicine/hstrainingprogram/aequanimitas. html.
2. Shedlock, J., 2002. Osler's "A Way of Life" and other addresses, with commentary and annotations, Sir William Osler, *Journal of the Medical Library Association*, 90(3): 352–353, www.ncbi.nlm.nih.gov/ pmc/articles/PMC116415/.
3. Anders, D., 1989. Aequanimitas centennial, *Southern Medical Journal*, 82(11): 1403–1404, http:// journals.lww.com/smajournalonline/Citation/1989/11000/Aequanimitas_Centennial.14.aspx.
4. Osler, W., 1997. *Aequanimitas*, New York University School of Medicine, http://litmed.med.nyu.edu/ Annotation?action=view&annid=66.
5. Swensen, S., et al., 2009. Quality: The mayo clinic approach, *American Journal of Medical Quality*, 24: 428.
6. Fry, J., 2007. What's Going on at Your Hospital Emotional Intelligence Development, Evancarmichael. com, retrieved from www.evancarmichael.com/Leadership/3726/Whats-Going-on-at-Your-Hospital-Emotional-Intelligence-Development.html.
7. Chen, P., 2008. Healing the doctor-patient divide, *New York Times*, September 11, www.nytimes. com/2008/09/11/health/chen9-11.html?_r=3&oref=slogin.
8. Watkins, T., 2010. Study tracks effects of interruptions on doctors, *CNNHealth*, May 12, retrieved from www.cnn.com/2010/HEALTH/05/12/doctors.interrupted/.
9. Chen, P., 2010. An unforeseen complication of electronic medical records, *New York Times*, April 22, www.nytimes.com/2010/04/22/health/22chen.html?src=me&ref=health.
10. Bryan, C., 1999. Caring carefully: Sir William Osler on the issue of competence vs. compassion in medicine, *Baylor University Medical Center Proceedings*, 12: 277–284, www.baylorhealth.edu/pro-ceedings/12_4/12_4_bryan.html.
11. Routson, J., 2010. Emotional Intelligence: An Essential Skill for Nurses, MedHunters.com, retrieved on May 26, from www.medhunters.com/articles/emotionalIntelligenceNurses.html.
12. Güleryüz, G., et al., 2008. The mediating effect of job satisfaction between emotional intelligence and organizational commitment of nurses: A questionnaire survey, *International Journal of Nursing Studies*, 45(11): 1625–1635, www.ncbi.nlm.nih.gov/pubmed/18394625.
13. Deshpande, S., and Joseph, J., 2009. Impact of emotional intelligence, ethical climate, and behavior of peers on ethical behavior of nurses, *Journal of Business Ethics*, 85(3), www.springerlink.com/ content/213737457q568854/.

14. Girdharwal, N., 2007. A Study on Emotional Intelligence at Health Care Industry, Pharmainfo.net, Vol. 5, Issue 5, retrieved from www.phar-mainfo.net/reviews/study-emotional-intelligence-health-care-industry, www.pharmainfo.net/reviews/study-emotional-intelligence-health-care-industry.

15. Kravvariti, E., et al., 2010. Emotional intelligence and the coronary heart disease: How close is the link? *Global Journal of Health Science*, 2(1), www.ccsenet.org/journal/index.php/gjhs/article/viewFile/1507/4635.

16. Grewal, D., 2008. Emotional intelligence and the graduate medical education, *Journal of American Medical Association*, 300(10): 1200–1202, http://academy.clevelandclinic.org/LinkClick.aspx?fleticket=zuR3Fo0ZxQ0%3D&tabid=1846.

17. Gewertz, B., 2006. Emotional intelligence, *Archives of Surgery*, 141, http://depts.washington.edu/facdev/pdfs/Gewertz_emotionalIntelligence.pdf.

18. Ohio State College of Nursing, 2010. Emotional Intelligence for Nurses, A carrier service resource, retrieved on May 20, from www.con.ohio-state.edu/Attachments/Student_Affairs/einurses.pdf.

19. Beurteaux, D., 2010. Religious CEOs: Apple's Steve Jobs, Minyanville.com, May 19, retrieved from www.minyanville.com/businessmarkets/articles/steve-jobs/5/13/2010/id/28278?from=AOL.

20. KFSN-TV/DT, 2010. A television presentation, *Zen Hospital*, retrieved from http://abclocal.go.com/kfsn/story?section=news/health/health_watch&id=7340871.

21. Andrews, J., 2007. Zen and the art of hospital budget planning, *Healthcare Finance News*, July 26, retrieved from www.healthcarefinancenews.com/news/zen-and-art-hospital-budget-planning.

22. McDonald, C., 1996. Medical heuristics: The silent adjudicators of clinical practice, *Annals of Internal Medicine*, 124(1), Part 1: 56–62, www.annals.org/content/124/1_Part_1/56.full.

23. Osler, W., 1905. After twenty-five years. In W. Osler (Ed.), *Aequanimitas with Other Addresses to Medical Students, Nurses and Practitioners of Medicine* (pp. 197–215). Blakiston, Philadelphia, PA.

24. Blanks, M., et al., 1991. *Ray E. Brown: Lectures, Messages, and Memoirs*, Health Administration Press, Foundation of the American College of Healthcare Executives, www.ache.org/pdf/secure/gifts/Apr10-BrownMemoir.pdf.

25. Goleman, D., 1998. What makes a leader, *Harvard Business Review*, November–December.

26. Wilcox, R., 2004. The symbol of modern medicine, *Annals of Internal Medicine*, 140(4): 311–312.

Chapter 15

Healthcare Systems Engineering, the Powerful Quality Improvement Tool

Introduction

"Despite serious and widespread efforts to improve the quality of health care, many patients still suffer preventable harm every day. Hospitals find improvement difficult to sustain, and they suffer "project fatigue" because so many problems need attention. No hospitals or health systems have achieved consistent excellence throughout their institutions." These words of wisdom from the president of The Joint Commission Mark Chassin and Jerod Loeb [1] suggest that we need high quality and reliability in care. At one time, the doctor was in charge of the patient recovery at hospitals. This is no longer true. The care is divided by various people like nurses, nurse assistants, pharmacists, resident doctors, equipment maintenance technicians, patient transporters, and other support personnel. The care is further divided by inaccurate medical record systems, software in the medical devices, hackers that can disconnect life support equipment, and delays in lab tests. The complexity from technology is increasing all the time such as nurse hears about 1,000 alarms a day limiting her from responding to patients who need immediate help.

The healthcare system requires integration of interactions among all the components of a system mentioned above and anything else that can influence the quality, safety and reliability of care such as environmental hazards, unknown hazards from the changes in software and sudden loss of electric power. All these and more functions make up a so-called system. Unfortunately, the system requirements are often flawed. They sometimes fail to identify the key components, including what the system "shall not do." For example, in a California hospital, a radiology technician was delivering a high dose of radiation to a patient as a part of a therapeutic requirement. He forgot to turn down the level of radiation after delivering the high dose. For 6 months, most of the patients were harmed from receiving high radiation. The system requirement was obviously flawed. It depended on the memory of the technician to select the right levels instead of automatic reset to a safe radiation level after each use. The system did not specify that "patients shall not get the wrong level of radiation under any circumstance." Then the machine would have been designed to automatically turn off the high level for the next patient.

Some Progress Has Been Made

Although the progress is limited by the creativity and active participation by stakeholders, it has led way to new challenges for safety and quality. In 2005, the National Academy of Engineering (NAE) and the Institute of Medicine (IOM) highlighted the need for a systems approach to the healthcare system and the application of systems engineering tools to improve healthcare [2]. Each IOM dimension of the care system—efficiency, effectiveness, safety, access, equity, and patient-centeredness, can be improved by systems engineering. But despite the NAE/IOM's recommendations, only narrowly focused efforts to implement these recommendations have occurred, and no substantive systems approach has gained traction or success.

Later in 2014, the President's Council of Advisors on Science and Technology (PCAST) in May 2014 wrote a report [3] that systems engineering, widely used in manufacturing and aviation, is an interdisciplinary approach to analyze, design, manage, and measure a complex system, but in spite of excellent examples, systems methods and tools are not yet used on a widespread basis in U.S. healthcare.

Fortunately many hospitals are using systems engineering which originated in the Department of Defense. In healthcare, it is called the healthcare systems engineering. The purpose of this tool is to design the processes system-wide such that the system always works right for the patients and patients never get harmed even if the components of a system malfunction or caregivers make mistakes. For example, the lab results from a wrong patient should not harm a patient. This is accomplished by designing the lab result process such that there is no way the lab system can deliver wrong results. The solution requires creative brainstorming by the stakeholders so there is a least possibility of error or there is a robust solution. It may require two independent verifications (redundancy) that the right report is delivered. Sometimes three verifications may be needed (triple redundancy) if an employee overlooks verification or do not have time to verify it correctly. A review published in the *Journal of American Medical Association Internal Medicine* [4] adds to the growing body of evidence that physician burnout negatively impacts clinical outcomes, as burned-out doctors were twice as likely to be involved in patient-safety incidents, provide suboptimal care as a result of low professionalism and garner low patient satisfaction ratings. Another notable finding was that burned-out residents and early-career physicians were 3.4 times more likely than their more experienced colleagues to deliver poor care attributed to low professionalism—defined as suboptimal adherence to guidelines, reduced professional integrity, poor communication to patients, and low empathy. These challenges require urgent implementation of healthcare systems engineering methods.

Significant progress has been made at hospitals such Johns Hopkins Hospital and Mayo Clinic which will be covered in this chapter.

Understanding Healthcare Systems Engineering

The International Council of Systems Engineering (INCOSE) describes the history of the field and offers this comprehensive definition of a system as follows [5]:

> …a construct or collections of different elements that together produce results not obtainable by the elements alone. The elements, or parts, can include people, hardware, software, facilities, policies, and documents; that is, all things required to produce systems-level results. The results include system-level qualities, properties, characteristics, functions, behavior, and performance. The value added by the system as a whole, beyond that contributed independently by the parts, is primarily created by the relationship among the parts; that is, how they are interconnected.

Healthcare Systems Engineering (HSE) methods range from creative brainstorming to using risk analysis tools, to using advanced mathematical modeling to analyze real-time decision-making such as to determine optimal time to transplant organs and tissues from living donors to maximize the life expectancy of the patients. In most cases, it can be practiced without mathematical modeling. This will become clear with a detailed example of an Intensive Care Unit (ICU) at Johns Hopkins Hospital. One does not have to be an engineer to practice HSE although it helps to have an engineer on the team such as a clinical engineer.

Reference 5 further sums up the following: We hypothesize that the application of systems engineering can significantly improve patient safety. Recently, the Centers for Medicare and Medicaid Services launched a national effort to reduce nine types of patient harm. These harms include adverse drug events, catheter-associated urinary tract infections, central-line-associated bloodstream infections, fall injuries, pressure ulcers, surgical site infections, venous thromboembolisms, ventilator-associated pneumonias, and obstetric adverse events. This is only a limited list, because healthcare experts have identified several other patient harms. The healthcare industry is addressing these harms as if each one occurs in isolation or independently, when they are interdependent. For example, patients who do not receive early and frequent mobilization are at risk for both pressure ulcers and venous thromboembolism, and it is no surprise that patient harms cluster. Yet nobody wants these harms to occur: not patients, not clinicians, not insurers, not technology companies. Still, the approach of healthcare to reduce harm relies on ever-increasing heroism of clinicians rather than designing safe systems. Current approaches at harm reduction often rely on brute force efforts and clinicians work on preventing one or two harms, although patients are at risk for many more harms.

Healthcare Systems Engineering at Johns Hopkins Medicine

Johns Hopkins Medicine with the help of Applied Physics Laboratories used systems engineering principles and best practices with clinical expertise to develop innovative approaches to the socio-technical features involved in patient care. This work focuses on understanding the interactions among people (clinicians, patients, families, and other stakeholders), processes (institutional, regulatory, professional ethics, etc.), and technology (medical devices including infusion pumps and instrumentation) to formulate a systems approach to innovations that lead to improved patient outcomes. Reference 2 describes the following approach at Johns Hopkins ICU.

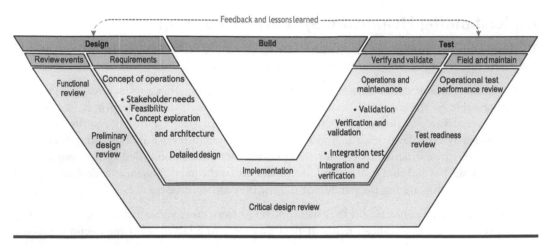

Figure 15.1 V-model for the project design and tests.

The hospital chose ICU because it addresses the combination of high burdens of illness, personal stress, and technology involving the integration of people, technologies, and the environment. They expanded on the systems concept by requiring the following:

a. Definition of the objectives/goals of the system
b. Elaboration of the interdependencies between the processes of the system
c. Clarification of the roles of the constituent system elements necessary to achieve objectives
d. Definition of the system's capabilities
e. Establishment of performance expectations
f. Measurement and evaluation of performance

Armed with this knowledge, a proposed system is developed for the healthcare in the form of a V-model shown in Figure 15.1 which includes tests and evaluations to prove the system is working correctly. This originated in the Department of Defense but is appropriate for all the industries including healthcare. The left side of the V-model shows the system requirements; the right side shows the evaluations for all the requirements before the system is implemented. Therefore, this model is proactive instead of reactive.

The workshop was for thought-provoking topics to stir discussion and assess which interactions within the ICU the assembled subject matter experts considered most important. The topics were split into segments, where each segment was intended to provoke discussion and produce information about interactions among technology, patients, people, and other entities. Two large screen displays in front of the room displayed the current topic and set of questions, as shown in Table 15.1.

A separate workshop was held to improve performance of medication infusion pumps in the ICU. Table 15.2 shows the issues discussed.

Then a workshop was held to determine the best practices. At least 30 stakeholders participated. The project team drew a threshold of 75% to define "consensus"; in other words, if the 75% or more respondents agreed with the project team's assessment, the project team declared that these items were indeed best practices for pump design. Table 15.3 summarizes the results of the best practices portion of the survey.

Table 15.1 Issues and questions for the ICU performance

Interaction Type and Definition	Questions for Discussion
Clinician-to-Nonpatient Interactions	
You are stranded on an island with 20 injured survivors and can call for five personnel with various types of expertise to help. Who would they be (i.e., what role) and why?	• Who do you interact with? • Why do you interact with that person? • What information does that person give you, or do you give him/her? • How do you interact with that person? • When and how frequently do you interact with this person? • If this interaction did not occur, what would be the consequence on quality of care and patient safety?
Clinician-to-Patient Interactions	
The survivors have suffered different types of injuries and conditions, and your team is checking on them. What are the main things the team must look for in (newly) admitted patients?	• Why does this interaction take place? What do you learn from it? • What tools and resources do you need during this interaction? • If this interaction did not occur, what would be the consequence on quality of care and patient safety?
People-to-Equipment Interactions	
If a limited amount of resources* can be brought onto the island, or be built from airplane scraps, what would you need?	• What equipment or devices do you use for your job? • Why do you use this device? • What information does this device give you or help you to acquire? • How do you use this device? • When and how frequently do you interact with this device? • If you could no longer use this device or equipment, what would be the consequence on quality of care and patient safety?
ICU-to-Resource Interactions	
The ICU island has connections to other resources.* Which resources would you select for connection to your ICU island and why?	• Who do you interact with? • Why do you interact with that resource? • What information does that resource give you or do you give the resource? • How do you interact with that resource? • When and how frequently do you interact with this resource? • If this interaction did not occur, what would be the consequence on quality of care and patient safety?

Table 15.2   Issues and questions for the medication infusion pumps

• Frequent alarms fatigue users [Sum]
• Ability to easily override safety features [Sum]
• Difficult to manage multiple infusion lines [CT4]
• Same alarm cues for critical and noncritical events [TA]
• Misinterpretation of a physician's order [TA]; 7.1-1 Most pumps are not interoperable with a host of data systems, including medication orders, drug library, electronic medical administration records, bar code medication administration, and reporting [CT2]
• Bypassing and forgetting to reset programming after a bolus [Sum]
• Errors in calculating conversions [Sum]
• Drug concentration options are not prominently displayed (e.g., need to scroll down for some). User reverts to non-DERS (Drug Error Reduction System) administration by bypassing safety functions [CT3]
• No maximum rate feature for bolus dosing for specific drugs
• Pump workflow does not match the user workflow. The sequence for programming the pump differs from the user's sequence of tasks for medication delivery [Sum]
• Inadequate/nonstandard visual cues for different classes of drugs [Sum]
• Can hang two bags of the same drug on pumps with more than one pump channel. [TA] Inability to know total dose of medication being infused if two or more pumps are infusing the same medication
• Inadequate notification of approaching out-of-tolerance conditions
• Inadequate display field sizes, line break position, and use of bolding to differentiate selection options [Sum]
• Prompts to enter rate or volume to be infused (VTBI) come before prompts on dose [CT3]
• Takes too much time to read pump status during use (e.g., indication of med being infused) [CT3]; rate information is displayed rather than more important dose information [CT3]
• Insufficient alerts when input errors have been made [Sum]
• Pump interface features associated with high risk control functions are not standardized across pumps (e.g. control/ label placement, color coding or order of data entry) [Sum]
• Use of weight data that varies from the primary source (medical records versus bed scales versus memory)
• Pump does not provide adequate indication of need for additional medication product in time for pharmacy to provide it. [TA]; 8.1.2. Sometimes notifications from the pump indicating infusions are nearing completion do not occur until after infusion is complete, interrupting continuous medication delivery [TA]
• Lack of forcing function to confirm/check important data entries [CT3]
• Some pumps allow users to edit the rate even if pulled from the library [Sum]
• Program too much VTBI
• Display content and format make it difficult to read in different settings (e.g., lighting, distance, angles) [TA]
• Pump fails and a replacement is not available [Sum]

Table 15.3 Best practices determined by the stakeholders

Best Practice	Agreement (%)
Items above 75 Agreement Threshold	
• Adequate control size and separation per human factors criteria	94.3
• Conventional and consistent use of data entry cursor	88.6
• Means to easily determine control labels in dark environments	86.1
• Reliable indication of battery status that allows enough time for users to change pump or plug into a power source	86.1
• Medication identification cues per pharmacy best practices, e.g., Tall Man lettering	85.7
• Standardized keypad control layout to include decimal point placement	83.3
• Functional grouping of controls and display, e.g., through use of color and spatial proximity	82.9
• Indication if audio alarm is disabled	80.6
• Access to standardized training, embedded training, or opportunities to practice use with feedback	80.6
• Ready indication of the drug library version presently loaded	77.1
• Consistent use of alarm characteristics	75.0
Items below 75 Agreement Threshold	
• Standardized concentrations and dosing units for drugs	52.8
• Alarm test feature	61.1
• Cues to indicate intravenous occlusion	63.9
• A forcing function to prevent the previous patient's profile from being used on a new patient	65.7
• Consistency in labeling across media	72.2

The lesson to be learned from this project is that there must be almost all the stakeholders involved and there must be consensus on what are the best practices. These best practices must be verified through process documents reviews/inspections and validated through testing.

Healthcare Systems Engineering at Mayo Clinic

The Healthcare Systems Engineering Program in the Mayo Clinic Robert D. and Patricia E. Kern Center for the Science of Healthcare Delivery brings together expertise from data-driven and mathematical sciences as well as human-focused sciences. Together, these researchers provide solutions to today's complex healthcare problems. The program carries out its mission by the following [6]:

- Identifying practice stakeholders within and outside Mayo Clinic and establishing long-term research collaborations
- Leveraging scientific knowledge to transform healthcare delivery
- Sharing knowledge between the healthcare and systems engineering communities
- Educating healthcare practitioners about systems engineering and engineering students about healthcare
- Leading the Mayo Clinic Kern Center for the Science of Health Care Delivery's Clinical Engineering Learning Laboratories initiative

An example of using healthcare systems engineering would be that the Mayo Clinic strives to improve the healthcare for patients and staff while making blood transfusions safer. Healthcare system engineers at the Mayo Clinic have developed many tactics to enhance the safety and efficiency of blood product transfusions. These strategies include the following:

- Developing and organizing models to predict adverse reactions prior to the actual blood transfusion
- Initiating a clinical trial to precisely measure the impact of red blood cell transfusions on home functional standing using an advanced mobile health technology solution
- Recognizing patient subgroups that may have different responses to blood transfusions. And emerging a clinical algorithmic outline for enhancing patient-specific blood transfusion triggers

The Mayo Clinic also focuses healthcare systems engineering toward their goal to improve healthcare for patients and staff members. Data and decision engineering projects stem from award winning care delivery and discoveries and established developments in practice. Engineered solutions come into play with patient's safety and access and timely patient-centered care while services are rendered in emergency medicine radiology and inpatient services. The resolutions confirm condensed problems with staff, with better preparation and resource utilization. In addition to patient care, the Mayo Clinic has also used systems engineering to help their operating room physicians. Operations can take a physical toll on surgeons over time. The Mayo Clinc's systems engineering program developed the OR-Stretch Program that acts as a buffer to the physical demands in the operating room. "The results of the OR-Stretch Pilot intervention to reduce intraoperative fatigue and discomfort are being integrated into operating rooms at Mayo Clinic, across the country and around the world" [6]. The results of this program add value to the quality of patient care and the quality of a physician's work.

Another area in which the Mayo clinic is working to reduce the risk of patient injury is with blood transfusions. They are using analytics to develop models that predict the adverse patient reactions prior to transfusion. Analytics are also being used to identify subgroups of patients who have different responses to blood transfusions and algorithms to show specific blood transfusion triggers. The Mayo Clinic is using clinical trials to measure the impact of red blood cell transfusion on the member's everyday functions. By analyzing this data, they can find solutions that can make a difference in the patient's day-to-day life.

Healthcare systems engineering will be used in the patient diagnosis process. Electronic information is often used in helping diagnose a patient. A provider may use the electronic medical records from another office to help diagnose a patient.

Figure 15.2 A view of the groupthink process. (*Source*: AllPosters.com.)

Summary

There are many benefits to systems engineering in the healthcare. Having the ability of integrating multiple systems and have better access to retrieve information, data, or records can greatly improve healthcare all around. Safety and quality is the goal and improving healthcare should come at no additional expense because the life of every patient is priceless.

The most useful paradigm to maximize the impact of improvements and summarize this chapter is: *If everyone votes "Yes" to a solution in the first try, your answer should be "No".* You must avoid the process of groupthink covered in the Chapter 3 where the team members are afraid to speak up or do not have time think system-wide solutions. Systems engineering is about thinking thorough and thinking outside the box for robust solutions. The cartoon in Figure 15.2 illustrates the groupthink process.

References

1. Chassin, M.R, and Loeb, J.M., 2013. High-reliability health care: Getting there from here, *The Milbank Quarterly*, 91(3): 459–490, www.ncbi.nlm.nih.gov/pmc/articles/PMC3790522/.
2. Ravitz, A.D., et al., 2013. Systems approach and systems engineering applied to health care: Improving patient safety and health care delivery, *Johns Hopkins APL Technical Digest*, 31(4), www.jhuapl.edu/techdigest/TD/td3104/31_04-Ravitz.pdf.
3. The President's Council of Advisors on Science and Technology, Report To The President, Better Health Care And Lower Costs: Accelerating Improvement Through Systems Engineering, May 2014, www.whitehouse.gov/sites/default/files/microsites/ostp/PCAST/pcast_systems_engineering_in_healthcare_-_may_2014.pdf.

4. Allar, D., 2018. Burned-out physicians twice as likely to compromise patient safety, *Cardiovascular Business*, September 07, www.cardiovascularbusiness.com/topics/practice-management/burned-out-physicians-compromise-patient-safety.

5. Tropello, S.P., et al., 2013. Enhancing the quality of care in the intensive care unit, a systems engineering approach, *Critical Care Clinics Journal*, 29(1), Article downloaded from the web on December 8, 2018, www.criticalcare.theclinics.com/article/S0749-0704(12)00086-3/pdf.

6. Mayo Clinic website, Robert D. and Patricia E. Kern Center for the Science of Health Care Delivery. Research Centers and Programs. *Health Care Systems Engineering*, Downloaded on December 26, 2018 from www.mayo.edu/research/centers-programs/robert-d-patricia-e-kern-center-science-health-care-delivery/research-activities/health-care-systems-engineering-program.

Appendix A: The Swiss Cheese Model

The Swiss Cheese Model is covered in the report below.
Obtained from the U.S. Department of Transportation Document
DOT/FAA/AM 00/7
Office of Aviation Medicine, Washington DC 20591 (February 2000)
Available at www.nific.gov/safety/reports/humanfactors_class&anly.pdf

The Human Factors Analysis and Classification System—HFACS

The Swiss Cheese Model of Accident Causation February 2000

Introduction

Sadly, the annals of aviation history are littered with accidents and tragic losses. Since the late 1950s, however, the drive to reduce the accident rate has yielded unprecedented levels of safety to a point where it is now safer to fly in a commercial airliner than to drive a car or even walk across a busy New York City street. Still, while the aviation accident rate has declined tremendously since the first flights nearly a century ago, the cost of aviation accidents in both lives and dollars has steadily risen. As a result, the effort to reduce the accident rate still further has taken on new meaning within both military and civilian aviation.

Even with all the innovations and improvements realized in the last several decades, one fundamental question remains generally unanswered: "Why do aircraft crash?" The answer may not be as straightforward as one might think. In the early years of aviation, it could reasonably be said that, more often than not, the aircraft killed the pilot. That is, the aircraft was intrinsically unforgiving and, relative to their modern counterparts, mechanically unsafe. However, the modern era of aviation has witnessed an ironic reversal of sorts. It now appears to some that the aircrew themselves are more deadly than the aircraft they fly (cited in Reference [1]). In fact, estimates in the literature indicate that between 70% and 80% of aviation accidents can be attributed, at least in part, to human error [2]. Still, to off-handedly attribute accidents solely to aircrew error is like telling patients they are simply "sick" without examining the underlying causes or further defining the illness.

So what really constitutes that 70%–80% of human error repeatedly referred to in the literature? Some would have us believe that human error and "pilot" error are synonymous. Yet simply writing off aviation accidents merely to pilot error is an overly simplistic, if not naive, approach to accident causation. After all, it is well established that accidents cannot be attributed to a single cause or, in most instances, even to a single individual [3]. In fact, even the identification of a "primary" cause is fraught with problems. Rather, aviation accidents are the end result of a number of causes, only the last of which are the unsafe acts of the aircrew [3–6].

The challenge for accident investigators and analysts alike is how best to identify and mitigate the causal sequence of events, in particular that 70%–80% associated with human error. Armed with this challenge, those interested in accident causation are left with a growing list of investigative schemes to choose from. In fact, there are nearly as many approaches to accident causation as there are those involved in the process [7]. Nevertheless, a comprehensive framework for identifying and analyzing human error continues to elude safety professionals and theorists alike. Consequently, interventions cannot be accurately targeted at specific human causal factors nor can their effectiveness be objectively measured and assessed. Instead, safety professionals are left with the status quo. That is, they are left with interest/fad-driven research resulting in intervention strategies that peck around the edges of accident causation, but do little to reduce the overall accident rate. What is needed is a framework around which a needs-based, data-driven safety program can be developed [8].

Reason's "Swiss Cheese" Model of Human Error

One particularly appealing approach to the genesis of human error is the one proposed by James Reason [5]. Generally referred to as the Swiss Cheese Model of human error, Reason describes four levels of human failure, each influencing the next (Figure A.1). Working backward in time from the accident, the first level depicts those unsafe acts of operators that ultimately led to the accident [4]. More commonly referred to in aviation as aircrew/pilot error, this level is where most accident investigations have focused their efforts and, consequently, where most causal factors are uncovered. After all, it is typically the actions or inactions of aircrew that are directly linked to the accident. For instance, failing to properly scan the aircraft's instruments while in instrument meteorological conditions (IMCs) or penetrating IMC when authorized only for visual meteorological conditions (VMCs) may yield relatively immediate and, potentially, grave consequences. Represented as "holes" in the cheese, these active failures are typically the last unsafe acts committed by aircrew.[1]

However, what makes the Swiss Cheese Model particularly useful in accident investigation is that it forces investigators to address latent failures within the causal sequence of events as well. As their name suggests, latent failures, unlike their active counterparts, may lie dormant or undetected for hours, days, weeks, or even longer, until one day they adversely affect the unsuspecting aircrew. Consequently, they may be overlooked by investigators with even the best intentions.

Within this concept of latent failures, Reason described three more levels of human failure. The first involves the condition of the aircrew as it affects performance. Referred to as preconditions for unsafe acts, this level involves conditions such as mental fatigue and poor communication and coordination practices, often referred to as crew resource management (CRM).

---

[1] Reason's original work involved operators of a nuclear power plant. However, for the purposes of this manuscript, the operators here refer to aircrew, maintainers, supervisors, and other humans involved in aviation.

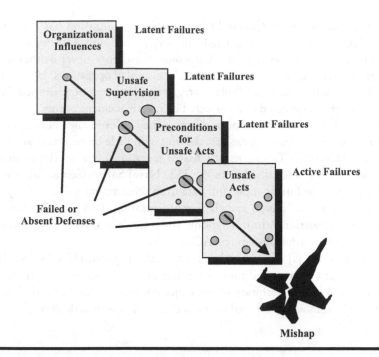

Figure A.1 The "Swiss Cheese Model" of human error causation. (Adapted from Reason, J. (1990). *Human Error.* **New York: Cambridge University Press.)**

Not surprising, if fatigued aircrew fail to communicate and coordinate their activities with others in the cockpit or individuals external to the aircraft (e.g., air traffic control, maintenance), poor decisions are made and errors often result.

But exactly why did communication and coordination breakdown in the first place? This is perhaps where Reason's work departed from more traditional approaches to human error. In many instances, the breakdown in good CRM practices can be traced back to instances of unsafe supervision, the third level of human failure. If, for example, two inexperienced (and perhaps even below-average pilots) are paired with each other and sent on a flight into known adverse weather at night, is anyone really surprised by a tragic outcome? To make matters worse, if this questionable manning practice is coupled with the lack of quality CRM training, the potential for miscommunication and, ultimately, aircrew errors, is magnified. In a sense then, the crew was "set up" for failure as crew coordination and ultimately performance would be compromised. This is not to lessen the role played by the aircrew, only that intervention and mitigation strategies might lie higher within the system.

Reason's model did not stop at the supervisory level either; the organization itself can impact performance at all levels. For instance, in times of fiscal austerity, funding is often cut, and as a result, training and flight time are curtailed. Consequently, supervisors are often left with no alternative but to task "nonproficient" aviators with complex tasks. Not surprisingly, then, in the absence of good CRM training, communication and coordination failures will begin to appear as will a myriad of other preconditions, all of which will affect performance and elicit aircrew errors. Therefore, it makes sense that, if the accident rate is going to be reduced beyond current levels, investigators and analysts alike must examine the accident sequence in its entirety and expand it beyond the cockpit. Ultimately, causal factors at all levels within the organization must be addressed if any accident investigation and prevention system is going to succeed.

In many ways, Reason's Swiss Cheese Model of accident causation has revolutionized common views of accident causation. Unfortunately, however, it is simply a theory with few details on how to apply it in a real-world setting. In other words, the theory never defines what the "holes in the cheese" really are, at least within the context of everyday operations. Ultimately, one needs to know what these system failures, or "holes," are, so that they can be identified during accident investigations or better yet, detected and corrected before an accident occurs.

The balance of this book will attempt to describe the "holes in the cheese." However, rather than attempt to define the holes using esoteric theories with little or no practical applicability, the original framework (called the Taxonomy of Unsafe Operations) was developed using more than 300 Naval aviation accidents obtained from the U.S. Naval Safety Center [6]. The original taxonomy has since been refined using input and data from other military (U.S. Army Safety Center and the U.S. Air Force Safety Center) and civilian organizations (National Transportation Safety Board and the Federal Aviation Administration). The result was the development of the human factors analysis and classification system (HFACS).

Drawing upon Reason's [5] concept of latent and active failures, HFACS describes four levels of failure: (1) unsafe acts, (2) preconditions for unsafe acts, (3) unsafe supervision, and (4) organizational influences. A brief description of the major components and causal categories follows; beginning with the level most closely tied to the accident, that is, unsafe acts.

Unsafe Acts

The unsafe acts of aircrew can be loosely classified into two categories: errors and violations [5]. In general, errors represent the mental or physical activities of individuals that fail to achieve their intended outcome. Not surprising, given the fact that human beings by their very nature make errors, these unsafe acts dominate most accident databases. Violations, on the other hand, refer to the willful disregard for the rules and regulations that govern the safety of flight. The bane of many organizations, the prediction and prevention of these appalling and purely "preventable" unsafe acts, continue to elude managers and researchers alike.

Still, distinguishing between errors and violations does not provide the level of granularity required of most accident investigations. Therefore, the categories of errors and violations were expanded here (Figure A.2), as elsewhere [5, 9], to include three basic error types (skill-based, decision, and perceptual) and two forms of violations (routine and exceptional).

In contrast to attention failures, memory failures often appear as omitted items in a checklist, as place losing, or as forgotten intentions. For example, most of us have experienced going to the refrigerator only to forget what we went for. Likewise, it is not difficult to imagine that when under stress during inflight emergencies, critical steps in emergency procedures can be missed. However, even when not particularly stressed, individuals have forgotten to set the flaps on approach or lower the landing gear—at a minimum, embarrassing gaffes.

The third, and final, type of skill-based errors identified in many accident investigations involves technique errors. Regardless of one's training, experience, and educational background, the manner in which one carries out a specific sequence of events may vary greatly. That is, two pilots with identical training, flight grades, and experience may differ significantly in the manner in which they maneuver their aircraft. While one pilot may fly smoothly with the grace of a soaring eagle, others may fly with the darting, rough transitions of a sparrow. Nevertheless, while both may be safe and equally adept at flying, the techniques they employ could set them up for specific failure modes. In fact, such techniques are as much a factor of innate ability and aptitude as they

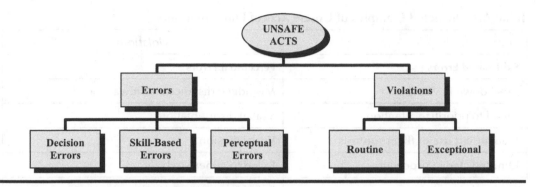

Figure A.2 Categories of unsafe acts committed by aircrews.

are an overt expression of one's own personality, making efforts at the prevention and mitigation of technique errors difficult, at best.

Decision errors. The second error form, decision errors, represents intentional behavior that proceeds as intended, yet the plan proves inadequate or inappropriate for the situation. Often referred to as "honest mistakes," these unsafe acts represent the actions or inactions of individuals whose "hearts are in the right place," but they either did not have the appropriate knowledge or just simply chose poorly.

Perhaps the most heavily investigated of all error forms, decision errors can be grouped into three general categories: procedural errors, poor choices, and problem-solving errors (Table A.1). Procedural decision errors [10], or rule-based mistakes, as described by Rasmussen [9], occur during highly structured tasks of the sort, "If X, then do Y." Aviation, particularly within the military and commercial sectors, by its very nature is highly structured, and consequently, much of pilot decision-making is procedural. There are very explicit procedures to be performed at virtually all phases of flight. Still, errors can, and often do, occur when a situation is either not recognized or misdiagnosed, and the wrong procedure is applied. This is particularly true when pilots are placed in highly time-critical emergencies like an engine malfunction on takeoff.

However, even in aviation, not all situations have corresponding procedures to deal with them. Therefore, many situations require a choice to be made among multiple response options. Consider the pilot flying home after a long week away from the family who unexpectedly confronts a line of thunderstorms directly in his path. He can choose to fly around the weather, divert to another field until the weather passes, or penetrate the weather, hoping to quickly transition through it. Confronted with situations such as this, choice decision errors [10], or knowledge-based mistakes as they are otherwise known, may occur. This is particularly true when there is insufficient experience, time, or other outside pressures that may preclude correct decisions. Put simply, sometimes we choose well, and sometimes we do not.

Finally, there are occasions when a problem is not well understood, and formal procedures and response options are not available. It is during these ill-defined situations that the invention of a novel solution is required. In a sense, individuals find themselves where no one has been before, and in many ways, must literally fly by the seat of their pants. Individuals placed in this situation must resort to slow and effortful reasoning processes where time is a luxury rarely afforded. Not surprisingly, while this type of decision-making is more infrequent than other forms, the relative proportion of problem-solving errors committed is markedly higher.

Table A.1 Selected Examples of Unsafe Acts of Pilot Operators

Errors	*Violations*
Skill-Based Errors	**Perceptual Errors**
Breakdown in visual scan	Misjudged distance/altitude/airspeed
Failed to prioritize attention	Spatial disorientation
Inadvertent use of flight controls	Visual illusion
Omitted step in procedure	Failed to adhere to brief
Omitted checklist item	Failed to use the radar altimeter
Poor technique	Flew an unauthorized approach
Overcontrolled the aircraft	Violated training rules
Decision Errors	Flew an overaggressive maneuver
Improper procedure	Failed to properly prepare for the flight
Misdiagnosed emergency	Briefed unauthorized flight
Wrong response to emergency	Not current/qualified for the mission
Exceeded ability	Intentionally exceeded the limits of the aircraft
Inappropriate maneuver	Continued low-altitude flight in VMC
Poor decision	Unauthorized low-altitude canyon running

Perceptual errors. Not unexpectedly, when one's perception of the world differs from reality, errors can, and often do, occur. Typically, perceptual errors occur when sensory input is degraded or "unusual," as is the case with visual illusions and spatial disorientation, or when aircrew simply misjudge the aircraft's altitude, attitude, or airspeed (Table A.1). Visual illusions, for example, occur when the brain tries to "fill in the gaps" with what it feels belongs in a visually impoverished environment, like that seen at night or when flying in adverse weather. Likewise, spatial disorientation occurs when the vestibular system cannot resolve one's orientation in space and therefore makes a "best guess"—typically when visual (horizon) cues are absent at night or when flying in adverse weather. In either event, the unsuspecting individual often is left to make a decision that is based on faulty information, and the potential for committing an error is elevated.

It is important to note, however, that it is not the illusion or disorientation that is classified as a perceptual error. Rather, it is the pilot's erroneous response to the illusion or disorientation. For example, many unsuspecting pilots have experienced "black-hole" approaches, only to fly a perfectly good aircraft into the terrain or water. This continues to occur, even though it is well known that flying at night over dark, featureless terrain (e.g., a lake or field devoid of trees), will produce the illusion that the aircraft is actually higher than it is. As a result, pilots are taught to rely on their primary instruments, rather than the outside world, particularly during the approach phase of flight. Even so, some pilots fail to monitor their instruments when flying at night. Tragically, these aircrew and others who have been fooled by illusions and other disorienting flight regimes may end up involved in a fatal aircraft accident.

Violations

By definition, errors occur within the rules and regulations espoused by an organization, typically dominating most accident databases. In contrast, violations represent a willful disregard for the rules and regulations that govern safe flight and, fortunately, occur much less frequently since they often involve fatalities [11].

While there are many ways to distinguish between types of violations, two distinct forms have been identified, based on their etiology, that will help the safety professional when identifying accident causal factors. The first, routine violations, tend to be habitual by nature and often tolerated by governing authority [5]. Consider, for example, the individual who drives consistently 5–10 mph faster than allowed by law or someone who routinely flies in marginal weather when authorized for VMCs only. While both are certainly against the governing regulations, many others do the same thing. Furthermore, individuals who drive 64 mph in a 55 mph zone, almost always drive 64 in a 55 mph zone. That is, they "routinely" violate the speed limit. The same can typically be said of the pilot who routinely flies into marginal weather.

What makes matters worse, these violations (commonly referred to as "bending" the rules) are often tolerated and, in effect, sanctioned by supervisory authority (i.e., you are not likely to get a traffic citation until you exceed the posted speed limit by more than 10 mph). If, however, the local authorities started handing out traffic citations for exceeding the speed limit on the highway by 9 mph or less (as is often done on military installations), then it is less likely that individuals would violate the rules. Therefore, by definition, if a routine violation is identified, one must look further up the supervisory chain to identify those individuals in authority who are not enforcing the rules.

On the other hand, unlike routine violations, exceptional violations appear as isolated departures from authority, not necessarily indicative of individual's typical behavior pattern nor condoned by management [5]. For example, an isolated instance of driving 105 mph in a 55 mph zone is considered an exceptional violation. Likewise, flying under a bridge or engaging in other prohibited maneuvers, like low-level canyon running, would constitute an exceptional violation. However, it is important to note that, while most exceptional violations are appalling, they are not considered "exceptional" because of their extreme nature. Rather, they are considered exceptional because they are neither typical of the individual nor condoned by authority. Still, what makes exceptional violations particularly difficult for any organization to deal with is that they are not indicative of an individual's behavioral repertoire and, as such, are particularly difficult to predict. In fact, when individuals are confronted with evidence of their dreadful behavior and asked to explain it, they are often left with little explanation. Indeed, those individuals who survived such excursions from the norm clearly knew that, if caught, dire consequences would follow. Still, defying all logic, many otherwise model citizens have been down this potentially tragic road.

Preconditions for Unsafe Acts

Arguably, the unsafe acts of pilots can be directly linked to nearly 80% of all aviation accidents. However, simply focusing on unsafe acts is like focusing on a fever without understanding the underlying disease causing it. Thus, investigators must dig deeper into why the unsafe acts took place. As a first step, two major subdivisions of unsafe aircrew conditions were developed: substandard conditions of operators and the substandard practices they commit (Figure A.3).

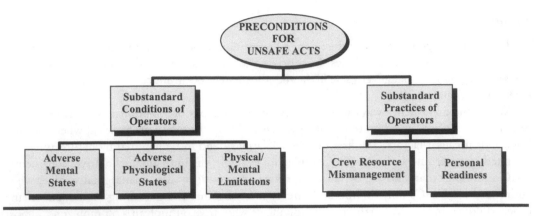

Figure A.3   Categories of preconditions of unsafe acts.

Substandard Conditions of Operators

Adverse mental states. Being prepared mentally is critical in nearly every endeavor, but perhaps even more so in aviation. As such, the category of adverse mental states was created to account for those mental conditions that affect performance (Table A.2). Principal among these are the loss of situational awareness, task fixation, distraction, and mental fatigue due to sleep loss or other stressors. Also included in this category are personality traits and pernicious attitudes such as overconfidence, complacency, and misplaced motivation.

Predictably, if an individual is mentally tired for whatever reason, the likelihood increases that an error will occur. In a similar fashion, overconfidence and other pernicious attitudes such as arrogance and impulsivity will influence the likelihood that a violation will be committed. Clearly then, any framework of human error must account for preexisting adverse mental states in the causal chain of events.

Adverse physiological states. The second category, adverse physiological states, refers to those medical or physiological conditions that preclude safe operations (Table A.2). Particularly important to aviation are such conditions as visual illusions and spatial disorientation as described earlier, as well as physical fatigue, and the myriad of pharmacological and medical abnormalities known to affect performance.

The effects of visual illusions and spatial disorientation are well known to most aviators. However, less well known to aviators, and often overlooked are the effects on cockpit performance of simply being ill. Nearly all of us have gone to work ill, dosed with over-the-counter medications, and have generally performed well. Consider, however, the pilot suffering from the common head cold. Unfortunately, most aviators view a head cold as only a minor inconvenience that can be easily remedied using over-the counter antihistamines, acetaminophen, and other nonprescription pharmaceuticals. In fact, when confronted with a stuffy nose, aviators typically are only concerned with the effects of a painful sinus block as cabin altitude changes. Then, again, it is not the overt symptoms that local flight surgeons are concerned with. Rather, it is the accompanying inner ear infection and the increased likelihood of spatial disorientation when entering IMCs that is alarming—not to mention the side effects of antihistamines, fatigue, and sleep loss on pilot decision-making. Therefore, it is incumbent upon any safety professional to account for these sometimes subtle medical conditions within the causal chain of events.

Physical/Mental Limitations. The third, and final, substandard condition involves individual physical/mental limitations (Table A.2). Specifically, this category refers to those instances

Table A.2 Selected Examples of Unsafe Aircrew Conditions

Substandard Conditions of Operators	*Substandard Practice of Operators*
Adverse Mental States	**CRM**
Channelized attention	Failed to backup
Complacency	Failed to communicate/coordinate
Distraction	Failed to conduct adequate brief
Mental fatigue	Failed to use all available resources
Get-home-itis	Failure of leadership
Haste	Misinterpretation of traffic calls
Loss of situational awareness	**Personal Readiness**
Misplaced motivation task saturation	Excessive physical training self-medicating
Adverse Physiological States	Violation of crew rest requirement
Impaired physiological state	Violation of bottle-to-throttle requirement
Medical illness	
Physiological incapacitation	
Physical fatigue	
Physical/mental limitation	
Insufficient reaction time	
Visual limitation	
Incompatible intelligence/aptitude	
Incompatible physical capability	

when mission requirements exceed the capabilities of the individual at the controls. For example, the human visual system is severely limited at night; yet, when driving a car, drivers do not necessarily slow down or take additional precautions. In aviation, while slowing down is not always an option, paying additional attention to basic flight instruments and increasing one's vigilance will often increase the safety margin. Unfortunately, when precautions are not taken, the result can be catastrophic, as pilots will often fail to see other aircraft, obstacles, or power lines due to the size or contrast of the object in the visual field.

Similarly, there are occasions when the time required to complete a task or maneuver exceeds an individual's capacity. Individuals vary widely in their ability to process and respond to information. Nevertheless, good pilots are typically noted for their ability to respond quickly and accurately. It is well documented, however, that if individuals are required to respond quickly (i.e., less time is available to consider all the possibilities or choices thoroughly), the probability of making an error goes up markedly. Consequently, it should be no surprise that when faced with the need for rapid processing and reaction times, as is the case in most aviation emergencies, all forms of error would be exacerbated.

In addition to the basic sensory and information processing limitations described above, there are at least two additional instances of physical/mental limitations that need to be addressed, albeit they are often overlooked by most safety professionals. These limitations involve individuals who simply are not compatible with aviation, because they are either unsuited physically or do not possess the aptitude to fly. For example, some individuals simply do not have the physical strength to operate in the potentially high-G environment of aviation, or for anthropometric reasons, simply have difficulty reaching the controls. In other words, cockpits have traditionally not been designed with all shapes, sizes, and physical abilities in mind. Likewise, not everyone has the mental ability or aptitude for flying aircraft. Just as not all of us can be concert pianists or NFL linebackers, not everyone has the innate ability to pilot an aircraft—a vocation that requires the unique ability to make decisions quickly and respond accurately in life-threatening situations. The difficult task for the safety professional is identifying whether insufficient aptitude might have contributed to the accident causal sequence.

Substandard Practices of Operators

Clearly then, numerous substandard conditions of operators can, and do, lead to the commission of unsafe acts. Nevertheless, there are a number of things that we do to ourselves that set up these substandard conditions. Generally speaking, the substandard practices of operators can be summed up in two categories: crew resource mismanagement and personal readiness.

Crew Resource Mismanagement. Good communication skills and team coordination have been the mantra of industrial/organizational and personnel psychology for decades. Not surprising then, CRM has been a cornerstone of aviation for the last few decades [12]. As a result, the category of crew resource mismanagement was created to account for occurrences of poor coordination among personnel. Within the context of aviation, this includes coordination both within and between aircraft with air traffic control facilities and maintenance control, as well as with facility and other support personnel as necessary. But aircrew coordination does not stop with the aircrew in flight. It also includes coordination before and after the flight with the brief and debrief of the aircrew.

It is not difficult to envision a scenario where the lack of crew coordination has led to confusion and poor decision-making in the cockpit, resulting in an accident. In fact, aviation accident databases are replete with instances of poor coordination among aircrew. One of the more tragic examples was the crash of a civilian airliner at night in the Florida Everglades in 1972 as the crew was busily trying to troubleshoot what amounted to a burned-out indicator light. Unfortunately, no one in the cockpit was monitoring the aircraft's altitude as the altitude hold was inadvertently disconnected. Ideally, the crew would have coordinated the trouble-shooting task ensuring that at least one crewmember was monitoring basic flight instruments and "flying" the aircraft. Tragically, this was not the case, as they entered a slow, unrecognized, descent into the Everglades, resulting in numerous fatalities.

Personal Readiness. In aviation, or for that matter in any occupational setting, individuals are expected to show up for work ready to perform at optimal levels. Nevertheless, in aviation as in other professions, personal readiness failures occur when individuals fail to prepare physically or mentally for duty. For instance, violations of crew rest requirements, bottle-to-brief rules, and self-medicating all will affect performance on the job and are particularly detrimental in the aircraft. It is not hard to imagine that, when individuals violate crew rest requirements, they run the risk of mental fatigue and other adverse mental states, which ultimately lead to errors and accidents. Note, however, that violations that affect personal readiness are not considered "unsafe act, violation" since they typically do not happen in the cockpit, nor are they necessarily active failures with direct and immediate consequences.

Still, not all personal readiness failures occur as a result of violations of governing rules or regulations. For example, running 10 miles before piloting an aircraft may not be against any existing regulations, yet it may impair the physical and mental capabilities of the individual enough to degrade performance and elicit unsafe acts. Likewise, the traditional "candy bar and coke" lunch of the modern businessman may sound okay to some, but may not be sufficient to sustain performance in the rigorous environment of aviation. While there may be no rules governing such behavior, pilots must use good judgment when deciding whether they are "fit" to fly an aircraft.

Unsafe Supervision

Recall that in addition to those causal factors associated with the pilot/operator, Reason [5] traced the causal chain of events back up the supervisory chain of command. As such, we have identified four categories of unsafe supervision: inadequate supervision, planned inappropriate operations, failure to correct a known problem, and supervisory violations (Figure A.4). Each is described briefly in the text that follows.

Inadequate Supervision

The role of any supervisor is to provide the opportunity to succeed. To do this, the supervisor, no matter at what level of operation, must provide guidance, training opportunities, leadership, and motivation, as well as the proper role model to be emulated. Unfortunately, this is not always the case.

For example, it is not difficult to conceive of a situation where adequate CRM training was either not provided, or the opportunity to attend such training was not afforded to a particular aircrew member. Conceivably, aircrew coordination skills would be compromised and if the aircraft were put into an adverse situation (an emergency for instance), the risk of an error being committed would be exacerbated and the potential for an accident would increase markedly.

In a similar vein, sound professional guidance and oversight is an essential ingredient of any successful organization. While empowering individuals to make decisions and function independently is certainly essential, this does not divorce the supervisor from accountability. The lack of guidance and oversight has proven to be the breeding ground for many of the violations that have crept into the cockpit. As such, any thorough investigation of accident causal factors must consider the role supervision plays (i.e., whether the supervision was inappropriate or did not occur at all) in the genesis of human error (Table A.3).

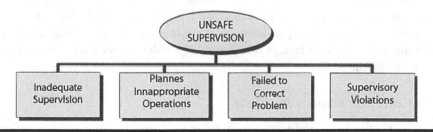

Figure A.4   Categories of unsafe supervision.

Table A.3   Selected Examples of Unsafe Supervision

Inadequate Supervision	Failed to Correct a Known Problem
Failed to provide guidance	Failed to correct document in error
Failed to provide operational doctrine	Failed to identify an at-risk aviator
Failed to provide oversight	Failed to initiate corrective action
Failed to provide training	Failed to report unsafe tendencies
Failed to track qualifications	**Supervisory Violations**
Failed to track performance	Authorized unnecessary hazard
Planned Inappropriate Operations	Failed to enforce rules and regulations
Failed to provide correct data	Authorized unqualified crew for flight
Failed to provide adequate brief time	
Improper manning	
Mission not in accordance with rules/regulations	
Provided inadequate opportunity for crew rest	

Planned Inappropriate Operations

Occasionally, the operational tempo and/or the scheduling of aircrew is such that individuals are put at unacceptable risk, crew rest is jeopardized, and ultimately performance is adversely affected. Such operations, though arguably unavoidable during emergencies, are unacceptable during normal operations. Therefore, the second category of unsafe supervision, planned inappropriate operations, was created to account for these failures (Table A.3).

Take, for example, the issue of improper crew pairing. It is well known that when very senior, dictatorial captains are paired with very junior, weak copilots, communication and coordination problems are likely to occur. Commonly referred to as the trans-cockpit authority gradient, such conditions likely contributed to the tragic crash of a commercial airliner into the Potomac River outside of Washington, DC, in January of 1982 [13]. In that accident, the captain of the aircraft repeatedly rebuffed the first officer when the latter indicated that the engine instruments did not appear normal. Undaunted, the captain continued a fatal takeoff in icing conditions with less than adequate takeoff thrust. The aircraft stalled and plummeted into the icy river, killing the crew and many of the passengers.

Clearly, the captain and crew were held accountable. They died in the accident and cannot shed light on causation, but what was the role of the supervisory chain? Perhaps crew pairing was equally responsible. Although not specifically addressed in the report, such issues are clearly worth exploring in many accidents. In fact, in that particular accident, several other training and manning issues were identified.

Failure to Correct a Known Problem

The third category of known unsafe supervision, failed to correct a known problem, refers to those instances when deficiencies among individuals, equipment, training, or other related safety areas are "known" to the supervisor, yet are allowed to continue unabated (Table A.3). For example, it is not uncommon for accident investigators to interview the pilot's friends, colleagues, and supervisors after a fatal crash only to find out that they "knew it would happen to him some day." If the supervisor knew that a pilot was incapable of flying safely, and allowed the flight anyway, he clearly did the pilot no favors. The failure to correct the behavior, either through remedial training or, if necessary, removal from flight status, essentially signed the pilot's death warrant—not to mention that of others who may have been on board.

Likewise, the failure to consistently correct or discipline inappropriate behavior certainly fosters an unsafe atmosphere and promotes the violation of rules. Aviation history is rich with reports of aviators who tell hair-raising stories of their exploits and barnstorming in low-level flights (the infamous "Been there, done that"). While entertaining to some, they often serve to promulgate a perception of tolerance and "one-upmanship" until 1 day someone ties the low-altitude flight record of ground level! Indeed, the failure to report these unsafe tendencies and initiate corrective actions is yet another example of the failure to correct known problems.

Supervisory Violations

Supervisory violations, on the other hand, are reserved for those instances when existing rules and regulations are willfully disregarded by supervisors (Table A.3). Although arguably rare, supervisors have been known occasionally to violate the rules and doctrine when managing their assets. For instance, there have been occasions when individuals were permitted to operate an aircraft without current qualifications or license. Likewise, it can be argued that failing to enforce existing rules and regulations or flaunting authority are also violations at the supervisory level. While rare and possibly difficult to cull out, such practices are a flagrant violation of the rules and invariably set the stage for the tragic sequence of events that predictably follow.

Organizational Influences

As noted previously, fallible decisions of upper-level management directly affect supervisory practices, as well as the conditions and actions of operators. Unfortunately, these organizational errors often go unnoticed by safety professionals, due in large part to the lack of a clear framework from which to investigate them. Generally speaking, the most elusive of latent failures revolve around issues related to resource management, organizational climate, and operational processes, as detailed in Figure A.5.

Figure A.5   Organizational factors influencing accidents.

Resource Management

This category encompasses the realm of corporate-level decision-making regarding the allocation and maintenance of organizational assets such as human resources (personnel), monetary assets, and equipment/facilities (Table A.4). Generally, corporate decisions about how such resources should be managed center around two distinct objectives—the goal of safety and the goal of on-time, cost-effective operations. In times of prosperity, both objectives can be easily balanced and satisfied in full. However, as we mentioned earlier, there may also be times of fiscal austerity that demand some give-and-take between the two. Unfortunately, history tells us that safety is often the loser in such battles and, as some can attest to very well, safety and training are often the first to be cut in organizations having financial difficulties. If cutbacks in such areas are too severe, flight proficiency may suffer, and the best pilots may leave the organization for greener pastures.

Table A.4 Selected Examples of Organizational Influences

Resource/Acquisition Management	*Organizational Process*
• Human Resources	• Operations
• Selection	• Operational tempo
• Staffing/manning	• Time pressure
• Training	• Production quotas
• Monetary/budget resources	• Incentives
• Excessive cost cutting	• Measurement/appraisal
• Lack of funding	• Schedules
• Equipment/facility resources	• Deficient planning
• Poor design	• Procedures
• Purchasing of unsuitable equipment	• Standards
Organizational Climate	**Clearly Defined Objectives**
• Structure	• Documentation
• Chain-of-command	• Instructions
• Delegation of authority	• Oversight
• Communication	• Risk management
• Formal accountability for actions	• Safety programs
• Policies	
• Hiring and firing	
• Promotion	
• Drugs and alcohol	
• Culture	
• Norms and rules	
• Values and beliefs	
• Organizational justice	

Excessive cost-cutting could also result in reduced funding for new equipment or may lead to the purchase of equipment that is suboptimal and inadequately designed for the type of operations flown by the company. Other trickle-down effects include poorly maintained equipment and workspaces, and the failure to correct known design flaws in existing equipment. The result is a scenario involving unseasoned, less-skilled pilots flying old and poorly maintained aircraft under the least desirable conditions and schedules. The ramifications for aviation safety are not hard to imagine.

Climate

Organizational climate refers to a broad class of organizational variables that influence worker performance. Formally, it was defined as the "situationally based consistencies in the organization's treatment of individuals" [14]. In general, however, organizational climate can be viewed as the working atmosphere within the organization. One telltale sign of an organization's climate is its structure, as reflected in the chain-of-command, delegation of authority and responsibility, communication channels, and formal accountability for actions (Table A.4). Just like in the cockpit, communication and coordination are vital within an organization. If management and staff within an organization are not communicating, or if no one knows who is in charge, organizational safety clearly suffers and accidents do happen [15].

An organization's policies and culture are also good indicators of its climate. Policies are official guidelines that direct management's decisions about such things as hiring and firing, promotion, retention, raises, sick leave, drugs and alcohol, overtime, accident investigations, and the use of safety equipment. Culture, on the other hand, refers to the unofficial or unspoken rules, values, attitudes, beliefs, and customs of an organization. Culture is "the way things really get done around here."

When policies are ill-defined, adversarial, or conflicting, or when they are supplanted by unofficial rules and values, confusion abounds within the organization. Indeed, there are some corporate managers who are quick to give "lip service" to official safety policies while in a public forum, but then overlook such policies when operating behind the scenes. However, the Third Law of Thermodynamics tells us that "order and harmony cannot be produced by such chaos and disharmony." Safety is bound to suffer under such conditions.

Operational Process

This category refers to corporate decisions and rules that govern the everyday activities within an organization, including the establishment and use of standardized operating procedures and formal methods for maintaining checks and balances (oversight) between the workforce and management. For example, such factors as operational tempo, time pressures, incentive systems, and work schedules are all factors that can adversely affect safety (Table A.4). As stated earlier, there may be instances when those within the upper echelon of an organization determine that it is necessary to increase the operational tempo to a point that overextends a supervisor's staffing capabilities. Therefore, a supervisor may resort to the use of inadequate scheduling procedures that jeopardize crew rest and produce suboptimal crew pairings, putting aircrew at an increased risk of a mishap. However, organizations should have official procedures in place to address such contingencies as well as oversight programs to monitor such risks.

Regrettably, not all organizations have these procedures nor do they engage in an active process of monitoring aircrew errors and human factor problems via anonymous reporting systems and safety audits. As such, supervisors and managers are often unaware of the problems before an accident occurs. Indeed, it has been said that "an accident is one incident to many" [16]. It is incumbent upon any organization to fervently seek out the "holes in the cheese" and plug them up, before they create a window of opportunity for catastrophe to strike.

Conclusion

It is our belief that the HFACS framework bridges the gap between theory and practice by providing investigators with a comprehensive, user-friendly tool for identifying and classifying the human causes of aviation accidents. The system, which is based on Reason's [5] model of latent and active failures [6], encompasses all aspects of human error, including the conditions of operators and organizational failure. Still, HFACS and any other framework only contributes to an already burgeoning list of human error taxonomies if it does not prove useful in the operational setting. In these regards, HFACS has recently been employed by the U.S. Navy, Marine Corps, Army, Air Force, and Coast Guard for use in aviation accident investigation and analysis. To date, HFACS has been applied to the analysis of human factors data from approximately 1,000 military aviation accidents. Throughout this process, the reliability and content validity of HFACS has been repeatedly tested and demonstrated [17].

Given that accident databases can be reliably analyzed using HFACS, the next logical question is whether anything unique will be identified. Early indications within the military suggest that the HFACS framework has been instrumental in the identification and analysis of global human factors safety issues (e.g., trends in aircrew proficiency [11]), specific accident types (e.g., controlled flight into terrain, CFIT [18]), and human factors problems such as CRM failures [19]. Consequently, the systematic application of HFACS to the analysis of human factors accident data has afforded the U.S. Navy/Marine Corps (for which the original taxonomy was developed) the ability to develop objective, data-driven intervention strategies. In a sense, HFACS has illuminated those areas ripe for intervention rather than relying on individual research interests not necessarily tied to saving lives or preventing aircraft losses.

Additionally, the HFACS framework and the insights gleaned from database analyses have been used to develop innovative accident investigation methods that have enhanced both the quantity and quality of the human factors information gathered during accident investigations. However, not only are safety professionals better suited to examine human error in the field, but using HFACS they can now track those areas (the holes in the cheese) responsible for the accidents as well. Only now is it possible to track the success or failure of specific intervention programs designed to reduce specific types of human error and subsequent aviation accidents. In so doing, research investments and safety programs can be either readjusted or reinforced to meet the changing needs of aviation safety.

Recently, these accident analysis and investigative techniques, developed and proven in the military, have been applied to the analysis and investigation of U.S. civil aviation accidents [20]. Specifically, the HFACS framework is currently being used to systematically analyze both commercial and general aviation accident data to explore the underlying human factors problems associated with these events. The framework is also being employed to develop improved methods and techniques for investigating human factors issues during actual civil aviation accident investigations by Federal Aviation Administration and National Transportation Safety Board officials. Initial results of this project have begun to highlight human factors areas in need of further safety research. In addition, like their military counterparts, it is anticipated that HFACS will provide the fundamental information and tools needed to develop a more effective and accessible human factors accident database for civil aviation.

In summary, the development of the HFACS framework has proven to be a valuable first step in the establishment of a larger military and civil aviation safety program. The ultimate goal of this, and any other, safety program is to reduce the aviation accident rate through systematic, data-driven investment.

References

1. Murray, S.R., 1997. Deliberate decision making by aircraft pilots: A simple reminder to avoid decision making under panic, *The International Journal of Aviation Psychology*, 7, 83–100.
2. Shappell, S.A., and Wiegmann, D.A., 1996. U.S. naval aviation mishaps 1977–92: Differences between single- and dual-piloted aircraft. *Aviation, Space, and Environmental Medicine*, 67, 65–69.
3. Heinrich, H.W., et al., 1980. *Industrial Accident Prevention: A Safety Management Approach*, Fifth Edition, McGraw-Hill, New York.
4. Bird, F., 1974. *Management Guide to Loss Control*, Institute Press, Atlanta, GA.
5. Reason, J., 1990. *Human Error*, Cambridge University Press, New York.
6. Shappell, S.A., and Wiegmann, D.A., 1997a. A human error approach to accident investigation: The taxonomy of unsafe operations, *The International Journal of Aviation Psychology*, 7, 269–291.
7. Senders, J.W., and Moray, N.P., 1991. *Human Error: Cause, Prediction and Reduction*, Erlbaum, Hillsdale, NJ.
8. Wiegmann, D.A., and Shappell, S.A., 1997. Human factors analysis of post-accident data: Applying theoretical taxonomies of human error, *International Journal of Aviation Psychology*, 7, 67–81.
9. Rasmussen, J., 1982. Human errors: A taxonomy for describing human malfunction in industrial installations, *Journal of Occupational Accidents*, 4, 311–333.
10. Orasanu, J.M., 1993. Decision-making in the cockpit. In E.L. Wiener, B.G. Kanki, and R.L. Helmreich (Eds.), *Cockpit Resource Management* (pp. 137–172). Academic Press, San Diego, CA.
11. Shappell, S., et al., 1999. Beyond mishap rates: A human factors analysis of U.S. Navy/Marine Corps TACAIR and rotary wing mishaps using HFACS, *Aviation, Space, and Environmental Medicine*, 70, 416–417.
12. Helmreich, R.L., and Foushee, H.C., 1993. Why crew resource management? Empirical and theoretical bases of human factors training in aviation. In E.L. Wiener, B.G. Kanki, and R.L. Helmreich (Eds.), *Cockpit Resource Management* (pp. 3–45). Academic Press, San Diego, CA.
13. National Transportation Safety Board, 1982. Air Florida, Inc., Boeing 737–222, N62AF, Collision with 14th Street bridge, near Washington National Airport, Washington, D.C., January 13, 1982 (Tech. Report NTSB-AAR-82–8). Washington: National Transportation Safety Board.
14. Jones, A.P., 1988. Climate and measurement of consensus: A discussion of "organizational climate." In Cole, S.G., Demaree, R.G., and W. Curtis (Eds.), *Applications of Interactionist Psychology: Essays in Honor of Saul B. Sells* (pp. 283–290). Erlbaum, Hillsdale, NJ.
15. Muchinsky, P.M., 1997. *Psychology Applied to Work*, Fifth Edition, Brooks/Cole Publishing Co, Pacific Grove, CA.
16. Reinhart, R.O., 1996. *Basic Flight Physiology*, Second Edition, McGraw-Hill, New York.
17. Shappell, S.A., and Wiegmann, D.A., 1997c. A reliability analysis of the Taxonomy of Unsafe Operations, *Aviation, Space, and Environmental Medicine*, 68, 620.
18. Shappell, S.A., and Wiegmann, D.A., 1997b. Why would an experienced aviator fly a perfectly good aircraft into the ground? In *Proceedings of the Ninth International Symposium on Aviation Psychology* (pp. 26–32). Ohio State University, Columbus, OH.
19. Wiegmann, D.A., and Shappell, S.A., 1999. Human error and crew resource management failures in Naval aviation mishaps: A review of U.S. Naval Safety Center data, 1990–96, *Aviation, Space, and Environmental Medicine*, 70, 1147–1151.
20. Shappell, S.A., and Wiegmann, D.A., 1999. Human error in commercial and corporate aviation: An analysis of FAR Part 121 and 135 mishaps using HFACS, *Aviation, Space, and Environmental Medicine*, 70, 407.

Index

Printed in the United States
by Baker & Taylor Publisher Services